PORTUGUESE
Phrase book

Alan Freeland

University of Southampton

Consultant: Graça Martins

D0921337

BBC Books

BBC Books publishes courses on the following languages:

ARABIC	ITALIAN
CHINESE	JAPANESE
FRENCH	PORTUGUESE
GERMAN	RUSSIAN
GREEK	SPANISH
HINDI & URDU	TURKISH

For further information write to:
BBC Books
Language Enquiry Service
Room A3116
Woodlands, 80 Wood Lane, London W12 0TT

Published by BBC Books,
a division of BBC Enterprises Limited,
Woodlands, 80 Wood Lane, London W12 0TT

First published 1992

Series editor: Carol Stanley
Editor: Philippa Goodrich

© Alan Freeland and Graça Martins 1992

ISBN 0 563 36296 0

Set in 8pt Itek Times by Ace Filmsetting Ltd, Frome
Printed and bound in Great Britain by Clays Ltd, St Ives Plc
Cover printed by Clays Ltd, St Ives Plc

Contents

HOW TO USE THIS BOOK

Communicating in a foreign language doesn't have to be diffi-cult – you can convey a lot with just a few words (plus a few ges-tures and a bit of mime). Just remember: keep it simple. Don't try to come out with long, grammatically perfect sentences when one or two words will get your meaning across.

Inside the back cover of this book is a list of All-purpose phrases. Some will help you to make contact – greetings, 'please' and 'thank you', 'yes' and 'no'. Some are to get people to help you understand what they're saying to you. And some are questions like 'do you have . . . ?' and 'where is . . . ?', to which you can add words from the Dictionary at the back of the book.

The book is divided into sections for different situations, such as Road travel, Shopping, Health and so on. In each section you'll find

- Useful tips and information
- Words and phrases that you'll see on signs or in print
- Phrases you are likely to want to say
- Things that people may say to you

Many of the phrases can be adapted by simply using another word from the Dictionary. For instance, take the question **O aeroporto fica longe?** (Is the airport far away?). If you want to know if the *station* is far away, just substitute **a estação** (the station) for **o aeroporto** to give **A estação fica longe?**

All the phrases have a simple pronunciation guide underneath based on English sounds – this is explained in Pronunciation (page 7).

If you want some guidance on how the Portuguese language works, see Basic grammar (page 175).

There's a handy reference section (starts on page 188) which contains lists of days and months, countries and nationalities, general signs and notices that you'll see, conversion tables, national holidays, useful addresses and numbers.

The 5,000-word Dictionary (page 210) comes in two sections – Portuguese–English and English–Portuguese.

A concise list of numbers is printed inside the front cover for easy reference, and right at the end of the book is an Emergencies section (which we hope you *won't* have to use).

Wherever possible, work out in advance what you want to say – if you're going shopping, for instance, write out a shopping list in Portuguese. If you're buying travel tickets, work out how to say where you want to go, how many tickets you want, single or return, etc.

Practise saying things out loud – the cassette that goes with this book will help you to get used to the sounds of Portuguese.

Above all – don't be shy! It'll be appreciated if you try to say a few words, even if it's only 'good morning' and 'goodbye' – and in fact those are the very sorts of phrases that are worth memorising, as you'll hear them and need to use them all the time.

If you'd like to learn more Portuguese, BBC Books also publishes *Get By in Portuguese* and *Discovering Portuguese*. BBC phrase books are also available for the following languages: French, German, Greek, Italian and Spanish. Future titles include Arabic and Turkish.

The authors would welcome any suggestions or comments about this book, but in the meantime, have a good trip – **boa viagem!**

PRONUNCIATION

You don't need perfect pronunciation to be able to communicate – it's enough to get the sounds approximately right and to stress the words in the correct place. If you want to hear real Portuguese voices and practise trying to sound like them, then listen to the cassette.

Portuguese pronunciation is fairly regular – you can usually tell how a word is pronounced from the way it's written, once you know what sound each letter (or group of letters) represents. A pronunciation guide is given with the phrases in this book – the system is based on English sounds, as described below.

Stress

In this book, a stressed syllable is shown in the pronunciation guide by bold type. Many Portuguese words are stressed on the last syllable but one: *obrigado*, *Lisboa*, *queria*, *ingleses*, *falam*. The main exceptions are:

1 When a word ends in a consonant (other than in the endings *-am* or *-em* or *-s*), the stress is on the last syllable: *Portugal*, *comer*, *assim*.

2 When there is a written accent, the stress is where the accent is: *itinerário*, *trânsito*. However, the main function of the *til* sign (˜) is to show that a vowel is nasalized (nasal vowels are explained below). Usually the stress coincides with the *til*: *estação*, *irmã*. If not, there is a second written accent: *órfão*.

Vowels

The pronunciation of Portuguese vowels can vary according to where the stress falls in the word. When the vowel is unstressed, it often almost disappears.

	Approx. English equivalent	Shown in book as	Example	
a stressed	a in 'father'	**ah**	**fado**	*fahdoo*
unstressed	a in 'about'	**a**	**tarifa**	*tareefa*
e stressed	e in 'get'	**e**	**hotel**	*otel*
	a in 'gate'	**ay**	**dizer**	*deezayr*
unstressed	e in 'other'	**i**	**começar**	*koomisar*
	hardly pronounced at end of word		**norte**	*nort*
i	ee in 'meet'	**ee**	**quilo**	*keeloo*
			viver	*veevayr*
o stressed	o in 'lot'	**o**	**loja**	*loja*
	o in 'note'	**oh**	**boca**	*bohka*
unstressed	oo in 'foot'	**oo**	**comer**	*koomayr*
	pronounced weakly at end of word		**cedo**	*sehdoo*
u	oo in 'foot'	**oo**	**azul**	*azool*
			mulher	*moolyer*

Vowel combinations

ai	ie in 'pie'	**iy**	**mais**	*miysh*
ao, au	ow in 'cow'	**ow**	**mau**	*mow*
ei	ay in 'say'	**ay**	**seis**	*saysh*
ia	ie in 'alien'	**ya**	**família**	*fameelya*
io	yu in 'yule'	**yoo**	**sócio**	*sosyoo*
oi	oy in 'toy'	**oy**	**dois**	*doysh*

ou	o in 'note'	**oh**	**outro**	*ohtroo*
ua	ua in 'aquatic'	**wa**	**água**	*ahgwa*
ui	ui in 'suite'	**wee**	**fui**	*fwee*

Nasal vowels

Portuguese vowels can have a nasal sound – say them through your nose and mouth at the same time, and as if followed by a short 'ng' as in 'gong'. Vowels are nasal when:

1 They are written with a *til* (˜): **não**.
2 They occur before **-m** or **-ns** at the end of a word: **sim**, **homens**. The **-m** or **-n** is not pronounced.
3 They are followed by **m** or **n** and another consonant: **comboio**, **andar**.

In the pronunciation guide in this book, an **m** or **n** with a *til* (**m̃**, **ñ**) tells you that you should make the vowel sound nasal. The most frequent situations in which nasal sounds occur are:

	Approx. English equivalent	Shown in book as	Example	
ã, an	a in 'Anne' + nasal sound	**añ**	**maçã**	*masañ*
			antes	*añtish*
ão, am	ow in 'cow' + nasal sound	**owñ, owm̃**	**nação**	*nasowñ*
			falam	*falowm̃*
ãe, em, en	ay in 'day' + nasal sound	**ayñ, aym̃**	**mãe**	*mayñ*
			homens	*omayñsh*
im, in	ee in 'meet' + nasal sound	**eem̃, eeñ**	**fim**	*feem̃*
			fins	*feeñsh*
õe	oy in 'toy' + nasal sound	**oyñ**	**põe**	*poyñ*
			nações	*nasoyñsh*
om, on	oh in 'note' + nasal sound	**ohm̃, ohñ**	**bom**	*bohm̃*
			bons	*bohñsh*
um, un	oo in 'foot' + nasal sound	**oom̃, ooñ**	**um**	*oom̃*
			uns	*ooñsh*

Consonants

Many Portuguese consonants are pronounced in a similar way to English. The main differences are with **c, g, h, j, q, r, s, x, z**.

	Approx. English equivalent	Shown in book as	Example	
b	b in 'but'	b	barco	*bahrkoo*
c followed by **e** or **i; ç**	s in 'set'	s	cidade	*seedahd*
			aço	*ahsoo*
c otherwise	c in 'can'	k	comer	*koomayr*
ch	sh in 'shut'	sh	chá	*shah*
d	d in 'dog'	d	donde	*dohñd*
f	f in 'feet'	f	faço	*fahsoo*
g followed by **e** or **i**	s in 'measure'	j	gente	*jayñt*
g otherwise	g in 'got'	g	grande	*grañd*
h	always silent		hotel	*otel*
j	s in 'measure'	j	já	*jah*
l	l in 'look'	l	livro	*leevroo*
lh	lli in 'million'	ly	olho	*olyoo*
m (See Nasal vowels)	m in 'mat'	m	metro	*metroo*
n (See Nasal vowels)	n in 'not'	n	nome	*nohm*
nh	ni in 'onion'	ny	vinho	*veenyoo*
p	p in 'pack'	p	pote	*pot*
qu followed by **e** or **i**	usually k in 'kit'	k	quilo	*keeloo*
qu otherwise	qu in 'quick'	kw	quando	*kwañdoo*
r	rolled as in Scottish accent	r	caro	*kahroo*

rr; r at beginning of a word	strongly rolled	**rr**	**carro**	*kahrroo*
			roda	*rroda*
s at beginning of a word and after a consonant; **ss**	s in 'set'	**s**	**saída**	*saeeda*
			classe	*klahs*
s between vowels	z in 'zoo'	**z**	**aviso**	*aveezoo*
s otherwise	sh in 'shut'	**sh**	**dois**	*doysh*
t	t in 'tin'	**t**	**tenho**	*taynyoo*
v	v in 'vet'	**v**	**vinho**	*veenyoo*
x often	sh in 'shut'	**sh**	**caixa**	*kiysha*
or	z in 'zoo'	**z**	**exemplo**	*eezaym̃ploo*
or	x in 'six'	**ks**	**táxi**	*tahksee*
or	s in 'set'	**s**	**próximo**	*proseemoo*
z at end of a word	sh in 'shut'	**sh**	**faz**	*fahsh*
z otherwise	z in 'zoo'	**z**	**fazer**	*fazayr*

11

Note

In Northern Portugal '**v**' is often pronounced as '**b**'.

THE PORTUGUESE ALPHABET

Portuguese uses the same alphabet as English, except that the letters **k**, **w** and **y** are only found in words borrowed from other languages. The names of the letters are given below in case you need to spell out a word.

Spelling

How is it spelt?
Como se escreve?
kohmoo si ishcrev

Portuguese is the national language of Portugal and Brazil and the official language of five African states – Angola, Mozambique, Cape Verde, Guinea Bissau and São Tomé and Príncipe. Just as English and American spelling differ slightly, so do Portuguese and Brazilian. Recently, the above seven countries agreed to reform their spelling to produce one common system, which is expected to take effect from the mid 1990s. This reform will particularly affect the way in which written accents are used. The spelling of some words will also be slightly different from the current European version used in this book. However, these changes are relatively minor and are unlikely to cause you any confusion.

Letter	Pronounced	Letter	Pronounced
A	*ah*	G	*jay*
B	*bay*	H (aga)	*agah*
C	*say*	I	*ee*
D	*day*	J (jota)	*jota*
E	*e*	K (capa)	*kahpa*
F	*efi*	L	*eli*

M	emi	T	tay
N	eni	U	oo
O	o	V (vê)	vay
P	pay	W (vê duplo)	vay *dooploo*
Q (quê)	kay	X (xix)	sheesh
R	erri	Y (ípsilon)	*eep*seelohn
S	esi	Z (zê)	zay

Note

The English name for **W** is also used in Portuguese. You may also hear **vê dobrado** – pronounced *vay doobrahdoo*.

GENERAL CONVERSATION

● The phrases **bom dia, boa tarde** and **boa noite** are used at different times of day. **Bom dia** means 'good morning' (or, literally, 'good day') and is used up to lunchtime. After that, until it gets dark, it's **boa tarde** – which can therefore mean either 'good afternoon' or 'good evening'. **Boa noite** is used as a greeting after nightfall, as well as to say 'goodnight'.

Olá means 'hello', and is often used together with one of the phrases above, e.g. **olá, bom dia.**

● The Portuguese shake hands when they meet and when they say goodbye. Women, and men and women (though not two men) often exchange kisses on both cheeks.

● When you're talking to someone in English, you vary your tone of voice and your way of saying things depending on whether you're addressing them formally, showing respect, or in a more casual way (as with a friend or member of the family).

In Portuguese, there's an extra way of making this distinction – by using different words to say 'you' and different endings on verbs. One way is more formal, the other more casual. There's a further explanation of this on page 181, but all you need to be aware of is that in this book we have used the more formal way, on the assumption that you will mostly be talking to people you don't know. The formal words for 'you' are **o senhor** (*oo sinyohr*) if talking to a man or **a senhora** (*a sinyohra*) if talking to a woman. However, the word for 'you' is usually omitted if the meaning is clear from the situation and the verb ending.

People may address *you* in the informal way (this is quite general among younger people). The informal word for 'you' is **tu** (*too*). You may notice an **s** on the ends of verbs, e.g. **queres?**

instead of **quer?** (would you like?); **tens?** instead of **tem?** (do you have?); and you may also hear **como te chamas?** instead of **como se chama?** (what's your name?).

You may also come across another word for 'you' – **você** (*vosay*). This is the normal word for 'you' in Brazil, but in Portugal its use is more complicated and best avoided.

Greetings

Hello
Olá
ohlah

(Hello), how are things?
(Olá), como vai?
(ohlah) kohmoo viy

Good morning
Bom dia
bohm deea

How are you?
Como está?
kohmoo istah

Good afternoon/evening
Boa tarde
boha tahrd

Fine, thanks
Bem, obrigado (*if you're male*)
baym ohbreegahdoo

Good evening/Goodnight
Boa noite
boha noyt

Bem, obrigada (*if you're female*)
baym ohbreegahda

Goodbye
Adeus
adayoosh

And you?
E o senhor? (*to a man*)
ee oo sinyohr

See you later
Até logo
ate logoo

E a senhora? (*to a woman*)
ee a sinyohra

Introductions

My name is ...
Chamo-me ...
shamoo-mi ...

This is ...
Este/Esta é ...
aysht/eshta e ...

This is Mr Brown
Este é o Senhor Brown
aysht e oo sinyohr ...

This is Mrs Clark
Esta é a Senhora Clark
eshta e a sinyohra ...

This is my husband/son
Este é o meu marido/filho
*aysht e oo mayoo mareedoo/
feelyoo*

This is my wife/daughter
Esta é a minha mulher/filha
*eshta e a meenya moolher/
feelya*

This is my boyfriend/fiancé
Este é o meu namorado
*aysht e oo mayoo
namoorahdoo*

This is my girlfriend/fiancée
Esta é a minha namorada
eshta e a meenya namoorahda

Pleased to meet you
Muito prazer
mweeñtoo prazayr

Talking about yourself and your family

(*see* Countries and nationalities, page 195)

I am English
Sou inglês (*if you're male*)
soh eeñglaysh
Sou inglesa (*if you're female*)
soh eeñglayza

I am Scottish
Sou escocês/escocesa
soh ishkoosaysh/ishkoosayza

I am Irish
Sou irlandês/irlandesa
soh eerlañdaysh/eerlañdayza

I am Welsh
Sou galês/galesa
soh galaysh/galayza

I live in London
Moro em Londres
moroo ayñ lohñdrish

We live in Newcastle
Moramos em Newcastle
mooramooz ayñ ...

I am a student
Sou estudante
soh ishtoodañt

I am a nurse
Sou enfermeiro *(male)*/
  enfermeira *(female)*
soh ayñfirmayroo/ayñfirmayra

I work . . .
Trabalho . . .
trabahlyoo . . .

I work in an office/in a
  factory
**Trabalho num escritório/
  numa fábrica**
*trabahlyoo noom
  ishkreetoryoo/nooma
  fahbreeka*

I work for a computer
  company
**Trabalho numa companhia de
  computadores**
*trabahlyoo nooma
  kohñpanyeea di
  koñpootadohrish*

I am unemployed
Estou desempregado *(male)*/
  desempregada *(female)*
*ishtoh dizayñprigahdoo/
  dizayñprigahda*

I am single
Sou solteiro *(male)*/**solteira**
  (female)
soh sohltayroo/sohltayra

I am married
Sou casado/casada
soh kazahdoo/kazahda

I am separated
Sou separado/separada
soh siparahdoo/siparahda

I am divorced
Sou divorciado/divorciada
*soh deevoorseeahdoo/
  deevoorseeahda*

I am a widower/widow
Sou viúvo/viúva
soh veeoovoo/veeoova

I have a son/a daughter
Tenho um filho/uma filha
*taynyoo ooñ feelyoo/ooma
  feelya*

I have three children
Tenho três filhos
taynyoo traysh feelyoosh

I don't have any children
Não tenho filhos
nowñ taynyoo feelyoosh

I have one brother
Tenho um irmão
taynyoo ooñ eermowñ

I have three sisters
Tenho três irmãs
taynyoo trayz eermañsh

I'm here with my husband
Estou aqui com o meu marido
ishtoh akee kohm̃ oo mayoo mareedoo

I'm here with my wife
Estou aqui com a minha mulher
ishtoh akee kohm̃ a meenya moolyer

I'm here with my family
Estou aqui com a minha família
ishtoh akee kohm̃ a meenya fameelya

I'm here on holiday
Estou aqui de férias
ishtoh akee di feryash

I'm here on business
Estou aqui em negócios
ishtoh akee aym̃ nigosyoosh

I speak very little Portuguese
Falo muito pouco português
fahloo mweeñtoo pohkoo poortoogaysh

My husband is/works . . .
O meu marido é/trabalha . . .
oo mayoo mareedoo e/ trabahlya . . .

My wife is/works . . .
A minha mulher é/trabalha . . .
a meenya moolyer e/trabahlya . . .

My husband is a bus-driver
O meu marido é motorista de autocarro
oo mayoo mareedoo e mootooreeshta di owtokahrroo

My wife is an accountant
A minha mulher é contabilista
a meenya moolyer e koñtabeeleeshta

My son is five years old
O meu filho tem cinco anos
oo mayoo feelyoo taym̃ seeñkoo anoosh

My daughter is eight years old
A minha filha tem oito anos
a meenya feelya taym̃ oytoo anoosh

You may hear

Como se chama?
kohmoo si shama
What is your name?

Donde é?
dohñdee e
Where are you from?

O que faz?
oo ki fahsh
What do you do?

Em que trabalha?
ayñ ki trabahlya
What job do you do?

O que estuda?
oo ki istooda
What do you study?

É casado/casada?
e kazahdoo/kazahda
Are you married?

Tem filhos?
tayñ feelyoosh
Do you have any children?

Quantos anos têm?/Que idade têm?
kwañtooz anoosh tayayñ/ki eedahd tayayñ
How old are they?

Quantos anos tem?/Que idade tem?
kwañtooz anoosh tayñ/ki eedahd tayñ
How old is he/she?

É muito engraçado
(*talking about a child*)
e mweeñtoo ayñgrasahdoo
He is very nice/good-looking

É muito engraçada
(*talking about a child*)
e mweeñtoo ayñgrasahda
She is very nice/pretty

Tem irmãos?
tayñ eermowñsh
Do you have any brothers and sisters?

Este é o seu marido/namorado?
aysht e oo sayoo mareedoo/namoorahdoo
Is this your husband, fiancé/boyfriend?

19

**Esta é a sua mulher/
namorada?**
*eshta e a sooa moolyer/
namoorahda*
Is this your wife, fiancée/
girlfriend?

**Este é o seu amigo?/Esta é a
sua amiga?**
*aysht e oo sayoo ameegoo/
eshta e a sooa ameega*
Is this your friend?

Para onde vai?
para ohñd viy
Where are you going?

**Onde está instalado/
instalada?**
*ohñd ishtah eeñshtalahdoo/
eeñshtalahda*
Where are you staying?

Onde mora?
ohñd mora
Where do you live?

Talking about Portugal and your own country

I like Portugal (very much)
Gosto (muito) de Portugal
*goshtoo (mweeñtoo) di
poortoogahl*

Portugal is very beautiful
Portugal é muito bonito
*poortoogahl e mweeñtoo
booneetoo*

It's the first time I've been to
Portugal
**É a primeira vez que venho a
Portugal**
*e a preemayra vaysh ki
vaynyoo a poortoogahl*

I come to Portugal often
Venho muito a Portugal
*vaynyoo mweeñtoo a
poortoogahl*

Are you from here?
É daqui?
e dakee

Have you ever been to
England/Scotland/
Ireland/Wales?
**Já foi alguma vez a
Inglaterra/Escócia/
Irlanda/Gales?**
*jah foy ahlgooma vayz a
eeñglaterra/ishkosya/
eerlañda/gahlish*

Did you like it?
Gostou?
gooshtoh

You may hear

Gosta de Portugal?
goshta di poortoogahl
Do you like Portugal?

É a primeira vez que vem a Portugal?
e a preemayra vaysh ki vaym a poortoogahl
Is this your first time in Portugal?

Quanto tempo fica aqui?
kwañtoo taympoo feeka akee
How long are you here for?

Fala muito bem português
fahla mweeñtoo baym poortoogaysh
Your Portuguese is very good

Likes and dislikes

I like . . .
Gosto de . . .
goshtoo di . . .

I like it
Gosto
goshtoo

I like swimming
Gosto de nadar
goshtoo di nadahr

I like football
Gosto de futebol
goshtoo di footbol

I don't like . . .
Não gosto de . . .
nowñ goshtoo di . . .

I don't like it
Não gosto
nowñ goshtoo

I don't like beer
Não gosto de cerveja
nowñ goshtoo di sirvayja

I don't like playing tennis
Não gosto de jogar ténis
nowñ goshtoo di joogahr teneesh

Do you like it?
Gosta?
goshta

Do you like ice-cream?
Gosta de gelado?
goshta di jilahdoo

Talking to a child

What's your name?
Como te chamas?
kohmoo ti shamash

How old are you?
Quantos anos tens?
kwañtooz anoosh tayñsh

Do you have any brothers
   and sisters?
Tens irmãos?
tayñz eermowñsh

Invitations and replies

Would you like a drink?
Quer beber alguma coisa?
ker bibayr ahlgooma koyza

Yes, please
Sim, por favor
seeñ poor favohr

No, thank you
Não, obrigado (*if you're male*)
nowñ ohbreegahdoo
Não, obrigada (*if you're
   female*)
nowñ ohbreegahda

I'd love to
Gostaria muito
gooshtareea mweeñtoo

That's very kind of you
É muito amável
e mweeñtoo amahvel

Please leave me alone
Deixe-me em paz
daysh-me ayñ pahsh

You may hear

Quer . . . ?
ker . . .
Would you like . . . ?

Quer beber alguma coisa?
ker bibayr ahlgooma koyza
Would you like a drink?

Quer comer alguma coisa?
ker koomayr ahlgooma koyza
Would you like something
to eat?

Que vai fazer esta noite?
ki viy fazayr eshta noyt
What are you doing tonight?

Quer ir/vir . . . ?
ker eer/veer . . .
Would you like to go/
come . . . ?

Quer ir dançar?
ker eer dañsahr
Would you like to go dancing?

Quer ir ao cinema?
ker eer ow seenayma
Would you like to go to the
cinema?

Quer vir jantar?
ker veer jañtahr
Would you like to come to
dinner?

**A que horas nos
encontramos?**
*a ki orash nooz
ayñkohñtramoosh*
What time shall we meet?

Onde nos encontramos?
ohñd nooz ayñkohñtramoosh
Where shall we meet?

Tem lume?
taym loom
Have you got a light?

Good wishes and exclamations

Congratulations!/Happy
Birthday!
Parabens!
parabayñsh

Merry Christmas!
Feliz Natal!
fileesh natahl

Happy New Year!
Bom ano novo!
bohm anoo nohvoo

Merry Christmas and a
Happy New Year!
Boas Festas!
bohash feshtash

Good luck!
Boa sorte!
boha sort

Enjoy yourself!
Divirta-se!
deeveerta-si

Have a good journey!
Boa viagem!
boha veeahjaym

Cheers!
Saúde!
saood

Enjoy your meal
Bom apetite!
bohm apiteet

Bless you! (*when someone sneezes*)
Santinho!
sañteenyoo

If only!/I wish I could!
Oxalá!
ohshalah

What a pity!
Que pena!
ki payna

Talking about the weather

The weather's very good
O tempo está muito bom
oo taympo ishtah mweeñtoo bohm

The weather's very bad
O tempo está muito mau
oo taympoo ishtah mweeñtoo mow

It's a wonderful day
Está um dia lindo
ishtah ooñ deea leeñdoo

It's hot, (isn't it?)
Está calor, (não está?)
ishtah kalohr (nowñ ishtah)

It's cold, (isn't it?)
Está frio, (não está?)
ishtah freeoo (nowñ ishtah)

Phew, it's hot!
Que calor!
ki kalohr

I (don't) like the heat
(Não) gosto do calor
(nowñ) goshtoo doo kalohr

It's very windy
Está muito vento
ishtah mweeñtoo vayñtoo

Is it going to rain?
Vai chover?
viy shoovayr

ARRIVING IN THE COUNTRY

● Whether you arrive by air, road or sea, the formalities (passport control and Customs) are quite straightforward; the only document you need is a valid passport.

● You will probably not need to say anything in Portuguese unless you are asked the purpose of your visit, or have something to declare at Customs. If you need to say what you have to declare (rather than just showing it), look up the words you need in the Dictionary. EC duty-free allowances apply – you can get a leaflet with the details at your point of departure.

You may see

Alfândega	Customs
Benvindo/Bem-vindo	Welcome
CEE	EEC
Mercadorias a declarar	Goods to declare
Nada a declarar	Nothing to declare
Outros passaportes	Other passports
Passageiros	Passengers
Passaportes	Passports

You may want to say

I am here on holiday
Estou aqui de férias
ishtoh akee di feryash

I am here on business
Estou aqui em negócios
ishtoh akee aym nigosyoosh

It's a joint passport
É um passaporte familiar
e oom pahsaport fameeleeahr

I have something to declare
Tenho algo que declarar
taynyoo ahlgoo ki diklarahr

I have this
Tenho isto
taynyoo eeshtoo

I have two bottles of whisky
Tenho duas garrafas de whisky
taynyoo dooash garrahfash di weeshkee

I have two cartons of cigarettes
Tenho duas caixas de cigarros
taynyoo dooash kiyshash di seegahrroosh

I have a receipt (for this)
Tenho um recibo (para isto)
taynyoo oom rriseeboo (para eeshtoo)

You may hear

O seu passaporte, por favor
oo sayoo pahsaport poor favohr
Your passport, please

Os seus documentos, por favor
oosh sayoosh dookoomayñtoosh poor favohr
Your documents, please

Qual é o objectivo da sua visita?
kwahl e oo ohbjeteevoo da sooa veezeeta
What's the purpose of your visit?

Está aqui de férias ou em negócios?
istah akee di feryash oh aym nigosyoosh
Are you here on holiday or business?

Quanto tempo fica em Portugal?
kwañtoo taympoo feeka aym poortoogahl
How long are you staying in Portugal?

Por favor, abra este saco/esta mala
poor favohr ahbra aysht sahkoo/eshta mahla
Please open this bag/this suitcase

Por favor, abra o porta-bagagens
poor favohr ahbra oo porta-bagahjayñsh
Please open the boot

Temos de revistar o carro
taymoosh di rriveeshtahr oo kahrroo
We have to search the car

Tem mais bagagem?
taym miysh bagahjaym
Do you have any other
  luggage?

**Tem de pagar imposto por
  isto**
*taym di pagahr eempohshtoo
  poor eeshtoo*
There is duty to pay on this

Venha comigo/connosco
vaynya koomeegoo/konoshkoo
Come with me/with us

DIRECTIONS

● Some general maps are available from the Portuguese National Tourist Office and the **Instituto de Promoção Turística** (addresses, page 206). Road maps are obtainable from bookshops. Local tourist offices can provide town plans and regional maps.

● You may notice that the words for 'the', **o** or **a**, are used in front of the names of most Portuguese regions, e.g. **o Algarve, o Minho, a Madeira.** This also happens with the names of some cities and towns, e.g. **o Porto, o Estoril, a Covilhã.**

● When you need to ask the way to somewhere, the easiest thing is to say **Por favor** to attract attention, and then add **para . . . ?** and the name of the place, e.g. **Por favor, para Coimbra?**

● If you're looking for a bank or petrol station, for example, the simplest way to ask is: **Há um banco/uma estação de serviço aqui perto?** ('Is there a bank/petrol station around here?').

● If you're looking for a particular address, have it written down. In Portugal, addresses are written with the street name first and the number afterwards, e.g. **Rua da Alegria, 7.** An address for an office or flat may also show the number of the floor, and whether it is on the left or right, e.g. **Rua Castilho, 18–2º Dto.** Here **2º** means '2nd', i.e. 2nd floor, and **Dto.** is short for **direito**, 'right'. (**Esq.** is short for **esquerdo**, 'left'.)

● When you're being given directions, listen out for the important bits (such as whether to turn left or right), and try to repeat each bit to make sure you've understood it correctly. If you can't understand anything, ask the person to say it again more slowly: **Podia repetir mais devagar?**

You may see

Avenida	Avenue
Bairro	District (*of town, city*)
Beco	Alley
Câmara Municipal	Town Hall
Castelo	Castle
Estação	Station
Igreja	Church
Largo	Square
Mercado	Market
Metro	Underground
Miradouro	Vantage point
Museu	Museum
Palácio	Palace
Para o/a ...	To the ...
Passagem subterrânea	Subway
Peões	Pedestrians
Praça	Square
Rua	Street
Sé	Cathedral
Travessa	Lane between two larger streets

You may want to say

Excuse me please . . . ?
Por favor . . . ?
poor favohr . . .

Pardon?
Como?
kohmoo

Could you repeat that, please?
Podia repetir, por favor?
poodeea rripiteer poor favohr

More slowly
Mais devagar
miysh divagahr

Again
Outra vez
ohtra vaysh

I am lost
Estou perdido/perdida
ishtoh pirdeedoo/pirdeeda

Where are we?
Onde estamos?
ohñd ishtahmoosh

Where does this road/street
lead to?
**Para onde vai esta estrada/
rua?**
*para ohñd viy eshta ishtrahda/
rrooa*

Is this the right way to
Oporto?
**É este o caminho para o
Porto?**
*e aysht oo kameenyoo para oo
pohrtoo*

Could you show me on the
map?
Podia-me indicar no mapa?
*poodeea-mi eeñdeekahr noo
mahpa*

Excuse me please, which
way to the station?
Por favor, para a estação?
poor favohr para a ishtasowñ

Excuse me please, which
way to the (town) centre?
**Por favor, para o centro (da
cidade)?**
*poor favohr para oo sayntroo
(da seedahd)*

The road to Faro, please?
**A estrada para Faro, por
favor?**
*a ishtrahda para fahroo poor
favohr*

How do I/we get to . . . ?
Como se vai para . . . ?
kohmoo si viy para . . .

How do I/we get to Évora?
Como se vai para Évora?
kohmoo si viy para evoora

How do I/we get to the
airport?
**Como se vai para o
aeroporto?**
*kohmoo si viy para oo
aeropohrtoo*

How do I/we get to the
beach?
Como se vai para a praia?
kohmoo si viy para a priya

Where is . . .?
Onde é . . .?
ohñdee e . . .

Where are . . . ?
Onde são . . . ?
ohñd sowñ . . .

Where is this? (*if you've got an address written down*)
Onde é?
ohñdee e

Where is the tourist office?
Onde é o turismo?
ohñdee e oo tooreeshmoo

Where is the Post Office?
Onde é o Correio?
ohñdee e oo koorrayoo

Where is this office/this room?
Onde é este gabinete/esta sala?
ohñdee e aysht gabeenayt/ eshta sahla

Where are the toilets?
Onde é a casa de banho?
ohñdee e a kahza di banyoo

Is it far?
Fica longe?
feeka lohñj

Is the airport far away?
O aeroporto fica longe?
oo aeropohrtoo feeka lohñj

How many kilometres away?
A quantos quilómetros?
a kwañtoosh keelomitroosh

How long does it take (on foot/by car)?
Quanto tempo leva (a pé/de carro)?
kwañtoo taympoo leva (a pe/di kahrroo)

Is there a bus/train?
Há um autocarro/comboio?
ah oom owtokahrroo/ kohmboyoo

Can I/we get there on foot?
Pode-se ir a pé?
pod-si eer a pe

Can I/we get there by car?
Pode-se ir de carro?
pod-si eer di kahroo

31

Is there . . . ?
Há . . . ?
ah . . .

Is there a bank around here?
Há um banco aqui perto?
ah oom bañkoo akee pertoo

Is there a supermarket in the town?
Há um supermercado na vila?
ah oom soopermirkahdoo na veela

You may hear

Enganou-se
ayñganoh-si
You've made a mistake

Estamos aqui
ishtamooz akee
We are here

Aqui
akee
Here

Ali, Acolá
alee, akoolah
There

Por aqui
poor akee
This way

Por ali
poor alee
That way, Along there

(À) direita
(ah) deerayta
(To the) right

(À) esquerda
(ah) ishkayrda
(To the) left

(Sempre) em frente
(saympri) aym frayñt
Straight on

A primeira (rua/transversal)
a preemayra (rrooa/trañshvirsahl)
The first (street/turning)

A segunda (rua/transversal)
a sigooñda (rrooa/trañshvirsahl)
The second (street/turning)

A terceira (rua/transversal)
a tirsayra (rrooa/trañshvirsahl)
The third (street/turning)

Do lado direito
doo lahdoo deeraytoo
On the right-hand side

Do lado esquerdo
doo lahdoo ishkayrdoo
On the left-hand side

No fim da rua
noo feeñ da rrooa
At the end of the street

Do outro lado da praça
doo ohtroo lahdoo da prahsa
On the other side of the square

Na esquina
na ishkeena
On the corner

Lá em baixo
lah aym biyshoo
Down there/downstairs

Lá em cima
lah aym seema
Up there/upstairs

Debaixo de
dibiyshoo di
Under

Encima de
aynseema di
Over

Antes dos semáforos
antish doosh simahfooroosh
Before the traffic lights

Depois da Sé
dipoysh da se
After/Past the cathedral

A seguir ao Museu
a sigeer ow moozayoo
After/Past the Museum

Em frente a
aym fraynt a
Opposite/In front of

Atrás de
atrahsh di
Behind

Ao lado de
ow lahdoo di
Next to

Ao pé de/Perto de
ow pe di/pertoo di
Near, Close to

Fica no largo
feeka noo lahrgoo
It's in the square

Quando chegar à Rua do Carmo . . .
kwandoo shigahr ah rrooa doo kahrmoo . . .
When you get to the Rua do Carmo . . .

Em direcção à Sé
aym deeresown ah se
Towards the cathedral

Até aos semáforos
ate owsh simahfooroosh
As far as the traffic lights

(Não) fica longe
(nown) feeka lohnj
It's (not) far away

Muito longe, Bastante longe
mweentoo lohnj, bashtant lohnj
Very far, Quite far

Fica perto
feeka pertoo
It's close by

Muito perto, Bastante perto
mweentoo pertoo, bashtant pertoo
Very close, Quite close

Fica a cinco minutos
feeka a seenkoo meenootoosh
It's five minutes away

Fica a vinte quilómetros
feeka a veeñt keelomitroosh
It's twenty kilometres away

Tem de apanhar o autocarro/ comboio
taym di apanyahr oo owtokahrroo/kohmboyoo
You have to catch the bus/ train

Vá . . .
vah . . .
Go . . .

Siga . . .
seega . . .
Carry on/Go on . . .

Desça . . .
daysha . . .
Go down . . .

Suba . . .
sooba . . .
Go up . . .

Fica no terceiro andar
feeka noo tirsayroo añdahr
It's on the third floor

A primeira/segunda porta
a preemayra/sigooñda porta
The first/second door

Vá de elevador
vah di ilivadohr
Take the lift

Vire . . .
veeri . . .
Turn . . .

Tome . . .
tomi . . .
Take . . .

Vá por . . .
vah poor . . .
Go along/over . . .

Atravesse . . .
atravesi . . .
Cross . . .

ROAD TRAVEL

● Consult the motoring organisations or the Portuguese National Tourist Office for information on driving in Portugal. The Portuguese motoring organisation is the **Automóvel Club de Portugal** (address, page 206).

● If you drive in Portugal, take extra care. Road accident figures are among the highest in Europe.

● You drive on the right in Portugal. Traffic from the right has priority on roads, even on roundabouts. Seatbelts are compulsory outside towns. Crash helmets are compulsory for both drivers and passengers of motorbikes and scooters.

● Speed limits are generally:
60 km per hour in built-up areas, 90 km per hour on ordinary roads, and 120 km per hour on motorways.

● Main roads are labelled as follows:
A (Auto-estrada) Motorway
IP (Itinerário Principal) Primary Route
EN (Estrada Nacional) National Highway

● You have to pay a toll (**portagem**) on motorways. The road surface of unnumbered roads and some secondary roads can be very variable, and mountain roads can be dangerous in winter. Much of Portugal is mountainous, especially from the river Tagus northwards, so roads are often narrow and twisty – journeys can take much longer than you'd think from looking at a map.

● The main grades of petrol are **super** (4-star) and **normal** (2-star). Unleaded petrol (**gasolina sem chumbo**) is becoming more widely available. Diesel (**gasóleo** or **diesel**) is easily obtainable.

● Petrol stations are not generally self-service, so you'll need a few words of Portuguese. Many service stations close at 7.00 or 8.00 p.m. during the week and at 1.00 p.m. on Saturdays. Some stay open till midnight, and in large cities and on motorways a few offer a 24-hour service. Credit cards are not yet widely accepted.

● Parking in towns and cities can be difficult because of traffic congestion. Some car parks have an attendant, and there are meters and underground car parks in some cities. When parking in the street, you need to look out for No Parking signs, often placed on a building or near an entrance rather than at the edge of the pavement. The parking sign is a white 'P' on a dark blue background. But a word or initials added under the 'P' usually indicates that parking is reserved – e.g. 'P' with **Embaixada** underneath means that parking is reserved for a nearby embassy.

If you park illegally, you are likely to be fined and you may also have your car towed away by the police **reboque** (tow truck). If you do have it towed away, contact the police (**PSP – Polícia de Segurança Pública**) to find out where to collect it.

● You can arrange car hire in Britain and Ireland with the large international firms. They also have offices at airports and elsewhere in Portugal (and there will often be someone who speaks English). There are local companies too in most towns and cities – look for the sign **Aluguer de automóveis**.

● In case of breakdown, there are emergency telephones on motorways and some other main roads (see page 287).

If you have to tell a mechanic what's wrong with your vehicle, the easiest way is to indicate the part affected and say 'this isn't working': **isto não funciona**. Otherwise, look up the word for the appropriate part (see page 46).

You may see

Alfândega	Customs
Aluguer de automóveis	Car hire
Animais	Cattle
Atenção	Caution
Atenção ao comboio	Beware of the train
Auto-estrada (portagem)	(Toll) motorway
Bermas baixas	Low verges, no hard shoulder
Centro	Town/city centre
Circule com cuidado/ precaução	Drive with care
CP	Portuguese Railways
Curvas perigosas	Dangerous bends
Dar prioridade	Give way
Desvio	Diversion
Devagar	Slow
Entrada	Entrance
Escola	School
Estação de serviço	Service/petrol station
Estacionamento	Parking
Estrada em mau estado	Uneven road surface
Estrada vedada ao trânsito	Road closed
Fim de auto-estrada	End of motorway
Garagem	Garage
Importância a pagar	Amount due
Ligar os médios (no túnel)	Use dipped headlights (in tunnel)
Limite de velocidade	Speed limit
Mantenha o acesso livre	Keep access clear
Mantenha-se à direita	Keep right
Não impedir o acesso	Do not obstruct access
Não ultrapassar	No overtaking
Nevoeiro	Fog
Obras	Road works

Oficina	Repair shop
Outras direcções	Other directions
Pare	Stop
Passagem de nível	Level crossing
Peões	Pedestrians
Perigo	Danger
Portagem	Toll
Posto de primeiros socorros	First-aid post
Preço por litro	Price per litre
Prioridade à direita	Priority to the right
Proibido estacionar	No parking
Reduza a velocidade	Reduce speed
Rua sem saída	Cul de sac, no through road
Saída	Exit
Saída de camiões	Lorry exit
Saída de fábrica	Factory exit
Sentido proibido	No entry
Sentido único	One-way street
Trânsito local	Local traffic
Travessia de peões	Pedestrian crossing
Use os faróis	Use headlights
Uso obrigatório de cinto de segurança	Seatbelt compulsory
Veículos pesados	Heavy goods vehicles
Zona para peões	Pedestrian precinct

You may want to say

Petrol

Is there a petrol station around here?
Há uma estação de serviço aqui perto?
ah ooma ishtasowñ di sirveesoo akee pertoo

4-star
Super
sooper

2-star
Normal
normahl

Unleaded petrol
Gasolina sem chumbo
gazooleena saym shoomboo

Diesel
Gasóleo
gazolyoo

20 litres of 4-star, please
Vinte litros de super, por favor
veeñt leetroosh di sooper poor favohr

1,000 escudos' worth of unleaded petrol
Mil escudos de gasolina sem chumbo
meel ishkoodoosh di gazooleena saym shoomboo

Fill it up with 4-star/2-star
Encha com super/normal
ayñsha kohm sooper/normahl

A can of oil
Uma lata de óleo
ooma lahta di olyoo

Water, please
Água, por favor
ahgwa poor favohr

Could you check the pressure in the tyres?
Podia ver a pressão dos pneus?
poodeea ver a prisowñ doosh pnayoosh

Could you change the tyre?
Podia mudar o pneu?
poodeea moodahr oo pnayoo

Could you clean the windscreen?
Podia limpar oo pára-brisas?
poodeea leeñpahr oo pahra-breezash

Where is the air, please?
Onde é o ar, por favor?
ohñdee e oo ahr poor favohr

How does the car wash work?
Como funciona a lavagem automática?
kohmoo fooñsyona a lavahjaym owtoomahteeka

How much is it?
Quanto é?
kwañtoo e

Parking

Where can I/we park?
Onde se pode estacionar?
ohñd si pod ishtasyoonahr

Can I/we park here?
Pode-se estacionar aqui?
pod-si ishtasyoonahr akee

How long can I/we park here?
Por quanto tempo se pode estacionar aqui?
poor kwañtoo tayṁpoo si pod ishtasyoonahr akee

How much is it per hour?
Quanto é por hora?
kwañtoo e poor ora

Hiring a car

(*see* Days, months, dates, *page 188*)

I want to hire a car
Quero alugar um carro
keroo aloogahr ooṁ kahrroo

A small car, please
Um carro pequeno, por favor
ooṁ kahrroo pikaynoo poor favohr

A medium-sized car, please
Um carro médio, por favor
ooṁ kahrroo medyoo poor favohr

A large car, please
Um carro grande, por favor
ooṁ kahrroo grañd poor favohr

An automatic car, please
Um carro automático, por favor
ooṁ kahrroo owtoomahteekoo poor favohr

For three days
Por três dias
poor traysh deeash

For a week
Por uma semana
poor ooma simana

For two weeks
Por duas semanas
poor dooash simanash

From . . . to . . .
De . . . até . . .
di . . . ate . . .

From Monday to Friday
De segunda até sexta
di sigooñda ate sayshta

From 10th to 17th August
De dez até dezassete de Agosto
di dez ate dizaset di agohshtoo

How much is it?
Quanto é?
kwañtoo e

Per day/week
Por dia/semana
poor deea/simana

Per kilometre
Por quilómetro
poor keelomitroo

Is mileage (kilometrage) included?
Está incluída a quilometragem?
ishtah eeñklooeeda a keelohmitrahjayñ

Is petrol included?
Está incluída a gasolina?
ishtah eeñklooeeda a gazooleena

Is insurance included?
Está incluído o seguro?
ishtah eeñklooeedoo oo sigooroo

Comprehensive insurance cover
Seguro contra todos os riscos
sigooroo kohñtra tohdooz oosh rreeshkoosh

My husband/My wife is driving too
O meu marido/A minha mulher também vai conduzir
oo mayoo mareedoo/a meenya moolyer tambayñ viy kohñdoozeer

Do you take credit cards?
Aceita cartões de crédito?
asayta kartoyñsh di kredeetoo

Do you take traveller's cheques?
Aceita traveller's cheques?
asayta trahvilirs shekish

Can I leave the car in Oporto?
Posso deixar o carro no Porto?
posoo dayshahr oo kahrroo noo pohrtoo

Can I leave the car at the airport?
Posso deixar o carro no aeroporto?
posoo dayshahr oo kahrroo noo aeropohrtoo

How does it work?
Como é que funciona?
kohmoo e ki fooñsyona

Breakdowns and repairs

(*see* Car and bicycle parts, *page 46*)

My car has broken down
O meu carro está avariado
oo mayoo kahrroo ishtah avareeahdoo

Is there a garage around here?
Há uma garagem aqui perto?
ah ooma garahjaym̃ akee pertoo

Could you telephone a garage?
Podia telefonar para uma garagem?
poodeea tilifoonahr para ooma garahjaym̃

Could you send a mechanic?
Podia mandar um mecânico?
poodeea mañdahr oom̃ mikaneekoo

Could you tow me to a garage?
Podia-me rebocar para uma garagem?
poodeea-mi rribookahr para ooma garahjaym̃

Do you do repairs?
Faz reparações?
fahsh rriparasoyñsh

I don't know what's wrong
Não sei o que se passa
nowñ say oo ki si pahsa

I think . . .
Acho que . . .
ahshoo ki . . .

It's the clutch
É a embraiagem
e a aym̃briyahjaym̃

It's the radiator
É o radiador
e oo rrahdyadohr

It's the brakes
São os travões
sowñ oosh travoyñsh

The car won't start
O carro não pega
oo kahrroo nowñ pega

The battery is flat
A bateria está descarregada
a batireea ishtah dishkarrigahda

The engine is overheating
O motor está a aquecer muito
oo mootohr ishtah a akesayr mweeñtoo

It's losing water/oil
Está a perder água/óleo
ishtah a pirdayr ahgwa/olyoo

It has a puncture
Tem um furo
taym oom fooroo

I don't have any petrol
Não tenho gasolina
nown taynyoo gazooleena

The ... doesn't work
O/A ... não funciona
oo/a ... nown foonsyona

I need a ...
Preciso dum/duma ...
priseezoo doom/dooma ...

Is it serious?
É grave?
e grahv

Could you repair it (today)?
Podia repará-lo (hoje)?
poodeea rriparah-loo (ohj)

When will it be ready?
Quando está pronto?
kwandoo ishtah prohntoo

How much will it cost?
Quanto custa?
kwantoo kooshta

You may hear

Petrol

Que deseja?
ki dizayja
What would you like?

Quanto quer?
kwantoo ker
How much do you want?

A chave, por favor
a shahv, poor favohr
The key, please

Parking

Não pode estacionar aqui
nowñ pod ishtasyoonahr akee
You can't park here

**São cento e cinquenta
escudos por hora**
*sowñ sayñtoo ee seeñkwayñta
ishkoodoosh poor ora*
It's a hundred and fifty
escudos an hour

Não se paga
nowñ si pahga
You don't pay

É grátis
e grahteesh
It's free

**Há ali um parque de
estacionamento**
*ah alee ooñ pahrk di
ishtasyoonamayñtoo*
There's a car-park over
there

Hiring a car

Que tipo de carro deseja?
ki teepoo di kahrroo dizayja
What kind of car do you
want?

Por quanto tempo?
poor kwañtoo tayñpoo
For how long?

Por quantos dias?
poor kwañtoosh deeash
For how many days?

**(O preço) são dezoito mil/
noventa e um mil escudos**
*(oo praysoo) sowñ dizoytoo
meel/noovayñta ee ooñ meel
ishkoodoosh*
(The price) is 18,000/91,000
escudos

Por dia
poor deea
Per day

Por semana
poor simana
Per week

Quem conduz?
kayñ kohñdoosh
Who is driving?

A sua carta de condução, por favor
a sooa kahrta di kohñdoosowñ poor favohr
Your driving licence, please

Qual é a sua morada?
kwahl e a sooa moorahda
What is your address?

Aqui tem as chaves
akee taym ash shavish
Here are the keys

Por favor, devolva o carro com o depósito cheio
poor favohr divohlva oo kahrroo kohm oo dipozeetoo shayoo
Please return the car with a full tank

Por favor, devolva o carro antes das seis (horas)
poor favohr divohlva oo kahrroo añtish dash saysh (orash)
Please return the car before six o'clock

Breakdowns and repairs

Qual é o problema?
kwahl e oo prooblayma
What's wrong with it?

Podia abrir o capot?
poodeea abreer oo kahpoh
Could you open the bonnet?

Não tenho as peças necessárias
nowñ taynyoo ash pesash nisisahryash
I don't have the necessary parts

Tenho de encomendar as peças
taynyoo di ayñkoomayñdahr ash pesash
I will have to order the parts

Está pronto na próxima terça-feira
istah prohñtoo na proseema tayrsa-fayra
It will be ready by next Tuesday

São dez mil escudos
sowñ desh meel ishkoodoosh
It will cost 10,000 escudos

Car and bicycle parts

Accelerator	O acelerador	asiliradohr
Air filter	O filtro do ar	feeltroo doo ahr
Alternator	O alternador	ahltirnadohr
Battery	A bateria	batireea
Bonnet	O capot	kahpoh
Boot	O porta-bagagens	porta-bagahjaynsh
Brake cable	O cabo dos travões	kahboo doosh travoynsh
Brake fluid	O óleo dos travões	olyoo doosh travoynsh
Brakes (front/ rear)	Os travões (da frente/de trás)	travoyñsh (da frayñt/di trash)
Carburettor	O carburador	karbooradohr
Chain	A corrente	koorraynt
Choke	O regulador do ar	rrigooladohr doo ahr
Clutch	A embraiagem	aymbriyahjayñ
Cooling system	O sistema de arrefecimento	seeshtayma di arrefiseemayñtoo
Disc brakes	Os travões de disco	travoyñsh di deeshkoo
Distributor	O distribuidor	deeshtreebweedohr
Electrical system	O sistema eléctrico	seeshtayma ayletreekoo
Engine	O motor	mootohr
Exhaust pipe	O tubo de escape	tooboo di ishkahp
Fanbelt	A correia da ventoinha	koorraya da vayñtooeenya
Frame	O quadro	kwahdroo
Front fork	O garfo	gahrfoo
Fuel gauge	O indicador da gasolina	eeñdeekadohr da gazooleena
Fuel pump	A bomba da gasolina	bohṁba da gazooleena

Fuse/Fuses	O fusível/os fusíveis	*foozeevel/ foozeevaysh*
Gearbox	A caixa das velocidades	*kiysha dash vilooseedahdish*
Gear lever	A alavanca das mudanças	*alavañka dash moodañsash*
Gears	As mudanças	*moodañsash*
Handbrake	O travão de mão	*travowñ di mowñ*
Handlebars	O guiador	*geeadohr*
Headlights	Os faróis	*faroysh*
Heater	O aquecimento	*akeseemayñtoo*
Horn	A buzina	*boozeena*
Ignition	A ignição	*eegneesowñ*
Ignition key	A chave da ignição	*shahv da eegneesowñ*
Indicator	O pisca-pisca	*peeshka-peeshka*
Inner tube	A câmara de ar	*kamara di ahr*
Lights (front/ rear)	Os faróis (da frente/de trás)	*faroysh (da frayñt/di trahsh)*
Lock	A fechadura	*feshadoora*
Oil filter	O filtro de óleo	*feeltroo di olyoo*
Oil gauge	O indicador do óleo	*eeñdeekadohr doo olyoo*
Pedal/Pedals	O pedal/os pedais	*pidahl/pidiysh*
Points	Os platinados	*plateenahdoosh*
Pump	A bomba	*bohmba*
Radiator	O radiador	*rradyadohr*
Radiator hose (top/bottom)	O tubo (superior/ inferior) do radiador	*tooboo (soopireeohr/ eeñfireeohr) doo rradyadohr*
Reversing lights	As luzes de marcha atrás	*loozish di mahrsha atrahsh*
Saddle	O selim	*sileeñ*
Silencer	O silenciador	*seelayñsyadohr*
Spare wheel	A roda sobresselente	*rroda soobrisilayñt*

Spark plugs	As velas	*velash*
Speedometer	O velocímetro	*vilooseemitroo*
Spokes	Os raios	*riyoosh*
Starter motor	O motor de arranque	*mootohr di arrañk*
Steering	A direcção	*deeresowñ*
Steering wheel	O volante	*voolañt*
Transmission (automatic)	A transmissão (automática)	*trañshmeesowñ (owtoomahteeka)*
Tyre (front/rear)	O pneu (da frente/de trás)	*pnayoo (da frayñt/di trahsh)*
Valve	A válvula	*vahlvoola*
Warning light	A luz avisadora	*loosh aveezadohra*
Wheel (front/rear)	A roda (da frente/de trás)	*rroda (da frayñt/di trahsh)*
Wheel rim	O aro	*ahroo*
Window	A janela	*janela*
Windscreen	O pára-brisas	*pahra-breezash*
Windscreen washer	O lava vidros	*lahva veedroosh*
Windscreen wiper	O limpa pára-brisas	*leeḿpa pahra-breezash*

TAXIS

● You can hail taxis in the street, or find them at a taxi rank – look for a sign with a white T on a dark blue background. Taxis that are free have the sign **LIVRE**.

● Taxis have meters, but it's a good idea to ask what the fare will be approximately, especially if you are going some distance. Extras for luggage or for journeys between 10 p.m. and 6 a.m. may not be shown on the meter. A tip of 10% or so is usual.

● Write down clearly the address of your destination if it's at all complicated, so that you can show it to the taxi driver. In Portuguese, addresses are written with the street name first and the number afterwards, e.g. **Rua das Flores, 53**.

● On the island of Madeira, as well as the local taxis, you can still enjoy a more leisurely form of transport – the **carros de bois**, wickerwork sledges drawn by pairs of oxen through the cobbled streets of Funchal. For a more exciting toboggan ride, try the **carros de cesto** from Terreiro da Luta or Monte down to Funchal.

You may see

Feche devagar, obrigado	Close (door) gently, thank you
Importância a pagar	Amount due
Tomada de passageiros	Passenger pick-up

You may want to say

(see also Directions, page 28)

Is there a taxi rank around here?

Há uma praça de táxis aqui perto?

ah ooma prahsa di tahkseesh akee pertoo

I need a taxi

Preciso dum táxi

priseezoo doom tahksee

Could you call me a taxi?

Podia-me chamar um táxi?

poodeea-mi shamahr oom tahksee

Immediately

Imediatamente

eemidyahtamaynt

For tomorrow at nine o'clock

Para amanhã às nove horas

para ahmanyañ ahsh nov orash

To the airport, please

Para o aeroporto, por favor

para oo aeropohrtoo poor favohr

To the station, please

Para a estação, por favor

para a ishtasowñ poor favohr

To the Hotel Dom Pedro, please

Para o Hotel Dom Pedro, por favor

para oo otel dohm paydroo poor favohr

To this address, please

Para esta morada, por favor

para eshta moorahda poor favohr

Is it far?

Fica longe?

feeka lohñj

How much will it cost?

Quanto custa?

kwañtoo kooshta

I am in a hurry

Estou com pressa

ishtoh kohm presa

Stop here, please

Pare aqui, por favor

pahri akee poor favohr

Could you wait (a few minutes), please?

Podia esperar (alguns minutos), por favor?

poodeea ishpirahr (ahlgooñsh meenootoosh) poor favohr

How much is it?
Quanto é?
kwañtoo e

There is a mistake
Há um engano
ah ooñ ayñganoo

On the meter it says 500 escudos
No taxímetro diz quinhentos escudos
noo tahkseemitroo deesh keenyayñtooz ishkoodoosh

Keep the change
Fique com o troco
feeki kohñ oo trohkoo

That's all right
Está bem
ishtah baym

Could you give me a receipt?
Podia-me dar um recibo?
poodeea-mi dahr ooñ rriseeboo

For 1,000 escudos
De mil escudos
di meel ishkoodoosh

You may hear

Fica a dez quilómetros
feeka a desh keelomitroosh
It's 10 kilometres away

(São) mil e duzentos escudos
(sowñ) meel ee doozayñtooz ishkoodoosh
(It's) 1,200 escudos

Há um suplemento
ah ooñ sooplimayñtoo
There is a supplement

Para a bagagem
para a bagahjaym
For the luggage

Para cada mala
para kada mahla
For each suitcase

AIR TRAVEL

● Mainland Portugal and the islands of Madeira and the Azores have six main airports served by international and domestic flights, and a number of smaller regional airports.

● At airports and airline offices, you'll generally find someone who speaks English, but be prepared to say a few things in Portuguese.

● Approximate flight times from Lisbon to the other main airports:

Faro – 40 minutes
Oporto – 45 minutes
Funchal (Madeira) – 1½ hours
Ponta Delgada (Azores) – 2¼ hours
Terceira (Azores) – 2½ hours

You may see

Aeroporto	Airport
Alfândega	Customs
Aluguer de automóveis	Car hire
Apertar cintos	Fasten seatbelts
Atraso	Delay
Autocarros (para o centro)	Buses (to the town/city centre
Câmbio	Bureau de change
CEE	EEC
Check-in	Check-in
Chegadas	Arrivals
Colete salva-vidas	Life jacket
Embarque	Boarding
Entrada	Entrance
Free-shop	Duty-free shop

Greve	Strike
Hora local	Local time
Informações	Information
Lavatório	Toilet
Ligação voos domésticos	Domestic flight connections
Mercadorias a declarar	Goods to declare
Nada a declarar	Nothing to declare
Não fumar/Não fumadores	No smoking/Non-smoking
Outros passaportes	Other passports
Partidas	Departures
Passageiros	Passengers
Passaportes	Passports
Perdidos e achados	Lost property
Porta	Gate
Recolha de bagagens	Luggage reclaim
Saída (de emergência)	(Emergency) exit
Sala de embarque	Departure lounge
Transferências	Transfers
Voo	Flight
Voos domésticos/ internacionais	Domestic/international flights
WC	Toilets

You may want to say

(*see also* Numbers, *page 208*; Days, months, dates, *page 188*; Time, *page 192*)

Is there a flight (from Lisbon) to Oporto?
Há um voo (de Lisboa) para o Porto?
ah oom vohoo (di leeshboha) para oo pohrtoo

Today
Hoje
ohj

This morning/afternoon
Esta manhã/tarde
eshta manyañ/tahrd

Tomorrow (morning/
afternoon)
Amanhã (de manhã/à tarde)
*ahmanyañ (di manyañ/ah
tahrd)*

Do you have a timetable of
flights to Ponta Delgada?
**Tem um horário dos voos
para Ponta Delgada?**
*taym oom ohrahryoo doosh
vohoosh para pohñta
delgahda*

What time is the first flight
to Oporto?
**A que horas é o primeiro voo
para o Porto?**
*a ki oraz e oo preemayroo
vohoo para oo pohrtoo*

The next flight
O próximo voo
oo proseemoo vohoo

The last flight
O último voo
oo oolteemoo vohoo

What time does it arrive (at
Oporto)?
**A que horas chega (ao
Porto)?**
a ki orash shayga (ow pohrtoo)

A ticket/Two tickets to Faro,
please
**Um bilhete/Dois bilhetes
para Faro, por favor**
*oom beelyayt/doysh
beelyaytish para fahroo poor
favohr*

Single
Simples
seemplish

Return
Ida e volta
eeda ee volta

First class/Business class
**Primeira classe/Classe de
negócios**
*preemayra klahs/klahs di
nigosyoosh*

Economy class/Tourist class
**Classe económica/classe
turística**
*klahs ikoonomeeka/klahs
tooreeshteeka*

For the eleven o'clock flight
Para o voo das onze horas
para oo vohoo daz ohñzi orash

I want to change/cancel my
reservation
**Quero mudar/cancelar a
minha reserva**
*keroo moodahr/kañsilahr a
meenya rrizerva*

What is the number of the flight?

Qual é o número do voo?

*kwahl e oo **noomiroo** doo vohoo*

What time do I/we have to check in?

A que horas é o check-in?

a ki oraz e oo shek-een

Which gate is it?

Qual é a porta?

*kwal e a **porta***

Is there a delay?

Há atraso?

ah atrahzoo

Where is the luggage from the flight from London?

Onde está a bagagem do voo de Londres?

ohñd istah a bagahjaym̃ doo vohoo di loñdrish

My luggage is not here

A minha bagagem não está aqui

*a **meenya** bagahjaym̃ nowñ ishtah akee*

Is there a bus to the centre of town?

Há um autocarro para o centro?

*ah ooñ owtokahrroo **para** oo sayñtroo*

You may hear

Quer um lugar à janela?

ker ooñ loogahr ah janela

Would you like a seat by the window?

Quer um lugar junto ao corredor?

ker ooñ loogahr jooñtoo ow koorridohr

Would you like a seat on the aisle?

Fumadores ou não-fumadores?

foomadohrish oh nowñ-foomadohrish

Smoking or non-smoking?

O embarque é às . . .

oo aym̃bahrk e ahsh . . .

The flight will board at . . . (*time*)

Porta número sete

porta noomiroo set

Gate number seven

O seu bilhete, por favor
oo sayoo beelyayt poor favohr
Your ticket, please

O seu passaporte, por favor
oo sayoo pahsaport poor favohr
Your passport, please

O seu cartão de embarque, por favor
o sayoo kartowñ di ayñbahrk poor favohr
Your boarding card, please

Como é a sua bagagem?
kohmoo e a sooa bagahjayñ
What does your luggage look like?

Tem o talão de identificação?
tayñ oo talowñ di eedayñteefeekasowñ
Do you have the reclaim tag?

Announcements you may hear over the airport public address system

Words to listen for include:

Voo	vohoo	Flight
Destino	dishteenoo	Bound/destined for
Embarque (imediato)	ayñbahrk (eemideeahtoo)	Boarding (now)
Passageiro(s)	pasajayroo(sh)	Passenger(s)
Porta	porta	Gate
Atraso	atrahzoo	Delay
Partida	parteeda	Departure
Última chamada	oolteema shamahda	Last call

TRAVELLING BY TRAIN

● The Portuguese State railway company is the **CP** (*say pay*) – **Caminhos de Ferro Portugueses**. There are roughly 4,000 km of track and about 700 stations. Rail travel in Portugal can be an interesting way of seeing the countryside, and many older stations are attractively decorated with tiles (**azulejos**).

● You can travel to Portugal by train from Paris, either directly (the **Sud** express) or via Madrid, changing there to the **Lisboa** express or the **Lusitânia**.

● The fastest service within Portugal is the **Alfa** from Lisbon to Oporto (3¼ hours). For these trains, tickets with seat reservations must be booked in advance.

● Advance booking is advisable for other long-distance services too. Tickets may be bought up to ten days in advance at stations or travel agents. Don't try to buy your ticket on the train – the difference in price amounts to a heavy fine.

● Lisbon–Faro takes just over four hours, and starts with a short ferry-crossing from Terreiro do Paço to Barreiro, on the south bank of the Tagus. There is a frequent service westwards from Lisbon along the coast to Estoril and Cascais, starting from Cais do Sodré station. Trains for Sintra leave from Rossio station.

● Fares are cheaper on **Dias Azuis** (Blue Days). Other discounts are available through the **bilhete de família** (family ticket), **bilhete turístico** (tourist ticket), **cartão jovem** (youth card), etc. Information about European railcards is available from British Rail.

● Work out in advance what you're going to ask for (1st or 2nd class, single or return, adult or child tickets, etc.). If you just ask for 'a ticket' (**um bilhete**), it'll be assumed that you want a single (**ida**) unless you specify 'return' (**ida e volta**).

You may see

Acesso aos lugares . . . a . . .	Access to seats . . . to . . .
Atraso	Delay
Auto expresso	Car-train
Bilheteira	Ticket office
Bilhetes	Tickets
Cafeteria	Buffet
Camas	Sleepers
Caminhos de Ferro Portugueses (CP)	Portuguese Railways
Carruagem-cama	Sleeping-car
Chefe de estação	Station master
Chegadas	Arrivals
Comboios regionais	Main line trains
Comboios suburbanos	Suburban trains
Couchettes	Couchettes
Depósito de bagagem	Left-luggage
Destino	Destination
Diariamente	Daily
Dias azuis	Cheap travel days
Dias úteis	Weekdays
Entrada	Entrance
Fora de serviço	Out of service
Greve	Strike
Horário dos comboios	Train timetable
Intercidades	Intercity
Linha	Platform
Paragem em . . . e seguintes	Calling at . . . and following stations
Paragens	Calling at
Partidas	Departures
Penalidades por uso indevido	Penalties for improper use
Perdidos e achados	Lost property
Reserva com antecedência	Advance booking
Reservas	Reservations

Sábados, domingos e feriados	Saturdays, Sundays and holidays
Saída	Exit; departure
Sala de espera	Waiting room
Só para comboios de hoje	(Tickets) for today's trains
Venda de bilhetes	Tickets on sale here
WC Homens/Senhoras	Toilets Men/Women

You may want to say

Information

(*see* Time, *page 192*)

Is there a train to Covilhã?
Há um comboio para a Covilhã?
ah ooṁ kohṁboyoo para a kooveelyañ

Do you have a timetable of trains to Évora?
Tem um horário dos comboios para Évora?
taym ooṁ ohrahryoo doosh kohṁboyoosh para evoora

What time . . . ?
A que horas . . . ?
a ki orash . . .

What time is the train to Santarém?
A que horas é o comboio para Santarém?
a ki oraz e oo kohṁboyoo para sañtarayṁ

What time is the first train to Estoril?
A que horas é o primeiro comboio para o Estoril?
a ki oraz e oo preemayroo kohṁboyoo para oo ishtooreel

The next train
O próximo comboio
oo proseemoo kohṁboyoo

The last train
O último comboio
oo oolteemoo kohṁboyoo

What time does it arrive (at Guarda)?
A que horas chega (à Guarda)?
a ki orash shayga (ah gwahrda)

What time does the train from Oporto arrive?
A que horas chega o comboio do Porto?
a ki orash shayga oo kohm̃boyoo doo pohrtoo

The train to Coimbra, please?
O comboio para Coimbra, por favor?
oo kohm̃boyoo para kooeem̃bra poor favohr

Which platform does the train to Leiria leave from?
De que linha parte o comboio para Leiria?
di ki leenya pahrt oo kohm̃boyoo para layreea

Does this train go to Beja?
Este comboio vai para Beja?
aysht kohm̃boyoo viy para beja

Do I/Do we have to change trains?
É preciso mudar de comboio?
e priseezoo moodahr di kohm̃boyoo

Where?
Onde?
ohñd

Tickets

(*see* Time, *page 192*; Numbers, *page 208*)

One/Two to Sintra, please
Um/Dois para Sintra, por favor
oom̃/doysh para seeñtra poor favohr

One ticket/Two tickets to Cascais, please
Um bilhete/Dois bilhetes para Cascais, por favor
oom̃ beelyayt/doysh beelyaytish para kashkiysh poor favohr

Single
Simples
seem̃plish

Return
Ida e volta
eeda ee volta

For one adult/two adults
Para um adulto/dois adultos
para oom̃ adooltoo/doyz adooltoosh

(And) one child/two children
(E) uma criança/duas crianças
(ee) ooma kreeañsa/dooash kreeañsash

First/second class
Primeira/segunda classe
preemayra/sigoonda klahs

For the 10.00 train to Elvas
Para o comboio das dez horas para Elvas
para oo kohm̃boyoo dash dez orash para elvash

For the **Alfa** to Oporto
Para o Alfa para o Porto
para oo ahlfa para oo pohrto

I want to reserve a seat/two seats
Quero reservar um lugar/dois lugares
keroo rrizirvahr oom̃ loogahr/ doysh loogahrish

I want to reserve a sleeper
Quero reservar uma cama
keroo rrizirvahr ooma kama

I want to reserve a couchette
Quero reservar uma couchette
keroo rrizirvahr ooma kooshet

I want to book places on the car-train to Lisbon
Quero reservar lugares no auto expresso para Lisboa
keroo rrizirvahr loogahrish noo owtoshpresoo para leeshboha

For the car and two passengers
Para o carro e dois passageiros
para oo kahrroo ee doysh pasajayroosh

The car is a Renault 5
O carro é um Renault cinco
oo kahrroo e oom̃ rrinoh seeñkoo

Can I take my bicycle on the train?
Posso levar a minha bicicleta no comboio?
posoo livahr a meenya beeseekleta noo kohm̃boyoo

How much is it?
Quanto é?
kwañtoo e

Is there a supplement?
Há um suplemento?
ah oom̃ sooplimayñtoo

Left luggage

Can I leave this?
Posso deixar isto?
posoo dayshahr eeshtoo

Can I leave these two
suitcases until three o'clock?
**Posso deixar estas duas
malas até às três horas?**
*posoo dayshahr eshtash
dooash mahlash ate ahsh
trayz orash*

What time do you close?
A que horas fecha?
a ki orash fesha

On the train

I have reserved a seat
Tenho um lugar reservado
*taynyoo oofm loogahr
rrizirvahdoo*

I have reserved a sleeper/
couchette
**Tenho uma cama/couchette
reservada**
*taynyoo ooma kama/kooshet
rrizirvahda*

Is this seat taken?
Este lugar está ocupado?
*aysht loogahr ishtah
ohkoopahdoo*

Do you mind if I open the
window?
Importa-se que abra a janela?
eemporta-si ki ahbra a janela

Where is the restaurant car?
Onde é o restaurante?
ohñdee e oo rishtowrañt

Where is the sleeping-car?
Onde é a carruagem-cama?
vohñdee e a karrooahjaym̃-kama

Excuse me, may I get by?
Com licença
kohm̃ leesayñsa

May I smoke?
Posso fumar?
posoo foomahr

Where are we?
Onde estamos?
ohñd ishtamoosh

Are we at Entroncamento?
Estamos no Entroncamento?
*ishtamoosh noo
ayñtrohñkamayñtoo*

How long does the train
stop here?
**Quanto tempo é que o
comboio pára aqui?**
*kwañtoo taym̃poo e ki oo
kohm̃boyoo pahra akee*

Could you tell me when we
get to . . . ?
**Podia-me dizer quando
chegássemos a . . . ?**
*poodeea-mi deezayr kwañdoo
shegahsimooz a. . .*

You may hear

Information

(*see* Time, *page 192*)

Parte às dez e meia
*pahrt ahsh dez ee **maya***
It leaves at half past ten

Chega às dez para as quatro
*shayga ahsh desh **para** ash
kwahtroo*
It arrives at ten to four

**Tem de mudar de comboio
em . . .**
*taym̃ di moo**dahr** de
koh**m̃boyoo** aym̃ . . .*
You have to change trains
at . . .

É a linha número quatro
*e a **leen**ya noomiroo **kwahtroo***
It's platform number four

Tickets

(*see* Time, *page 192*; Numbers, *page 208*)

Para quando quer o bilhete?
*para **kwañdoo** ker oo bee**lyayt***
When do you want the
  ticket for?

Quando quer viajar?
*kwañdoo ker vee**a**jahr*
When do you want to travel?

Simples ou de ida e volta?
*see**m̃**pliz oh di **eeda** ee **volta***
Single or return?

Quando regressa?
*kwañdoo rri**gre**sa*
When are you coming back?

**(São) seiscentos e cinquenta
  escudos**
*(sowñ) saysh**sayñ**tooz ee
  seeñ**kwayñ**ta ish**koo**doosh*
(It's) 650 escudos

**Há um suplemento de mil e
  duzentos escudos**
*ah oom̃ sooplee**mayñ**too di meel
  ee doozayñtoosh
  ish**koo**doosh*
There is a supplement of
  1,200 escudos

BUSES, COACHES AND TRAMS

● As well as town and city bus services, there are many buses between towns and villages. In most cases you can pay the driver as you get on, though tickets for long-distance services can be bought at bus station ticket offices.

● If you intend to use the buses a lot in a town or city, you can buy **uma caderneta de módulos**, a multiple-journey ticket, or one of the various kinds of pass. These are available at bus company kiosks (**postos de venda**) and offices. In Lisbon, you can buy a combined bus/rail/underground travel card. Children under four travel free. There are no half-fares.

● On driver-only buses, you have to punch your own ticket in a machine as you move along the bus – otherwise the ticket is not valid.

● Lisbon's trams (**eléctricos**) deserve special mention – they are an efficient form of transport and a delightful way of seeing the city. Tram stops have the sign **PARAGEM** in large letters. Bus stops are also marked **PARAGEM** but the lettering is smaller, and the sign also carries the word **CARRIS**, the Lisbon bus company, and its logo – two overlapping circles.

You may see

Autocarro	Bus; coach
Bilheteira	Ticket office
Camioneta	Coach
Cobrança automatizada	Automatic ticket punch
Destino	Destination
Embarque	Boarding

Entrada	Entrance
Estação de autocarros	Bus station
Facilite os trocos	Have change ready
Horário	Timetable
Linha	Platform
Não distraia o motorista	Do not distract the driver's attention
Não fumar	No smoking
Paragem	Bus/tram stop
Partidas	Departures
Porta	Door; gate
Rodoviária Nacional (RN)	National Bus Company
Saída (de emergência)	(Emergency) exit
Venda de passes	Passes on sale

You may want to say

Information

(*for sightseeing bus tours, see* Sightseeing, *page 139*)

Where is the bus stop?
Onde é a paragem?
ohñdee e a parahjaym̃

Where is the bus station?
Onde é a estação de autocarros?
ohñdee e a ishtasowñ di owtokahrroosh

Is there a bus to the beach?
Há um autocarro para a praia?
ah oom̃ owtokahrroo para a priya

What number is the tram to the station?
Qual é o eléctrico para a estação?
kwahl e oo iletreekoo para a ishtasowñ

Do they go often?
São frequentes?
sowñ frikwayñtish

What time is the bus to Aljustrel?

A que horas é o autocarro para Aljustrel?

a ki oraz e oo owtokahrroo para aljooshtrel

What time is the first bus to Braga?

A que horas é o primeiro autocarro para Braga?

a ki oraz e oo preemayroo owtokahrroo para brahga

The next bus

O próximo autocarro

oo proseemoo owtokahrroo

The last bus

O último autocarro

oo oolteemoo owtokahrroo

What time does it arrive?

A que horas chega?

a ki orash shayga

Where does the bus to the town centre leave from?

De onde parte o autocarro para o centro?

dohñd pahrt oo owtokahrroo para oo sayñtroo

Does the bus to the airport leave from here?

É daqui que parte o autocarro para o aeroporto?

e dakee ki pahrt oo owtokahrroo para oo aeropohrtoo

Does this bus go to Aveiro?

Este autocarro vai para Aveiro?

aysht owtokahrroo viy para ahvayroo

I want to get off at the Museum

Quero sair no Museu

keroo saeer noo moozayoo

Could you tell me where to get off?

Podia-me dizer onde devo sair?

poodeea-mi deezayr ohñd dayvoo saeer

Is this the right stop for the cathedral?

É esta a paragem para a Sé?

e eshta a parahjaym para a se

The next stop, please

A próxima paragem, por favor

a proseema parahjaym poor favohr

Could you open the door,
please?
**Podia abrir a porta, por
favor?**
*poodeea abreer a porta poor
favohr*

Excuse me, may I get by?
Com licença!
kohm leesaynsa

Tickets

One/Two to the centre,
please
**Um/Dois para o centro, por
favor**
*oom/doysh para oo sayntroo
poor favohr*

A multiple-journey ticket,
please
**Uma caderneta de módulos,
por favor**
*ooma kadirnayta di
modooloosh poor favohr*

Where can I buy a multiple-
journey ticket?
**Onde posso comprar uma
caderneta de módulos?**
*ohnd posoo kohmprahr ooma
kadirnayta di modooloosh*

How much is it?
Quanto é?
kwantoo e

You may hear

**O autocarro para o centro
parte daquela paragem**
*oo owtokahrroo para oo
sayntroo pahrt dakela
parahjaym*
The bus to the centre leaves
from that stop there

**O cinquenta e sete vai para a
estação**
*oo seenkwaynta ee set viy para
a ishtasown*
The 57 goes to the station

Há um de dez em dez minutos
*ah oom di dez aym desh
meenootoosh*
There's one every ten
minutes

Parte às dez e meia
pahrt ahsh dez ee maya
It leaves at half past ten

Chega às três e vinte
shayga ahsh trayz ee veeñt
It arrives at twenty past three

Pode comprar uma caderneta de módulos no quiosque da CARRIS
pod kohm̃prahr ooma kadirnayta di modooloosh noo keeoshk da karreesh
You can buy a multiple-journey ticket at the bus company kiosk

Paga ao motorista
pahga ow mootooreeshta
You pay the driver

Vai sair aqui?
viy saeer akee
Are you getting off here?

Tem de sair na próxima (paragem)
taym̃ di saeer na proseema (parahjaym̃)
You have to get off at the next stop

Devia ter saído (uma paragem) antes
diveea tayr saeedoo (ooma parahjaym̃) añtish
You should have got off (one stop) before

UNDERGROUND TRAVEL

● Lisbon has an underground system, **o metro**. It is not very extensive, but it is a quick and convenient means of transport for the areas that it serves. It is very easy to find your way. There are plans of the system inside the stations, in the carriages, and on some maps of the city. Rush hours should be avoided.

● There is a fixed fare for any distance, so you only need to say how many tickets you want. You can buy ten tickets (**uma caderneta de dez**), at a reduced fare, at any **metro** ticket office. All stations have automatic ticket machines, with instructions in several languages, and tickets from these are cheaper. A combined rail/bus/underground travel card is available for use within the city of Lisbon.

● Children under four travel free. There are no half-fares.

● You have to punch your own ticket in a machine at the barrier leading from the ticket hall before you go down to the platform, otherwise the ticket is not valid.

You may see

Abertura emergência portas	To open doors in emergency
Átrio	Entrance concourse (*underground*)
Bilhetes	Tickets
Caminhe pela esquerda	Walk on the left
Correspondência ...	Change for ...
Destino	Destination
Entrada	Entrance
Mantenha-se à direita	Stand on the right
Metro/Metropolitano	Underground

Não fumar/Proibido fumar	No smoking
Não saia nem entre após aviso de fecho de portas	Do not get out or in after the signal that the doors are closing
Não se apoie na porta	Do not lean on the door
Não ultrapasse a faixa amarela	Do not cross the yellow line *(at edge of platform)*
Oblitere o seu bilhete	Punch your ticket
Penalidades por uso indevido	Penalties for improper use
Saída (de emergência)	(Emergency) exit
Só utilizar em caso de perigo	Use only if in danger
(Sinal de) alarme	Alarm (signal)
Validação de bilhetes	Ticket check

You may want to say

Is there an underground station around here?
Há uma estação de metro aqui perto?
ah ooma ishtasowñ di metroo akee pertoo

One/Two, please
Um/Dois, por favor
ooṁ/doysh poor favohr

Ten tickets, please
Uma caderneta de dez bilhetes, por favor
ooma kadirnayta di desh beelyaytish poor favohr

Which line is it for Sete Rios?
Qual é a linha para Sete Rios?
kwahl e a leenya para set reeoosh

Which stop is it for the Modern Art Centre?
Qual é a estaçâo para o Centro de Arte Moderna?
kwahl e a ishtasowñ para o sayñtroo di ahrt mooderna

Does this train go to Saldanha?
Este metro vai para o Saldanha?
aysht metroo viy para oo sahldanya

Where are we?
Onde estamos?
ohñd ishtamoosh

Is this the stop for the Luz stadium?
É esta a estação para o Estádio da Luz?
e eshta a ishtasowñ para oo ishtahdyoo da loosh

You may hear

É a linha do Colégio Militar
e a leenya doo koolejyoo meeleetahr
It's the Colégio Militar line

É a próxima estação
e a proseema ishtasowñ
It's the next stop

Devia ter saído (uma estação) antes
diveea tayr saeedoo (ooma ishtasowñ) añtish
You should have got off (one stop) before

BOATS AND FERRIES

● There are river ferries, some taking cars, on the Tagus, the Sado (Setúbal-Tróia), the Guadiana (between the Algarve and Spain), and the Minho. There is a hydrofoil service from Funchal (Madeira) to Porto Santo, and boat connections between some of the islands of the Azores.

You may see

Barcos	Boats
Cais	Quay
Colete salva-vidas	Life jacket
Embarque	Embarcation
Ferry-boat	Ferry
Passeios de barco	Boat trips
Porto	Port, harbour

You may want to say

Information
(*see* Time, *page 192*)

Is there a boat to the
   Berlengas (today)?
**Há um barco para as
   Berlengas (hoje)?**
*ah ooṁ bahrkoo para
   ash birlayñgash (ohj)*

Is there a car ferry to Tróia?
Há um ferry para Tróia?
ah ooṁ ferree para troya

Are there any boat trips?
Há passeios de barco?
ah pasayoosh di bahrkoo

What time is the boat to
   Faial?
**A que horas é o barco para o
   Faial?**
*a ki oraz e oo bahrkoo para
   oo faeeahl*

What time is the first boat?
A que horas é o primeiro barco?
a ki oraz e oo preemayroo bahrkoo

The next boat
O próximo barco
oo proseemoo bahrkoo

The last boat
O último barco
oo oolteemoo bahrkoo

What time does it arrive?
A que horas chega?
a ki orash shayga

What time does it return?
A que horas regressa?
a ki orash rrigresa

How long does the crossing take?
Quanto dura a travessia?
kwañtoo doora a traviseea

Where does the boat to Pico leave from?
De onde sai o barco para o Pico?
dohñd siy oo bahrkoo para oo peekoo

Where can I buy tickets?
Onde posso comprar os bilhetes?
ohñd posoo kohmprahr oosh beelyaytish

What is the sea like today?
Como está o mar hoje?
kohmoo ishtah oo mahr ohj

Tickets
(*see* Numbers, *page 208*)

Four tickets to Cacilhas, please
Quatro bilhetes para Cacilhas, por favor
kwahtroo beelyaytish para kaseelyash poor favohr

Two adults and two children
Dois adultos e duas crianças
doyz adooltooz ee dooash kreeañsash

Single
Simples
seemplish

Return
Ida e volta
eeda ee volta

I'd like to book tickets for the ferry to Tróia
Queria reservar bilhetes para o ferry para Tróia
kireea rrizirvahr beelyaytish para oo ferree para troya

For a car and two passengers
Para um carro e dois passageiros
para ooñ kahrroo ee doysh pasajayroosh

How much is it?
Quanto é?
kwañtoo e

You may hear

Há barcos às terças e sextas
ah bahrkooz ahsh tayrsaz ee sayshtash
There are boats on Tuesdays and Fridays

O barco para o Faial sai às nove
oo bahrkoo para oo faeeahl siy ahsh nov
The boat to Faial leaves at nine o'clock

Regressa às quatro e meia
rrigresa ahsh kwahtroo ee maya
It returns at half past four

O barco para o Montijo sai da estação do Terreiro do Paço
oo bahrkoo para oo mohñteejoo siy da ishtasowñ doo tirrayroo doo pahsoo
The boat to Montijo leaves from Terreiro do Paço station

O mar está calmo
oo mahr ishtah kahlmoo
The sea is calm

O mar está bravo
oo mahr ishtah brahvoo
The sea is rough

AT THE TOURIST OFFICE

● There are tourist information offices in most towns and cities – look for the sign **Turismo**. There will often be someone who speaks English.

● Tourist offices have leaflets about sights worth seeing, lists of hotels, town plans and regional maps, and can supply information about opening times and local transport. They can also book hotel rooms for you.

● Tourist office opening hours in main towns are generally 9 a.m. to 7 p.m. Mondays to Fridays, and 9 a.m. to 5 p.m. on Saturdays and Sundays. Some close for lunch from 12.30 until 2 p.m.

You may want to say

(*see* Directions, *page 28*; Sightseeing, *page 139*;
Time, *page 192*)

Where is the tourist office?
Onde é o posto de turismo?
ohñdee e oo pohshtoo di tooreeshmoo

Do you speak English?
Fala inglês?
fahla eeñglaysh

Do you have . . . ?
Tem . . . ?
tayñ . . .

Do you have a plan of the city?
Tem um mapa da cidade?
tayñ ooñ mahpa da seedahd

Do you have a map of the area?
Tem um mapa da região?
*tayñ ooñ **mahp**a da **rrijeeowñ***

Do you have a list of hotels?
Tem uma lista de hotéis?
*tayñ **ooma leesh**ta di otaysh*

Do you have a list of campsites?
Tem uma lista de parques de campismo?
*tayñ **ooma leesh**ta di **pahr**kish di **kañpeesh**moo*

Could you recommend a cheap hotel?
Podia recomendar um hotel barato?
*poodeea rrikoomayñ**dahr** ooñ otel **barah**too*

Could you book a hotel for me, please?
Podia-me reservar um hotel, por favor?
*poodeea-mi rrizir**vahr** ooñ otel poor fa**vohr***

Could you recommend a traditional restaurant?
Podia-me recomendar um restaurante típico?
*poodeea-mi rrikoomayñ**dahr** ooñ rishtow**rañt tee**peekoo*

Where can I/we hire a car?
Onde se pode alugar um carro?
*ohñd si pod aloo**gahr** ooñ **kahr**roo*

What is there to see here?
O que há aqui de interesse?
*oo ki ah a**kee** de eeñti**ray**si*

Do you have any leaflets?
Tem brochuras?
*tayñ broh**shoo**rash*

Do you have any information about . . . ?
Tem informações sobre . . . ?
*tayñ eeñfoorma**soyñsh sohb**ri . . .*

Where is the naval museum?
Onde é o Museu da Marinha?
ohñdee e oo moozayoo da mareenya

Could you show me on the map?
Podia-me indicar no mapa?
poodeea-mi eeñdeekahr noo mahpa

When is the museum open?
Quando é que o museu está aberto?
kwañdoo e ki oo moozayoo ishtah abertoo

Are there any excursions?
Há excursões?
ah ishkoorsoyñsh

You may hear

Posso ajudar?
posoo ajoodahr
Can I help you?

Quanto tempo cá vai ficar?
kwañtoo taympoo kah viy feekahr
How long are you going to be here?

Precisa de ajuda?
priseeza di ajooda
Do you need help?

Em que hotel está?
* aym ki otel ishtah*
What hotel are you in?

É inglês/inglesa?
e eeñglaysh/eeñglayza
Are you English?

Que categoria de hotel queria?
ki katigooreea di otel kireea
What kind of hotel would you like?

Donde é?
dohñdee e
Where are you from?

É/Fica na parte antiga da cidade
e/feeka na pahrt añteega da seedahd
It's in the old part of town

Aqui tem
akee taym
Here you are

ACCOMMODATION

● Portugal offers a wide range of accommodation. For fuller details of what is available, in Britain contact the Portuguese National Tourist Office, and in Portugal the **Instituto de Promoção Turística** (addresses, page 206).

● Hotels and guest houses usually have a plaque at the door with an initial for the type of establishment and the grade.

Hotels (**hotel – H**) are graded from one to five stars according to facilities. The **pensão (P)**, graded from one to four stars, is a more modest guest house. Hotels and guest houses that call themselves **residência** or **residencial (R)** offer bed and breakfast only.

For motorists there are also a few roadside motels (**motel**), graded either two or three stars.

Youth hostels are **pousadas de juventude**.

● There is a network of over 30 State-owned luxury hotels called **pousadas**, many of them in restored historical buildings (castles, palaces and monasteries). In the high season, stays are limited to three days, but at other times of year you can stay for longer. Advance booking is advisable, through a travel agent or **ENATUR** (address, page 206).

● In country areas, especially in the north, there are various types of private accommodation where you are treated as a more personal family guest: manor houses (**Turismo de Habitação**), local houses typical of the area (**Turismo Rural**), and farms (**Agroturismo**). Houses licensed by the tourist authorities have a plaque at the door with the letters **TER – Turismo no Espaço Rural**.

● If you're travelling around, you can get lists of hotels from local tourist offices, and they will probably also be able to make a booking for you.

● There are plenty of campsites all over Portugal, especially along the coasts. They are graded from one to four stars. Tourist offices have lists, or you can buy a complete guide (**O Roteiro Campista**), written in several languages. It is advisable to have a Camping Carnet.

If you want to camp elsewhere, check the local regulations – for instance, camping may not be allowed in forest areas because of the danger of fire.

● When you book in somewhere, you will usually be asked for your passport and may be asked to fill in a registration card.

You may see

Abrigo	Mountain shelter
Água potável	Drinking water
1º andar	1st floor
2º andar	2nd floor
Banho	Bath
Camas	Beds
Casa de banho	Toilet; bathroom
Cave	Basement
Chuveiros	Showers
Completo	Full up, no vacancies
Corrente eléctrica	Electricity
Elevador	Lift
Entrada	Entrance
Estalagem	Inn
Garagem	Garage
Hotel (H)	Hotel
Hotel Residência (HR)	Hotel, guest house (*no restaurant*)
Lavandaria	Laundry

Lixo	Rubbish
Meia pensão	Half board
Não deitar lixo	Do not dump rubbish
Parque de Campismo	Campsite
Pensão (P)	Guest house
Pensão completa	Full board
Piscina	Swimming pool
Pousada	State-owned luxury hotel
Pousada de juventude	Youth hostel
Proibido acampar	No camping
Proibido acampar com caravana	No caravans
Proibido fazer lume	Do not light fires
Quartos (vagos)	Rooms (vacant)
Recepção	Reception
Rés-do-chão (R/C)	Ground floor
Residência (R)	Hotel, guest house (*no restaurant*)
Restaurante	Restaurant
Saída (de emergência)	(Emergency) exit
Sala	Lounge
Sala de jantar	Dining-room
Sala de televisão	Television room
Serviço de quartos	Room service
Tarifa	Charge, tariff
Toque a campainha	Please ring the bell

You may want to say

Booking in and out

I've reserved a room
Tenho um quarto reservado
*taynyoo oom kwahrtoo
rrizirvahdoo*

I've reserved two rooms
**Tenho dois quartos
reservados**
*taynyoo doysh kwahrtoosh
rrizirvahdoosh*

I've reserved a place/space
Tenho um lugar reservado
taynyoo ooᵐ loogahr rrizirvahdoo

My name is . . .
Chamo-me . . .
shamoo-mi . . .

Do you have a room?
Tem um quarto?
tayᵐ ooᵐ kwahrtoo

A single room
Um quarto individual
ooᵐ kwahrtoo eeñdeeveedwahl

A double room
Um quarto duplo
ooᵐ kwahrtoo dooploo

For one night
Para uma noite
para ooma noyt

For two nights
Para duas noites
para dooash noytish

With bath/shower
Com banho/duche
kohᵐ banyoo/doosh

Can I see the room?
Posso ver o quarto?
posoo vayr oo kwahrtoo

Do you have space for a tent?
Tem lugar para uma tenda?
tayᵐ loogahr para ooma tayñda

Do you have space for a caravan?
Tem lugar para uma caravana?
tayᵐ loogahr para ooma karavana

How much is it?
Quanto é?
kwañtoo e

Per night
Por noite
poor noyt

Per week
Por semana
poor simana

Is there a reduction for children?
Há desconto para crianças?
ah dishkohñtoo para kreeañsash

Is breakfast included?
O pequeno almoço está incluído?
oo pikaynoo ahlmohsoo ishtah eeñklooeedoo

It's too expensive
É muito caro
e mweeñtoo kahroo

Do you have anything cheaper?
Tem algo mais barato?
tayᵐ ahlgoo miysh barahtoo

Do you have anything
bigger/anything smaller?
**Tem algo maior/algo mais
pequeno?**
*taym ahlgoo miyor/ahlgoo
miysh pikaynoo*

I'd like to stay another night
Queria ficar mais uma noite
kireea feekahr miyz ooma noyt

I am leaving tomorrow
morning
Saio amanhã de manhã
siyoo ahmanyañ di manyañ

The bill, please
A conta, por favor
a kohñta poor favohr

Do you take credit cards?
Aceita cartões de crédito?
asayta kartoyñsh di kredeetoo

Do you take traveller's
cheques?
Aceita traveller's cheques?
asayta trahvilirs shekish

Could you recommend a
hotel in Tomar?
**Podia-me recomendar um
hotel em Tomar?**
*poodeea-mi rrikoomayñdahr
ooñ otel ayñ toomahr*

Could you phone them to
make a booking, please?
**Podia-lhes telefonar para
fazer uma reserva, por
favor?**
*poodeea-lyish tilifoonahr para
fazayr ooma rrizerva poor
favohr*

In hotels

(*see* Problems and complaints, *page 166*; Time, *page 192*)

Where can I/we park?
Onde se pode estacionar?
ohñd si pod ishtasyoonahr

Do you have a cot for the
baby?
Tem um berço para o bebé?
taym ooñ bayrsoo para oo bebe

Is there room service?
Há serviço de quartos?
ah sirveesoo di kwahrtoosh

Do you have facilities for
the disabled?
**Há facilidades para
deficientes?**
*ah faseeleedahdish para
difeesyayñtish*

What time is breakfast?
**A que horas é o pequeno
almoço?**
*a ki oraz e oo pikaynoo
ahlmohsoo*

Can I/we have breakfast in the room?
Pode-se tomar o pequeno almoço no quarto?
pod-si toomahr oo pikaynoo ahlmohsoo noo kwahrtoo

What time is dinner?
A que horas é o jantar?
a ki oraz e oo jañtahr

What time does the hotel close?
A que horas fecha o hotel?
a ki orash fesha oo otel

I'll be back very late
Voltarei muito tarde
vohltaray mweeñtoo tahrd

(Key) number 42, please
(A chave) número quarenta e dois, por favor
(a shahv) noomiroo kwarayñta ee doysh poor favohr

Are there any messages for me?
Há algum recado para mim?
ah ahlgooñ rrikahdoo para meeñ

Where is the bathroom?
Onde é a casa de banho?
ohñdee e a kahza di banyoo

Where is the dining-room?
Onde é a sala de jantar?
ohñdee e a sahla di jañtahr

Can I leave this in the safe?
Posso deixar isto no cofre?
posoo dayshahr eeshtoo noo kofri

Could you get my things from the safe?
Podia-me tirar as coisas do cofre?
poodeea-mi teerahr ash koyzash doo kofri

Could you call me at eight o'clock?
Podia-me chamar às oito horas?
poodeea-mi shamahr ahz oytoo orash

Could you call me a taxi?
Podia-me chamar um táxi?
poodeea-mi shamahr ooñ tahksee

For right now
Para agora mesmo
para agora mayshmoo

For tomorrow at nine o'clock
Para amanhã às nove
para ahmanyañ ahsh nov

Could you clean a suit for me?
Podia-me limpar um fato?
poodeea-mi leeñpahr ooñ fahtoo

Could you find me a babysitter?
Podia-me arranjar uma ama?
poodeea-mi arrañjahr ooma ama

Could you put it on the bill?
Podia pôr na conta?
poodeea pohr na kohñta

I need another pillow
Preciso de outra almofada
priseezoo dohtra ahlmoofahda

Room number 21
Quarto número vinte e um
kwahrtoo noomiroo veeñt ee oom

I need a towel
Preciso duma toalha
priseezoo dooma tooahlya

At campsites

Is there a campsite around here?
Há um parque de campismo aqui perto?
ah oom pahrk di kaṁpeeshmoo akee pertoo

Where are the dustbins?
Onde são os contentores do lixo?
ohñd sowñ oosh kohñtayñtohrish doo leeshoo

Can I/we camp here?
Pode-se acampar aqui?
pod-si akaṁpahr akee

Is the water drinkable?
A água é potável?
a ahgwa e potahvel

Where can I/we park?
Onde se pode estacionar?
ohñd si pod ishtasyoonahr

Where is the laundry-room?
Onde é a lavandaria?
ohñdee e a lavandareea

Where are the showers?
Onde são os chuveiros?
ohñd sowñ oosh shoovayroosh

Where is there an electric point?
Onde há uma tomada?
ohñdee ah ooma toomahda

Where are the toilets?
Onde são as casas de banho?
ohñd sowñ ash kahzash di banyoo

Self-catering accommodation

(*see* Directions, *page 28*; Problems and complaints, *page 166*)

I have rented a villa
Aluguei uma casa
aloogay ooma kahza

It's called Casa do Moinho
Chama-se Casa do Moinho
shama-si kahza doo mooeenyoo

I have rented an apartment
Aluguei um apartamento
aloogay oom apartamayñtoo

We're in number 11
Estamos no número onze
ishtahmoosh noo noomiroo ohñz

My name is . . .
Chamo-me . . .
shamoo-mi . . .

What is the address?
Qual é a morada?
kwahl e a moorahda

How do I/we get there?
Como se vai para lá?
kohmoo si viy para lah

Could you give me the key?
Podia-me dar a chave?
poodeea-mi dahr a shahv

Where is . . .
Onde é . . .
ohñdee e . . .

Where is the stopcock?
Onde é a torneira de segurança?
ohñdee e a toornayra di sigoorañsa

Where is the fusebox?
Onde é a caixa dos fusíveis?
ohñdee e a kiysha doosh foozeevaysh

How does the cooker work?
Como funciona o fogão?
kohmoo fooñsyona oo foogowñ

How does the water-heater work?
Como funciona o esquentador?
kohmoo fooñsyona oo ishkayñtadohr

Is there air conditioning?
Há ar condicionado?
ah ahr kohñdeesyoonahdoo

Is there a spare gas bottle?
Há outra garrafa de gás?
ah ohtra garrahfa di gahsh

Is there any more bedding?
Há mais roupa de cama?
ah miysh rrohpa di kama

What day do they come to clean?

Em que dia fazem a limpeza?

aym̃ ki deea fahzaym̃ a leem̃payza

Where do I/we put the rubbish?

Onde se deixa o lixo?

ohñd si daysha oo leeshoo

When do they come to collect the rubbish?

Quando vêm recolher o lixo?

kwañdoo vayaym̃ rrikoolyayr oo leeshoo

Where can I contact you?

Onde o posso contactar?
  (to a man)

ohñdi oo posoo kohñtaktahr

Onde a posso contactar?
  (to a woman)

ohñdi a posoo kohñtaktahr

You may hear

Posso ajudar?

posoo ajoodahr

Can I help you?

Qual é o seu nome, por favor?

kwahl e oo sayoo nohm poor favohr

Your name, please?

Por quantas noites?

poor kwañtash noytish

For how many nights?

Para quantas pessoas?

para kwañtash pisohash

For how many people?

Com (casa de) banho ou sem (casa de) banho?

kohm̃ (kahza di) banyoo oh saym̃ (kahza di) banyoo

With bath(room) or without bath(room)?

É uma tenda grande ou pequena?

e ooma tayñda grañd oh pikayna

Is it a large or a small tent?

Lamento, está cheio

lamayñtoo ishtah shayoo

I'm sorry, we're full

O passaporte, por favor
oo pahsaport poor favohr
Your passport, please

Assine aqui, por favor
aseen akee poor favohr
Sign here, please

Liga-se assim
leega-si aseem
You switch it on like this

Apaga-se assim
apahga-si aseem
You switch it off like this

Vêm todos os dias
vayaym tohdooz oosh deeash
They come every day

Vêm às sextas(-feiras)
vayaym ahsh sayshtash(-fayrash)
They come on Fridays

TELEPHONES

● There are telephone boxes in the streets, and also in many cafés. You can telephone abroad from any public telephone, and instructions are in English as well as Portuguese. You can also make long-distance calls from post offices.

● Public telephones take 10-, 20-, and 50-escudo coins. There's a groove on the top of the telephone where you line up coins. Lift the receiver, dial the number, and the coins will drop into the slot when the call is answered.

Telephones operated by phone-cards are becoming widely available.

● To call abroad, first dial **00** (for Europe), then the code for the country – for the UK it's **44**. Follow this with the town code minus the initial **0**, and then the number you want. For example: for a Central London number, dial **00 44 71**, then the number.

● If you want to make a reverse charge call to the UK, dial **0505 00 44** and you will get straight through to the UK operator. The number for the local international operator is 099.

Instructions you may see in a phone box:

Coloque na calha as moedas necessárias	Place the necessary coins in the groove
Levante o auscultador	Lift the receiver
Aguarde o sinal de marcar	Wait for the dialling tone
Marque o número desejado	Dial the number you want
Coloque moedas quando a lâmpada piscar	Add more coins when the light flashes
Use moedas de …	Use coins of…

And on older equipment:

Tire o auscultador Lift the receiver
Introduza na caixa uma ou Insert one or more coins in
  mais moedas the box

You may see

Avariado Out of order
Chamadas internacionais International calls
Chamadas locais Local calls
Chamadas nacionais Long-distance calls
  interurbanas
Indicativo Code
Lista telefónica Telephone directory
Páginas amarelas Yellow pages
Telefone Telephone

You may want to say

Is there a telephone?
Há um telefone?
ah oom tilifon

Where is the telephone?
Onde é o telefone?
ohñdee e oo tilifon

Do you have change for the
  telephone, please?
Tem moedas para o telefone,
  por favor?
taym mwedash para oo tilifon
  poor favohr

A telephone card, please
Um credifone, por favor
oom kredeefon poor favohr

Do you have a telephone
  directory?
Tem uma lista telefónica?
taym ooma leeshta tilifoneeka

I want to call England
Quero ligar para a Inglaterra
keroo leegahr para a eeñglaterra

Mr Garcia, please
O senhor Garcia, por favor
oo sinyohr garseea poor favohr

Extension number 121, please
Extensão número cento e vinte e um, por favor
ishtayñsowñ noomiroo sayñtoo ee veeñt ee ooñ poor favohr

My name is . . .
Chamo-me . . .
shamoo-mi . . .

It's . . . speaking
Fala . . .
fahla . . .

When will he/she be back?
Quando volta?
kwañdoo volta

I'll call later
Ligo mais tarde
leegoo miysh tahrd

Can I hold, please?
Posso esperar, por favor?
posoo ispirahr poor favohr

Can I leave a message?
Posso deixar um recado?
posoo dayshahr ooñ rrikahdoo

Please tell him/her that . . . called
Por favor, diga-lhe que telefonou . . .
poor favohr deega-lyi ki tilifoonoh . . .

I am in the Hotel da Praia
Estou no Hotel da Praia
ishtoh noo otel da priya

My telephone number is . . .
O meu número de telefone é o . . .
oo mayoo noomiroo di tilifon e oo . . .

Could you ask him/her to call me?
Podia-lhe pedir que me telefonasse?
poodeea-lyi pideer ki mi tilifoonahsi

Could you repeat that, please?
Podia repetir, por favor?
poodeea rripiteer poor favohr

More slowly, please
Mais devagar, por favor
miysh divagahr poor favohr

Sorry, I've got the wrong number
Desculpe, é engano
dishkoolpi e ayñganoo

We have been cut off/The line has gone dead
A chamada caiu
a shamahda kaeeoo

How much is the call?
Quanto é a chamada?
kwañtoo e a shamahda

What is the number for calling a taxi?
Qual é o número para chamar um táxi?
kwahl e o noomiroo para shamahr oom tahksee

You may hear

Está?
ishtah
Hello?

Estou
ishtoh
Hello

Quem fala?
kaym fahla
Who's calling?

Um momento, por favor
oom moomayñtoo poor favohr
One moment, please

Não desligue
nowñ dishleegi
Hold the line

Espere, por favor
ishperi poor favohr
Please wait

Estou a fazer a ligação
ishtoh a fazayr a leegasowñ
I'm putting you through

A linha está impedida
a leenya ishtah eeṁpideeda
The line's engaged

Quer esperar?
ker ishpirahr
Do you want to hold on?

Ninguém responde
neeñgayṁ rrishpohñd
There's no answer

Não está
nowñ ishtah
He/She is not in

É engano
e ayñganoo
You've got the wrong
    number

CHANGING MONEY

● The Portuguese unit of currency is the **escudo**, made up of 100 **centavos**. The symbol used is the dollar sign **$**, placed between the escudos and the centavos, e.g. **2$50** (two escudos fifty centavos), **250$00** (two hundred and fifty escudos). There are coins of $50 (50 centavos) and 1, 2$50, 5, 10, 20, 50, 100 and 200 escudos. There are banknotes of 100, 500, 1,000, 5,000 and 10,000 escudos.

● You can change money, traveller's cheques or Eurocheques into escudos at banks and other places (hotels, travel agencies, etc.) where you see a **câmbio** sign.

● Banks are open from 8.30 a.m. to 3 p.m. Mondays to Fridays, and are closed on Saturdays.

● In banks, you go first to the **câmbio** desk, where a form is filled in for you to sign. You then get your money from the cashier (**caixa**). You may be asked for the name of your hotel or the address you're staying at. In Portugal, addresses are given with the street name first and the number afterwards, e.g. **Rua de Camões, 73**.

● There is an extensive network of cash dispensers outside banks, many of which can be operated with credit cards or Eurocheque cards – check with your British bank for details. Instructions are in English as well as Portuguese.

Instructions you may see on a cash dispenser:

Introduza o seu cartão	Insert your card
Cartão não introduzido na posição correcta	Card not correctly inserted
Marque o código pessoal	Key in your PIN number

Escolha a operação no teclado	Select the service you require
Qual é a importância que deseja levantar?	How much do you want to withdraw?
Operação em curso	Your transaction is being processed
Deseja continuar?	Do you want another transaction?
Sim/Não	Yes/No
Retire o cartão	Take your card
Espere um momento, por favor	Please wait
Retire o seu dinheiro e o talão	Take your cash and receipt

You may see

Aberto	Open
Banco	Bank
Caixa	Cashier
Caixa automática	Cash dispenser
Câmbio	Exchange, Bureau de change
Encerrado	Closed
Entrada	Entrance
Fechado	Closed
Saída	Exit

You may want to say

I'd like to change some pounds sterling
Queria cambiar libras esterlinas
kireea kambyahr leebraz ishtirleenash

I'd like to change some traveller's cheques
Queria cambiar traveller's cheques
kireea kambyahr trahvilirs shekish

I'd like to change a Eurocheque
Queria cambiar um Eurocheque
kireea kambyahr oom ayooroshek

I'd like to get some money with this credit card
Queria levantar dinheiro com este cartão de crédito
kireea livañtahr deenyayroo kohm aysht kartowñ di kredeetoo

What's the exchange rate today?
Qual é o câmbio de hoje?
kwahl e oo kambyoo di ohj

Could you give me some change, please?
Podia-me dar trocos, por favor?
poodeea-mi dahr trokoosh poor favohr

Could you give me five 1,000-escudo notes?
Podia ser em cinco notas de mil escudos?
poodeea sayr aym seeñkoo notash di meel ishkoodoosh

I'm at the Hotel Boa Vista
Estou no Hotel Boa Vista
ishtoh noo otel boha veeshta

I'm at the Sol apartments
Estou nos apartamentos Sol
ishtoh nooz apartamayñtoosh sol

I'm staying with friends
Fico em casa de amigos
feekoo aym kahza di ameegoosh

The address is Rua do Campo Alegre, 25
A morada é Rua do Campo Alegre, 25
a moorahda e rrooa doo kampoo alegri veeñt ee seeñkoo

You may hear

Quanto quer cambiar?
kwañtoo ker kambyahr
How much do you want to change?

O seu passaporte, por favor
oo sayoo pahsaport poor favohr
Your passport, please

A sua morada, por favor?
a sooa moorahda poor favohr
Your address, please?

Como se chama o hotel, por favor?
kohmoo si shama oo otel poor favohr
What's the name of your hotel, please?

Assine aqui, por favor
aseen akee poor favohr
Sign here, please

Por favor, vá à caixa
poor favohr vah ah kiysha
Please go to the cashier

EATING AND DRINKING

● To order something, all you need do is name it, and say 'please', adding 'for me', 'for him' or 'for her' if you're ordering for several people, to show who wants what.

If you're ordering more than one of something, in most cases add -s to the end of the word to make it plural, e.g. café – cafés, sopa – sopas, bife – bifes. (For the plural of words ending in -ão, -l or -m, see page 175.)

● The various kinds of cafés and bars serve both alcoholic and soft drinks. Opening hours vary according to local demand – closing earlier in small towns or rural areas, later in cities. There are no age restrictions for going into bars, only for being served alcohol. The usual arrangement is that you pay for all your drinks and so on when you're ready to leave, but in some self-service cafés, canteens, and ice-cream parlours, you will see the sign pré-pagamento, indicating that you need to pay at the till in advance, before collecting what you want.

● There is an official classification system for restaurantes, which reflects the range and prices of the dishes offered. The four categories are luxury, 1st class, 2nd class and 3rd class. The class of the restaurant is indicated at the entrance, often on a ceramic tile, and the menu, too, is normally posted near the door.

Restaurant prices include VAT (IVA) and service, but an extra tip of about 5% is appreciated.

● Portuguese breakfast is likely to consist of bread rolls or croissants, butter and jam, and cheese or cooked ham. The jams may include marmelada, quince jelly, which is particularly delicious when home made. (The word for quince is

marmelo, and **marmelada** is the origin of the English word 'marmalade'.)

Lunch is usually served between 12.30 p.m. and 2.00 p.m., and dinner between 7.30 p.m. and 9.30 p.m. The Portuguese often have a late afternoon snack (**lanche**).

● Helpings tend to be generous, and you may sometimes find that it is adequate to ask for two portions to share between three. Occasionally menus offer the option of either a full portion (**uma dose**) or half (**meia dose**).

● Snack-bars often serve **pratos combinados**, which are set dishes of things like ham and eggs or chicken and chips. These are numbered on the menu, and you just ask for the number you want.

● Coffee is usually the espresso type, very strong and served in small cups. If you want a small black coffee ask for **um café** (you may also hear it called **uma bica**, especially in the Lisbon area). A small white coffee is **um garoto**, or, in Oporto and the north, **um pingo**. If you want a larger white coffee (tea-cup size), ask for **uma meia de leite**. A glass of hot milk with a little coffee is **um galão**.

● Tea (**chá**) comes on its own – you usually have to ask if you want it with milk (**chá com leite**) or lemon (**chá com limão**). Herbal teas are also available. For a wider choice of teas, look out for a tea-room, **salão de chá**.

● A refreshing alternative to tea is **chá de limão** or 'lemon tea', an infusion of lemon.

● There are about 30 wine-producing areas in Portugal, including Madeira and the Azores. Ten of these are officially 'demarcated' regions – Bairrada, Dão, Vinho Verde, etc. – where the definition and quality of the product is carefully controlled. In addition to the demarcated regions, there are also many excellent local wines at reasonable prices. The house wine (**o vinho da casa**) in restaurants is usually good quality and value – all you need specify is red (**tinto**) or white (**branco**).

You may find that the wine list (**a lista dos vinhos**) makes a distinction between **vinhos maduros** (mature wines) and **vinhos verdes** (young or 'green' wines). The familiar **vinho verde** is a white, slightly sparkling wine, that goes well with fish and seafood. The **verde** in the name refers to the wine's youth rather than its colour – it is ready for drinking a few months after the vintage, and does not mature with age. In the **vinho verde** region, in the north-east of Portugal, you can find both white and red 'green' wines! Both are very acidic.

● Port wine is world famous. The grapes are grown on the terraced slopes of the upper Douro valley, between Peso da Régua and the Spanish border. In the spring following the vintage, the wine is taken down to mature for many years in the port cellars of Vila Nova da Gaia. This is situated on the south bank of the Douro facing Oporto, the city which gives the wine its name – **vinho do Porto**. The cellars themselves are well worth a visit, or you can select from the many types of port available in the elegant surroundings of the **Solar do Vinho do Porto** in either Oporto or Lisbon.

● Portugal's other famous fortified wine is Madeira, which takes its name from the island that produces it. There are four main types: **Boal** and **Malmsey** or **Malvasia**, both of which are sweet, **Verdelho**, which is slightly sweet, and **Sercial**, which is dry.

● Beer (**cerveja**) is of the light lager type, though sometimes a dark version is available (**cerveja preta**). If you order **uma cerveja**, you will be brought a bottle. You may be asked which of two or three brands you want. For a glass of draught lager, ask for **uma imperial** (or, if you want two, **duas imperiais**). If you want a glass of draught lager in Oporto or the north of Portugal, ask for **um fino**.

• There is enormous regional variety in Portuguese cooking, and the full range can be found in Lisbon and other main cities. In smaller towns, menus may offer more local fare.

On menus, you will come across the words **à . . .** or **à moda de . . .** in the names of many dishes. Both phrases mean 'in the style of . . .', e.g. **Leitão assado à Bairrada** (Roast sucking pig Bairrada style), **Tripas à moda do Porto** (Tripe Oporto style).

In restaurants you will often be served immediately with one or two small cheeses to nibble at while your order is being prepared.

In the south and along the coasts, there is usually excellent fish and seafood. For a combination of fish and shellfish, try one of the many variations of **caldeirada** – fish stew. In the Algarve, some seafood dishes are cooked in and served from a **cataplana**, a round copper pan that can be tightly closed to seal in the flavours during cooking. Portuguese cooking makes ample use of fresh coriander, **coentro**, particularly with certain fish and seafood dishes.

In the interior, especially in the centre and north, fresh fish may not be readily available. Typical dishes here are often based on meat, especially pork, or on some of the many varieties of spiced sausage. There are a number of traditional stews of meat and vegetables, e.g. **cozido à portuguesa**.

Dried salt cod, **bacalhau**, is a Portuguese speciality. However, the claim that there are 365 different **bacalhau** dishes, one for every day of the year, may be a slight exaggeration!

• There is an impressive range of tempting sweet dishes, pastries and cakes in the **pastelarias**, or cafés that specialise in pastries. Common ingredients are eggs, almonds (grown particularly in the Algarve) and cinnamon. As you travel round, it is worth looking out for local specialities such as **pastéis de Belém** (custard tarts) in the Belém district of Lisbon and **queijadas** (cheesecakes) in Sintra and Madeira.

You may see

Aberto diariamente/todos os dias	Open every day
Adega	Wine cellar
Cervejaria	Bar, pub
Comida regional	Regional specialities
Cozinha portuguesa/ internacional	Portuguese/international cuisine
Ementa turística	Tourist menu, set-price menu
Encerra à segunda-feira	Closed on Mondays
Lista	Menu
Marisqueira	Seafood restaurant
Casa de banho	Toilet
Prato do dia	Dish of the day
Pratos combinados	Set dishes
Pré-pagamento	Payment in advance
Restaurante	Restaurant
Salão de chá	Tea-room
Sala de jantar	Dining-room
Tasca	Bar; cheap restaurant
Taverna	Tavern, bar

You may want to say

General phrases

Is there an inexpensive restaurant around here?
Há algum restaurante não muito caro aqui perto?
ah ahlgoom rrishtowrañt nowñ mweeñtoo kahroo akee pertoo

A (one) . . . , please
Um/Uma . . . , por favor
oom/ooma . . . poor favohr

Another . . . , please
Outro/Outra . . . , por favor
ohtroo/ohtra . . . poor favohr

More . . . , please
Mais . . . , por favor
miysh . . . poor favohr

For me
Para mim
para meem

For him/her
Para ele/ela
para ayl/ela

For them
Para eles/elas
para aylish/elash

This one, please
Este, por favor
aysht poor favohr

Two of these, please
Dois destes, por favor
doysh dayshtish poor favohr

Do you have . . . ?
Tem . . . ?
taym . . .

Is/Are there any . . . ?
Há . . . ?
ah . . .

What is there to eat?
O que há para comer?
oo ki ah para koomayr

What is there for dessert?
O que há para sobremesa?
oo ki ah para soobrimayza

What do you recommend?
O que aconselha?
oo ki akohñsaylya

Do you have any typical
  local dishes?
Tem algum prato regional?
*taym ahlgoom prahtoo
  rrijyoonahl*

What is this?
Que é isto?
ki e eeshtoo

How do you eat this?
Como se come isto?
kohmoo si kom eeshtoo

Cheers!
Saúde!
saood

Enjoy your meal!
Bom apetite!
bohm apiteet

Nothing else, thanks
Mais nada, obrigado/a
miysh nahda ohbreegahdoo/a

The bill, please
A conta, por favor
a kohñta poor favohr

Where is the toilet?
Onde é a casa de banho?
ohndee e a kahza di banyoo

Cafés and bars

A black coffee, please
Um café, por favor
ooṁ kafe poor favohr

Two white coffees, please
Dois garotos, por favor
doysh garohtoosh poor favohr
Dois pingos, por favor
(Oporto and the north)
doysh peeṅgoosh poor favohr

A tea with milk/lemon, please
Um chá com leite/limão, por favor
ooṁ shah kohṁ layt/leemowṅ poor favohr

A lemon tea, please
Um chá de limão, por favor
ooṁ shah di leemowṅ poor favohr

Mineral water, please
Uma água mineral, por favor
ooma ahgwa meenirahl poor favohr

Fizzy/Still
Com gás/Sem gás
kohṁ gahsh/sayṁ gahsh

A fizzy orange, please
Uma laranjada, por favor
ooma laraṅjahda poor favohr

What fruit juices do you have?
Que sumos de fruta tem?
ki soomoosh di froota tayṁ

An orange juice, please
Um sumo de laranja, por favor
ooṁ soomoo di laraṅja poor favohr

A beer, please
Uma cerveja, por favor
ooma sirvayja poor favohr

Two draught beers, please
Duas imperiais, por favor
dooash eeṁpireeiysh poor favohr
Dois finos, por favor
(in the north)
doysh feenoosh poor favohr

A glass of red wine, please
Um copo de vinho tinto, por favor
ooṁ kopoo di veenyoo teeṅtoo poor favohr

A gin and tonic, please
Um gin-tónico, por favor
ooṁ jeeṅ-toneekoo poor favohr

With ice
Com gelo
kohṁ jayloo

What bar snacks do you have?
Que petiscos tem?
ki piteeshkoosh taym

Some olives, please
Azeitonas, por favor
azaytohnash poor favohr

Some crisps, please
Batatas fritas, por favor
batahtas freetash poor favohr

A (large) portion of grilled squid
Uma dose de lulas grelhadas
ooma doz di loolash grilyahdash

What sandwiches do you have?
Que sandes tem?
ki sañdish taym

A ham sandwich, please
Uma sandes de fiambre, por favor
ooma sañdish di feeambri poor favohr

Boiled ham/Cured ham
Fiambre/Presunto
feeambri/prizooñtoo

Two cheese sandwiches, please
Duas sandes de queijo, por favor
dooash sañdish di kayjoo poor favohr

Do you have ice-creams?
Tem gelados?
taym jilahdoosh

What flavours do you have?
Que sabores tem?
ki sabohrish taym

A chocolate/vanilla one, please
Um de chocolate/baunilha, por favor
oom di shookoolaht/ bowneelya poor favohr

Booking a table

I want to reserve a table for two people
Quero reservar uma mesa para duas pessoas
keroo rrizirvahr ooma mayza para dooash pisohash

For eight o'clock
Para as oito
para az oytoo

For tomorrow at half past seven
Para amanhã às sete e meia
para ahmanyañ ahsh set ee maya

I have booked a table
Tenho uma mesa reservada
*taynyoo ooma mayza
rrizirvahda*

The name is . . .
Em nome de . . .
aym nohm di . . .

In restaurants

A table for four, please
**Uma mesa para quatro,
por favor**
*ooma mayza para kwahtroo
poor favohr*

On the terrace, if possible
Na esplanada, se possível
na ishplanahda si pooseevel

Waiter!/Waitress!
Faz favor!
fahsh favohr

The menu, please
A lista, por favor
a leeshta poor favohr

The wine list, please
A carta de vinhos, por favor
*a kahrta di veenyoosh poor
favohr*

Do you have a set menu?
Tem ementa turística?
taym imaynta tooreeshteeka

Do you have vegetarian
dishes?
Tem pratos vegetarianos?
*taym prahtoosh
vijitareeanoosh*

Set dish number three,
please
**O prato número três, por
favor**
*oo prahtoo noomiroo traysh
poor favohr*

The set menu, please
A ementa turística, por favor
*a imaynta tooreeshteeka poor
favohr*

For the first course . . .
Para o primeiro prato . . .
para oo preemayroo prahtoo . . .

Fish soup, please
Sopa de peixe, por favor
sohpa di paysh poor favohr

Two mixed hors-d'œuvres,
please
**Dois aperitivos variados, por
favor**
*doysh apireeteevoosh
vareeahdoosh poor favohr*

For the second course . . .
Para o segundo prato . . .
para oo sigooñdoo prahtoo . . .

Pork chop, please
Costeleta de porco, por favor
kooshtilayta di pohrkoo poor favohr

Scabbard fish, please
Peixe-espada, por favor
paysh-ishpahda poor favohr

Are vegetables included?
Os legumes estão incluídos?
oosh ligoomish ishtowñ eeñklooeedoosh

With chips
Com batatas fritas
kohm batahtash freetash

And a mixed/lettuce salad
E uma salada mista/de alface
ee ooma salahda meeshta/di ahlfahs

For dessert . . .
Para sobremesa . . .
para soobrimayza . . .

Crème caramel, please
Pudim flan, por favor
poodeem flañ poor favohr

A peach, please
Um pêssego, por favor
ooñ paysigoo poor favohr

What cheeses do you have?
Que queijos tem?
ki kayjoosh taym

Excuse me, where is my steak?
Desculpe, onde está o meu bife?
dishkoolp ohñd ishtah oo mayoo beef

More bread, please
Mais pão, por favor
miysh powñ poor favohr

More chips, please
Mais batatas fritas, por favor
miysh batahtash freetash poor favohr

A glass/A bottle of water
Um copo/Uma garrafa de água
ooñ kopoo/ooma garrahfa di ahgwa

A bottle of red house wine
Uma garrafa de vinho tinto da casa
ooma garrahfa di veenyoo teeñtoo da kahza

Half a bottle of white wine
Meia garrafa de vinho branco
maya garrahfa di veenyoo brañkoo

It's very good
Está muito bom
ishtah mweeñtoo bohm

It's really delicious
Está delicioso
ishtah dileeseeyohzoo

This is burnt
Isto está queimado
eeshtoo ishtah kaymahdoo

This is not cooked
Isto está cru
eeshtoo ishtah kroo

No. I ordered the chicken
Não. Pedi o frango
nown pidee oo frañgoo

The bill, please
A conta, por favor
a kohñta poor favohr

Do you accept credit cards?
Aceita cartões de crédito?
asayta kartoyñsh di kredeetoo

Do you accept traveller's cheques?
Aceita traveller's cheques?
asayta trahvilirs shekish

Excuse me, there is a mistake here
Desculpe, há aqui um engano
dishkoolp ah akee oom ayñganoo

You may hear

Cafés and bars

Que deseja(m)?
ki dizayja/dizayjowñ
What would you like?

Que quer(em) tomar?
ki ker/kerayñ toomahr
What would you like to have?

Com gelo?
kohñ jayloo
With ice?

Fresco ou natural?
frayshkoo oh natoorahl
Chilled or room-temperature?

Com ou sem gás?
kohñ oh sayñ gahsh
Fizzy or still?

Grande ou pequeno?
grañd oh pikaynoo
Large or small?

Qual prefere?
kwahl prifer
Which do you prefer?

Temos . . .
taymoosh . . .
We have . . .

Restaurants

Quantos são?
kwañtoosh sowñ
How many are you?

Para quantas pessoas?
para kwañtash pisohash
For how many people?

Só um momento
so oofñ moomayñtoo
Just a moment

Tem uma mesa reservada?
tayñ ooma mayza rrizirvahda
Have you booked a table?

Tem de esperar dez minutos
tayñ di ishpirahr desh meenootoosh
You will have to wait ten minutes

Não se importa de esperar?
nowñ si eeñporta di ishpirahr
Would you mind waiting?

Que deseja(m)?
ki dizayja/dizayjowñ
What would you like?

Deseja(m) um aperitivo?
dizayja/dizayjowñ oofñ apireeteevoo
Would you like an aperitif?

Recomendamos . . .
rrikoomayñdamoosh . . .
We recommend . . .

Para o primeiro prato
para oo preemayroo prahtoo
For the first course

Para o segundo prato
para oo sigooñdoo prahtoo
For the second course

Para beber?
para bibayr
To drink?

Quer o bife bem passado ou mal passado?
ker oo beef bayñ pasahdoo oh mahl pasahdoo
Do you want your steak well done or rare?

Para quem é o/a . . . ?
para kayñ e oo/a . . .
Who is the . . . for?

Terminou?/Terminaram?
tirmeenoh/tirmeenahrowñ
Have you finished?

Deseja(m) sobremesa? E café?
dizayja/dizayjowñ soobrimayza ee kafe
Would you like dessert? And coffee?

Mais alguma coisa?
miyz ahlgooma koyza
Anything else?

MENU READER

General phrases

Acepipes	Tit-bits
Adega	Wine cellar
Águas minerais	Mineral waters
Almoço	Lunch
Aves e caça	Poultry and game
Bebidas (alcoólicas)	(Alcoholic) drinks
C/ = com	With
Carnes	Meat dishes
Cervejas	Beers
Conta	Bill
Couvert	Cover charge
Cozinha	Kitchen; cooking, cuisine
Doces	Sweets, desserts
Dose	Portion
Ementa	Menu
Ementa turística	Set menu
Entradas	Starters
Frutas	Fruit
IVA incluído	Including VAT
Jantar	Dinner
Lanche	Afternoon snack
Licores	Spirits, liqueurs
Lista	Menu
Lista de vinhos	Wine list
Mariscos	Seafood
Meia dose	Half portion
Ovos	Egg dishes
Pão e manteiga	Bread and butter
Peixes	Fish

Pequeno almoço	Breakfast
Petiscos	Snacks
Prato do dia	Dish of the day
Pratos combinados	Set dishes
Pré-pagamento	Payment in advance
Queijos	Cheeses
Refeições	Meals
Refrigerantes	Soft drinks
Saladas	Salads
Sandes	Sandwich(es)
Sanduíches	Sandwiches
Serviço (não) incluído	Service (not) included
Sobremesas	Desserts
Sopas	Soups
Sumos	Fruit juices
Vinhos (brancos/tintos/rosés)	Wines (white/red/rosé)

Drinks

Água mineral	Mineral water
com gás/sem gás	fizzy/still
Água tónica	Tonic water
Aguardente	Spirit
Bagaceira	Grape spirit
Batido de leite	Milkshake
Bica	Small black coffee
Brandy	Brandy
Café	Coffee
com leite	white
descafeinado	decaffeinated
instantâneo	instant
Carioca	Weak coffee
Cerveja	Beer
de barril	draught
preta	dark

Chá	Tea
com leite/limão	with milk/lemon
de ervas	herb
de limão	lemon infusion
de tília	linden blossom
Champanhe	Champagne
Cimbalino	Small black coffee
Colheita	Vintage
Conhaque	Cognac, brandy
Doce	Sweet
Engarrafado	Bottled
Galão	Large milky coffee
Garoto	Small white coffee
Garrafa	Bottle
Garrafeira	Specially selected *(on wine labels)*
Gelo	Ice
Gin	Gin
Ginjinha	Cherry liqueur
Gin-tónico	Gin and tonic
Laranjada	Orange squash
Leite	Milk
Limonada	Lemonade
Medronho	Arbutus berry liqueur
Mosto	Grape juice
Região demarcada	Demarcated area *(on wine labels)*
Reserva	Specially selected *(on wine labels)*
Sangria	Wine and fruit punch
Seco	Dry
Sidra	Cider
Soda	Soda
Sumo	Juice
de alperce/ananás/laranja/	apricot/pineapple/orange/

limão/maracujá/pera/	lemon/passion fruit/pear/
pêssego/tomate/toranja	peach/tomato/grapefruit
Uísque	Whisky
Vermute	Vermouth
Vinho	Wine
branco	white
da Madeira	Madeira
do Porto	Port
espumante	sparkling
maduro	mature
moscatel	muscatel
rosé	rosé
tinto	red
verde	'green', young
Vodka	Vodka
Whisky	Whisky

Food

Abacate	Avocado
Abóbora	Pumpkin
Açafrão	Saffron
Açorda	Bread soup
à alentejana	Alentejo style *(with garlic)*
de marisco	with seafood
Agrião (*pl.* **agriões**)	Watercress
Aipo	Celery
Alcachofra	Artichoke
Alface	Lettuce
Alheira	Garlic sausage
Alho	Garlic
Almôndegas	Meatballs
Alperce	Apricot

Amêijoas	Clams; cockles
à Bulhão Pato	with garlic and coriander
à portuguesa	cooked in olive oil with garlic and parsley
na cataplana	with cured ham and spiced sausage
Ameixa	Plum
Amêndoa	Almond
Amendoim (*pl.* amendoins)	Peanut
Amora	Blackberry; mulberry
Ananás	Pineapple
Anchova	Anchovy
Anona	Custard apple
Arenque	Herring
Arroz	Rice
de atum	with tuna
de frango	with chicken
de marisco	with seafood
doce	rice pudding with lemon and cinnamon
Assado/a	Roast
Atum	Tuna
Aveia	Oats
Avelã	Hazelnut
Azeite	Olive oil
Azeite e vinagre	Oil and vinegar
Azeitonas	Olives
Bacalhau	Salt cod
à Brás	with eggs, potatoes and onions
à Gomes de Sá	with onions, potatoes and black olives
Bacon	Bacon
Banana	Banana
Batata doce	Sweet potato

Batatas	Potatoes
fritas	chips; crisps
Baunilha	Vanilla
Beringela	Aubergine
Besugo	Bream
Beterraba	Beetroot
Bifanas	Small steak in sandwich
Bife	Steak
Biqueirões	Anchovies
Biscoito	Biscuit
Bitoque	Steak and fried egg
Bolacha	Biscuit
Bolo	Cake
podre	spiced honey cake
rei	Portuguese Christmas cake
Boqueirões	Anchovies
Borrego	Lamb
Brasa: na brasa	Barbecued
Broa	Maize bread; cornmeal cake
Cabrito	Kid
Cachorro-quente	Hot dog
Caju	Cashew nut
Calamar	Squid
Calda: em calda	In syrup
Caldeirada	Fish stew
Caldo	Consommé
de galinha	Chicken consommé
verde	Green cabbage and potato broth
Camarão (*pl.* **camarões**)	Shrimp; prawn
Canela	Cinnamon
Canja de galinha	Chicken soup
Caracóis	Snails
Caranguejo	Crab
Carapau	Horse mackerel
Caril	Curry

Carne	Meat
de vaca	beef
de vitela	veal
picada	mince
de porco	pork
à alentejana	Alentejo style pork
	(*with cockles*)
Carneiro	Mutton
Casa: da casa	Of the house
Caseiro/a	Home-made
Castanha	Chestnut
Cataplana	Round, copper pan
	with tight-fitting lid
Cavala	Mackerel
Cebola	Onion
Cebolada	Onion sauce
Cenoura	Carrot
Centeio	Rye
Cereja	Cherry
Cesto de frutas	Basket of fruit
Cevada	Barley
Champignons	Mushrooms
Chanfana	Braised kid or lamb in red
	wine
Cherne	Bass
Chocolate	Chocolate
Chocos	Cuttlefish
com tinta	cooked in their ink
Chouriço	Garlic and paprika sausage
Churrasco: no churrasco	Barbecued
Churrasco de vaca	Barbecued steak
de porco	barbecued pork
Coco	Coconut
Codorniz	Quail
Coelho	Rabbit
Coentro	Coriander

Cogumelos	Mushrooms
Compota	Compote
Consomé	Consommé
Corvina	Type of fish
Coscorões	Fritters
Costeleta	Chop
Couve	Cabbage
Couves de Bruxelas	Brussels sprouts
Couve-flor	Cauliflower
Cozido/a	Boiled
Cozido à portuguesa	Meat and vegetable stew
Cravinhos	Cloves
Creme de camarão	Cream of shrimp/prawn soup
Crepes	Pancakes
Croquete	Croquette
Dia: do dia	Of the day
Dobrada	Tripe with chickpeas
Eirós	Eels
Enchido	Sausage
Enguias	Eels
Ensopado	Stew
de borrego	lamb stew
de enguias	eel stew
Entrecosto	Entrecôte
Época: da época	In season
Ervilhas	Peas
Escabeche	Marinade for fish
Escalfado/a	Poached
Escalope	Escalope
Espadarte	Swordfish
Espargos	Asparagus
Esparguete	Spaghetti
Espetada	Kebab
Espinafre	Spinach
Estufado/a	Stewed
Faisão	Pheasant

Farófias	Egg whites in milk (*dessert*)
Farturas	Fritters
Favas	Broad beans
Febras de porco	Lean pork slices
Feijão	Beans
Feijoada	Beans and meat stew
Fiambre	Boiled ham
Fígado	Liver
Figo	Fig
Filete	Fillet
Filhós	Fritters
Fios de ovos	Sugared threads of egg yolk
Flocos de aveia	Oatflakes
Folhado	Puff pastry
Forno: no forno	Baked
Framboesa	Raspberry
Frango	Chicken
assado	roast
no espeto	grilled on a spit
na púcara	casseroled
Fresco/a	Fresh; chilled
Frigideira: na frigideira	Fried
Frio/a	Cold
Frito/a	Fried
Fruta da época	Fruit in season
Fumado/a	Smoked
Galinha	Boiling fowl
Galinhola	Woodcock
Gamba	Prawn
Ganso	Goose
Gaspacho à alentejana	Chilled soup of tomato, peppers and cucumber
Gelado	Ice-cream
Gengibre	Ginger
Ginja	(Morello) cherry

Goraz	Bream
Grão de bico	Chickpeas
Grelhado/a	Grilled
Grelos	Turnip tops
Groselha	Currant; blackcurrant
Guisado	Stew
Hamburguer	Hamburger
Hortaliças	Green vegetables
Inhame	Yam, sweet potato
Iogurte	Yoghurt
Iscas	Liver marinated in wine
Jardineira: à jardineira	With mixed vegetables
Javali	Wild boar
Lagosta	Lobster
Lagostim	Crayfish
Lampreia	Lamprey
Laranja	Orange
Lavagante	Lobster
Lebre	Hare
Legumes	Vegetables
Leitão	Sucking pig
Leite	Milk
Leite creme	Dessert made with milk, egg yolks and vanilla flavouring
Lentilha	Lentil
Lima	Lime
Limão	Lemon
Língua	Tongue
Linguado	Sole
Linguiça	Spiced sausage
Lombo	Loin
Lulas	Squid
de caldeirada	in a stew
recheadas	stuffed

Maçã	Apple
assada	baked
Maçaroca	Corn cob
Macarrão	Macaroni
Macedónia de frutas	Fruit salad
Maionese	Mayonnaise
Manteiga	Butter
Mãos de vitela à jardineira	Calf's foot stew
Maracujá	Passion fruit
Marisco	Seafood
Marmelada	Quince jelly
Marmelo	Quince
Mel	Honey
Melancia	Water melon
Melão	Melon
Meloa	Melon
Merengue	Meringue
Mero	Grouper
Mexilhão (*pl.* mexilhões)	Mussel
Milho	Maize, corn
Miolos	Brains
Misto/a	Mixed
Miúdos	Offal
Molho	Sauce
béchamel	béchamel
ao Madeira	Madeira
Morangos	Strawberries
com chantilly	with whipped cream
Morcela	Black pudding with cumin
Mortadela	Garlic sausage
Mostarda	Mustard
Mousse de chocolate	Chocolate mousse
Nabo	Turnip
Nata	Cream
Natural	Natural; at room temperature

ao natural	cooked in its own juice
Nêspera	Medlar, loquat
Noz	Walnut
Noz-moscada	Nutmeg
Óleo	Oil
Omeleta	Omelette
de cogumelos	mushroom
de fiambre	cooked ham
simples	plain
Orelha de porco	Pig's ear
Ostras	Oysters
Ovo	Egg
cozido	boiled
escalfado	poached
estrelado	fried
mexido	scrambled
quente	soft-boiled
Ovos moles	'Soft eggs' – egg yolk dessert
Paio	Smoked ham sausage
Panado/a	Fried in breadcrumbs
Pão	Bread
de centeio	rye
de milho	maize
integral	wholemeal
Pão-de-ló	Sponge cake
Papaia	Pawpaw
Pargo	Sea bream
Passa	Raisin
Passado/a:	
bem passado/a	Well done (*steak*)
mal passado/a	Rare (*steak*)
Pastel (*pl.* **pastéis**)	Cake; pastry; rissole
pastel de nata	custard tart
pastéis de bacalhau	salt cod rissoles
Pato	Duck

Pato bravo	Wild duck
Peixe-espada	Scabbard fish
Pepino	Cucumber
Pêra	Pear
Perca	Perch
Percebes	Barnacles
Perdiz	Partridge
Perna	Leg
Pêro	Type of apple
Peru	Turkey
Pés de porco	Pig's trotters
Pescada	Hake
Pêssego	Peach
Pimenta	Pepper (*seasoning*)
Pimento	Pepper (*vegetable*)
Piripíri	Chilli and olive oil seasoning
Polvo	Octopus
Pombo	Pigeon
Prego (no pão)	Steak sandwich
Presunto	Cured ham
Púcara: na púcara	'In the pot' – casserole
Pudim flan	Crème caramel
Puré de batata	Mashed potato
Queijadas de Sintra	Sintra cheesecakes
Queijo	Cheese
da Ilha	type of Cheddar from the Azores
da Serra	soft ewe's milk cheese from the Estrela mountains
de Azeitão	similar to Serra, but stronger
de cabra	goat's milk cheese
Quente	Hot
Rabanadas	French toast

Rábanos	Radishes
Rabo de vaca	Oxtail
Raia	Skate
Recheado/a	Stuffed
Refogado	Oil for cooking in which onion, garlic, tomato, etc. have been fried
Refogado/a	Fried in oil
Repolho	White cabbage
Requeijão	Curd cheese
Rins	Kidneys
Rissol (*pl.* **rissóis**)	Rissole
Robalo	Bass
Rojões à moda do Minho	Casserole of marinated pork cubes
Romã	Pomegranate
Sal	Salt
Salada	Salad
de alface	lettuce
de tomate	tomato
mista	mixed
russa	Russian
Salmão	Salmon
Salmonete	Red mullet
Salpicão	Sausage made of smoked loin of pork
Salsa	Parsley
Salsicha	Sausage
Salteado/a	Sautéed
Sandes	Sandwich(es)
Sanduíche	Sandwich
Santola	Spider crab
Sapateira	Crab
Sardinhas	Sardines
Sargo	Bream

Savel	Shad
Simples	Plain (*omelette, etc.*)
Solha	Sole
Sopa	Soup
de ervas	green vegetable
Juliana	vegetable
Sorvete	Sorbet
Tâmara	Date
Tamboril	Monkfish
Tarte	Tart
de amêndoa	almond
de maçã	apple
Tempero	Dressing
Tinta: com tinta	In their ink (*cuttlefish, etc.*)
Tomate	Tomato
Toranja	Grapefruit
Torradas	Toast
Torrão	Nougat
Torta	Pie
Tosta	Toasted sandwich
de queijo	cheese
mista	ham and cheese
Toucinho	Bacon
do céu	'Bacon from heaven' – almond and egg sweet
Tripas	Tripe
Trufas	Truffles
Truta	Trout
Uvas	Grapes
Vaca	Beef
Veado	Venison
Vieiras	Scallops
Vinagre	Vinegar
Vitela	Veal

SHOPPING

● Shop opening hours vary a bit, but many shops close for two hours in the middle of the day. Exceptions are department stores and shops in city centres and tourist areas. General opening hours are 9 a.m. to 1 p.m. and 3 p.m. to 7 p.m. on weekdays, and 9 a.m. to 1 p.m. on Saturdays. Shopping centres stay open until midnight throughout the week.

● There are some chains of department stores with branches mainly in large towns and cities. There are also large, self-service supermarkets, especially in urban areas. On the whole, though, Portuguese shops are smaller, individual ones.

Many places have markets – some permanent, some only one day a week; some outdoor, some indoor. Some sell only fruit and vegetables; others sell almost anything.

● Chemists (**farmácia**) are generally open from 9 a.m. to 1 p.m. and 3 p.m. to 7 p.m. on weekdays, and 9 a.m. to 1 p.m. on Saturdays. Lists of duty chemists that are open late are displayed on the shop doors (and are printed in newspapers).

Chemists sell mainly medicines, baby products and health foods. For toiletries and cosmetics go to a **perfumaria** or **drogaria**.

● Post offices (**Correio**) are generally open from 8.30 a.m. to 6 p.m., Mondays to Fridays. They are closed on Saturdays. Letterboxes (**marco de correio**) are painted red with **Correio** in white lettering. There may be separate slots for airmail (**via aérea**), packages (**volumes**) and letters (**cartas**).

If you only want stamps, you can get them at some stationers (**papelaria**) and sometimes at hotels.

Smaller post offices are identifiable by their distinctive 'shop' sign – a red horse and rider in a white circle, against a green background.

If you want to receive mail at a *poste restante*, have it addressed to **Posta Restante**, with the name of the town or village you're staying in.

● To ask for something in a shop, all you need do is name it and add 'please' – or just point and say 'some of this, please' or 'two of those, please'.

Before you go shopping, try to make a list of what you need in Portuguese. If you're looking for clothes or shoes, work out what size to ask for and other things like colour, material and so on.

Shopkeepers and customers always exchange greetings and goodbyes, so check up on the correct phrases for the time of day (see inside back cover).

You may see

Aberto	Open
Antiguidades	Antiques
Artigos de desporto	Sports equipment
Artigos de pele/cabedal	Leather goods
Auto-serviço	Self-service
Barbeiro	Barber's
Boutique	Clothes, fashions
Brindes	Gifts
Brinquedos	Toys
Cabeleireiro/a	Hairdresser's
Caixa	Cashier
Calçado	Footwear
Cave	Basement
Centro comercial	Shopping centre
Confecções	Clothes, fashions

Confeitaria	Confectioner's
Correio	Post; Post Office
Discos	Records
Drogaria	Drugstore
Electrodomésticos	Electrical goods
Encerrado	Closed
Entrada	Entrance
Farmácia	Chemist's
Farmácias de serviço	Duty chemists
Fechado	Closed
Flores/Florista	Flowers/Florist's
Frutas/Frutaria	Fruit/Fruiterer's
Gabinete de provas	Fitting rooms
Hipermercado	Hypermarket
Joalharia	Jeweller's
Limpeza a seco	Dry-cleaning
Liquidação (total)	(Clearance) sale
Livraria	Bookshop
Loja de ferragens	Ironmonger's/Hardware store
Mercearia	Grocer's
Mobiliário	Furniture
Moda	Fashionwear
Móveis	Furniture
Oculista	Optician's
Ourivesaria	Goldsmith's, jeweller's
Padaria	Baker's
Papelaria	Stationer's
Pastelaria	Cake shop; Café
Peixaria	Fishmonger's
Perfumaria	Perfumery
Preço de revenda	Retail price
Promoção	Special offer
Pronto a vestir	Ready to wear clothes
Relojoaria	Watchmaker's

Roupa (de senhora/homem/criança)	Clothes (women's/men's/children's)
Saída (de emergência)	(Emergency) exit
Sapataria	Shoe shop
Supermercado	Supermarket
Tabacaria	Tobacconist's
Talho	Butcher's
Vestuário (de senhora/homem/criança)	Clothes (women's/men's/children's)

You may want to say

General phrases

(see also Directions, page 28; Problems and complaints, page 166; Numbers, page 208)

Which way is the town centre?
Como se vai para o centro da cidade?
kohmoo si viy para oo sayñtroo da seedahd

Where is the chemist's?
Onde é a farmácia?
ohñdee e a farmahsya

Is there a grocer's shop around here?
Há uma mercearia por aqui?
ah ooma mirsiareea poor akee

Where can I buy batteries?
Onde se pode comprar pilhas?
ohñd si pod kohmprahr peelyash

What time does the baker's open?
A que horas abre a padaria?
a ki oraz ahbri a pahdareea

What time does the post office close?
A que horas fecha o Correio?
a ki orash fesha oo koorrayoo

What time do you open in the morning?
A que horas abre de manhã?
a ki oraz ahbri de manyañ

What time do you close this evening?
A que horas fecha esta tarde?
a ki orash fesha eshta tahrd

Do you have . . . ?
Tem . . . ?
taym̃ . . .

Do you have stamps?
Tem selos?
taym̃ sayloosh

Do you have any wholemeal bread?
Tem pão integral?
taym̃ powñ eeñtigrahl

How much is it?
Quanto é?
kwañtoo e

Altogether
No total
noo tootahl

How much does this cost?
Quanto custa?
kwañtoo kooshta

How much do these cost?
Quanto custam?
kwañtoo kooshtowm̃

I don't understand
Não compreendo
nowñ kohm̃priayñdoo

Could you write it down, please?
Podia escrever, por favor?
poodeea ishkrivayr poor favohr

It's too expensive
É muito caro
e mweeñtoo kahroo

Haven't you got anything cheaper?
Não tem nada mais barato?
nowñ taym̃ nahda miysh barahtoo

I don't have enough money
Não tenho dinheiro que chegue
nowñ taynyoo deenyayroo ki shayg

Could you keep it for me?
Podia-mo guardar?
poodeea-moo gwardahr

I'm just looking
Estou só a ver
ishtoh so a vayr

This one, please
Este, por favor
aysht poor favohr

That one, please
Esse, por favor
aysi poor favohr

Three of these, please
Três destes, por favor
traysh dayshtish poor favohr

Two of those, please
Dois desses, por favor
doysh daysish poor favohr

Not that one – this one
Esse não – este
aysi nowñ – aysht

There's one in the window
Há um na montra
ah ooñ na mohñtra

That's fine
Está bem
ishtah baym̃

Nothing else, thank you
Mais nada, obrigado/a
miysh nahda ohbreegahdoo/a

I'll take it
Levo este
levoo aysht

I'll think about it
Vou pensar
voh payñsahr

Do you have a bag, please?
Tem um saco, por favor
taym̃ ooñ sahkoo poor favohr

Could you wrap it for me, please?
Podia-mo embrulhar, por favor?
poodeea-moo aym̃broolyahr poor favohr

With plenty of paper
Com muito papel
kohm̃ mweeñtoo papel

I'm taking it to England
Vou-o levar para Inglaterra
voh-oo livahr para eeñglaterra

It's a gift
É um presente
e ooñ prizayñt

Where do I/we pay?
Onde se paga?
ohñd se pahga

Do you take credit cards?
Aceita cartões de crédito?
asayta kartoyñsh di kredeetoo

Do you take traveller's cheques?
Aceita traveller's cheques?
asayta trahvilirs shekish

I'm sorry, I don't have any change
Desculpe, não tenho troco
dishkoolp nowñ taynyoo trohkoo

Could you give me a receipt please
Podia-me dar a factura, por favor
podeea-mi dahr a fahtoora poor favohr

Buying food and drink

A kilo of . . .
Um quilo de . . .
ooṁ keeloo di . . .

A kilo of grapes, please
Um quilo de uvas, por favor
ooṁ keeloo di oovash poor favohr

Two kilos of oranges, please
Dois quilos de laranjas, por favor
doysh keeloosh di larañjash poor favohr

Half a kilo of tomatoes, please
Meio quilo de tomate, por favor
mayoo keeloo di toomaht poor favohr

A hundred grams of . . .
Cem gramas de . . .
sayṁ gramash di . . .

A hundred grams of olives, please
Cem gramas de azeitonas, por favor
sayṁ gramash di azaytohnash poor favohr

Two hundred grams of spicy sausage, please
Duzentos gramas de chouriço, por favor
doozayṁtoosh gramash di shohreesoo poor favohr

In a piece
Inteiro
eeñtayroo

Sliced
Às fatias
ahsh fateeash

A piece of cheese, please
Um bocado de queijo, por favor
ooṁ bookahdoo di kayjoo poor favohr

Five slices of ham, please
Cinco fatias de fiambre, por favor
seeñkoo fateeash di feeaṁbri poor favohr

Boiled ham/Cured ham
Fiambre/Presunto
feeaṁbri/prizooñtoo

A bottle of white wine, please
Uma garrafa de vinho branco, por favor
ooma garrahfa di veenyoo brañkoo poor favohr

A carton of milk, please
Um pacote de leite, por favor
* oom pakot di layt poor favohr*

Two cans of beer, please
Duas latas de cerveja, por favor
dooash lahtash di sirvayja poor favohr

A bit of that, please
Um bocado daquele, por favor
oom bookahdoo dakayl poor favohr

A bit more
Mais um bocado
miysh oom bookahdoo

A bit less
Um pouco menos
oom pohkoo maynoosh

What is this?
O que é isto?
oo ki e eeshtoo

What is there in this?
O que é que isto leva?
oo ki e ki eeshtoo leva

Can I try it?
Posso provar?
posoo proovahr

At the chemist's

Aspirins, please
Aspirinas, por favor
ashpeereenash poor favohr

Plasters, please
Pensos rápidos, por favor
paynsoosh rrahpeedoosh poor favohr

Do you have something for . . .?
Tem algo para . . . ?
taym ahlgoo para . . .

Do you have something for diarrhoea?
Tem algo para a diarreia?
taym ahlgoo para a deearraya

Do you have something for insect bites?
Tem algo para mordeduras de insectos?
taym ahlgoo para moordidoorash di eeñsetoosh

Do you have something for period pains?
Tem algo para dores menstruais?
taym ahlgoo para dohrish meñshtrooiysh

Buying clothes and shoes

I'd like a skirt/a shirt
Queria uma saia/uma camisa
*kireea ooma siya/ooma
kameeza*

I'd like some sandals
Queria umas sandálias
kireea oomash sañdahlyash

Size 40
Número quarenta
noomiroo kwarayñta

Can I try it on?
Posso experimentar?
posoo ishpireemayñtahr

Is there a mirror?
Há um espelho?
ah ooḿ ishpaylyoo

I like it/them
Gosto
goshtoo

I don't like it/them
Não gosto
nowñ goshtoo

I don't like the colour
Não gosto da cor
nowñ goshtoo da kohr

Do you have it in other
colours?
Tem noutras cores?
tayñ nohtrash kohrish

It's too big
É muito grande
e mweeñtoo grañd

They're too big
São muito grandes
sowñ mweeñtoo grañdish

It's too small
É muito pequeno
e mweeñtoo pikaynoo

They're too small
São muito pequenos
sowñ mweeñtoo pikaynoosh

Have you got a smaller size?
Tem mais pequeno?
tayñ miysh pikaynoo

Have you got a bigger size?
Tem maior
tayñ miyor

Miscellaneous

Five stamps for England, please
Cinco selos para a Inglaterra, por favor
seeñkoo sayloosh para a eeñglaterra poor favohr

Three postcards, please
Três postais, por favor
traysh pooshtiysh poor favohr

Matches, please
Fósforos, por favor
foshfooroosh poor favohr

A film like this, please
Um rolo destes, por favor
ooṁ rrohloo dayshtish poor favohr

For this camera
Para esta máquina
para eshta mahkeena

Do you have any English newspapers?
Tem jornais ingleses?
tayṁ joorniyz eeñglayzish

You may hear

Posso ajudá-lo?
posoo ajoodah-loo
May I help you?

Que deseja?
ki dizayja
What would you like?

Quanto quer?
kwañtoo ker
How much do you want?

Quantos/Quantas quer?
kwañtoosh/kwañtash ker
How many do you want?

Está bem assim?
ishtah bayṁ aseeṁ
Is that all right?

Mais alguma coisa?
miyz ahlgooma koyza
Anything else?

Desculpe, está esgotado
dishkoolp ishtah ishgootahdoo
I'm sorry, we're sold out

Desculpe, estamos fechados/ encerrados
dishkoolp ishtamoosh fishahdoosh/ayñsirrahdoosh
I'm sorry, we're closed now

Quer que embrulhe?
ker ki ayṁbroolyi
Shall I wrap it?

Por favor, pague na caixa
poor favohr pahg na kiysha
Please pay at the cashier's
desk

Tem trocos?
taym trokoosh
Do you have any change?

Precisa de receita
priseeza di rrisayta
You need a prescription

Qual é o seu número?
kwahl e oo sayoo noomiroo
What size are you?

Que tipo de . . . ?
ki teepoo di . . .
What sort of . . . ?

Que tipo de rolo deseja?
ki teepoo di rrohloo dizayja
What sort of film would you
like?

Para que tipo de máquina?
para ki teepoo di mahkeena
What sort of camera is it
for?

BUSINESS TRIPS

● You'll probably be doing business with the help of interpreters or in a language everybody speaks, but you may need a few Portuguese phrases to cope at a company's reception desk.

● When you arrive for an appointment, all you need do is say who you've come to see and give your name or hand over your business card. However, if you're not expected, you may need to make an appointment or leave a message.

You may see

1º andar	1st floor
2º andar	2nd floor
Avariado	Out of order
Elevador	Lift
Entrada	Entrance
Entrada proibida	No entry
Entrada proibida a pessoas estranhas ao serviço	No entry to unauthorised persons
Escada	Stairs
Não fumar	No smoking
Recepção	Reception
Rés-do-chão (R/C)	Ground floor
SA = Sociedade Anónima	Limited company
Saída (de emergência)	(Emergency) exit

You may want to say

(see also Days, months, dates, *page 188*; Time, *page 192)*

Mr Garcia, please
O Senhor Garcia, por favor
oo sinyohr garseea poor favohr

Mrs/Miss Fernandes, please
A Senhora Fernandes, por favor
a sinyohra firnañdish poor favohr

The manager, please
O gerente, por favor
oo jirayñt poor favohr

My name is . . .
Chamo-me . . .
shamoo-mi . . .

My company is . . .
A minha companhia é . . .
a meenya kohm̃panyeea e . . .

I have an appointment with Mr João Rodrigues
Tenho uma entrevista marcada com o Senhor João Rodrigues
taynyoo ooma ayñtriveeshta markahda kohm̃ oo sinyohr jwowñ rroodreegish

I don't have an appointment
Não tenho entrevista marcada
nowñ taynyoo ayñtriveeshta markahda

I'd like to make an appointment with Miss/Mrs Gomes
Queria marcar uma entrevista com a Senhora Gomes
kireea markahr ooma ayñtriveeshta kohm̃ a sinyohra gohmish

I am free this afternoon at five o'clock
Estou livre esta tarde às cinco
ishtoh leevri eshta tahrd ahsh seeñkoo

I'd like to talk to the export manager
Queria falar com o director de exportação
kireea falahr kohm̃ oo deeretohr di ayshpoortasowñ

What is his/her name?
Como é que ele/ela se chama?
kohmoo e ki ayl/ela si shama

135

When will he/she be back?
Quando regressa?
kwañdoo rrigresa

Can I leave a message?
Posso deixar um recado?
posoo dayshahr ooñ rrikahdoo

Could you ask him/her to call me?
Podia-lhe pedir que me telefonasse?
poodeea-lyi pideer ki mi tilifoonahsi

My telephone number is . . .
O meu número de telefone é o . . .
oo mayoo noomiroo di tilifon e oo . . .

I am staying at the Hotel Palácio
Estou no Hotel Palácio
ishtoh noo otel palahsyoo

Where is his/her office?
Onde é o seu gabinete?
ohñdee e oo sayoo gabeenayt

I have come for the exhibition
Vim à exposição
veeñ ah ayshpoozisowñ

I have come for the trade fair
Vim à feira das indústrias
veeñ ah fayra dash eeñdooshtreeash

I have come for the conference
Vim ao congresso
veeñ ow kohñgresoo

I have to make a phone call (to Britain)
Tenho de fazer uma chamada (para a Grã-Bretanha)
taynyo di fazayr ooma shamahda (para a grañbritanya)

I have to send a telex
Tenho de mandar um telex
taynyoo di mañdahr ooñ teleks

I have to send this by fax
Tenho de mandar isto por fax
taynyoo di mañdahr eeshtoo poor fahks

I'd like to send this by post
Queria mandar isto por correio
kireea mañdahr eeshtoo poor koorrayoo

I'd like to send this by courier
Queria mandar isto por mensageiro especial
kireea mañdahr eeshtoo poor mayñsajayroo ishpiseeyahl

I need someone to type a letter for me
Preciso que alguém me escreva uma carta à máquina
priseezoo ki ahlgaym̃ mi ishkrayva ooma kahrta ah mahkeena

I need a photocopy (of this)
Preciso duma fotocópia (disto)
priseezoo dooma fohtohkopya (deeshtoo)

I need an interpreter
Preciso dum intérprete
priseezoo doom̃ eeñterprit

You may hear

O seu nome, por favor?
oo sayoo nohm poor favohr
Your name, please?

Como se chama, por favor?
kohmoo si shama poor favohr
What is your name, please?

O nome da sua companhia, por favor?
oo nohm da sooa kohm̃panyeea poor favohr
The name of your company, please?

Tem entrevista marcada?
taym̃ ayñtriveeshta markahda
Do you have an appointment?

Tem cartão?
taym̃ kartowñ
Do you have a card?

Está à sua espera?
istah ah sooa ishpera
Is he/she expecting you?

(Espere) um momento, por favor
(ishper) oom̃ moomayñtoo poor favohr
(Wait) one moment, please

Vou-lhe dizer que está aqui
voh-lyi deezayr que ishtah akee
I'll tell him/her you're here

Já vem
jah vaym̃
He/she is just coming

Sente-se, por favor
sayñti-si poor favohr
Please sit down

Não se quer sentar?
nowñ si ker sayñtahr
Wouldn't you like to sit down?

Entre, por favor
ayñtri poor favohr
Go in, please

Venha por aqui, por favor
vaynya poor akee poor favohr
Come this way, please

O Senhor Garcia não está
*oo sinyohr garseea nowñ
ishtah*
Mr Garcia is not in

A Senhora Gomes está fora
a sinyohra gohmish ishtah fora
Mrs/Miss Gomes is away

**A Senhora Fernandes
regressa às onze horas**
*a sinyohra firnañdish rrigresa
ahz ohñzi orash*
Mrs/Miss Fernandes will be
back at eleven o'clock

**Dentro de meia hora/uma
hora**
*dayñtroo di maya ora/ooma
ora*
In half an hour/an hour

**Apanhe o elevador para o
terceiro andar**
*apanyi oo ilivadohr para oo
tirsayroo añdahr*
Take the lift to the third
floor

Vá pelo corredor
vah payloo koorridohr
Go along the corridor

É a primeira/segunda porta
e a preemayra/sigooñda porta
It's the first/second door

À esquerda/direita
ah ishkayrda/deerayta
On the left/right

**É o gabinete número
trezentos e vinte**
*e oo gabeenayt noomiroo
trizayñtooz ee veeñt*
It's room number 320

Entre!
ayñtri
Come in!

SIGHTSEEING

● You can get information about all the sights worth seeing from the Portuguese National Tourist Office (address, page 206) and from local tourist offices. The latter can also tell you about the sightseeing tours by coach that are available in many cities and tourist areas, often with English-speaking guides.

● Opening hours vary for historic buildings, museums, galleries and so on, but most close for lunch. Most are shut on Mondays and public holidays.

● Portugal has over twenty nature parks and reserves. Information may be obtained from local tourist offices.

You may see

Aberto	Open
Encerrado	Closed
Fechado (para obras de restauro)	Closed (for restoration)
Horário de abertura ao público	Visiting hours
Não mexer	Do not touch
Não pisar a relva	Keep off the grass
Privado	Private
Proibida a entrada	No entry
Visitas guiadas	Guided tours

You may want to say

(see also At the tourist office, *page 75, for asking for information, brochures, etc.)*

Opening times

(see Time, *page 192)*

When is the museum open?
Quando é que o museu está aberto?
kwañdoo e ki oo moozayoo ishtah abertoo

What time does the convent open?
A que horas abre o convento?
a ki oraz ahbri oo kohñvayñtoo

What time does the palace close?
A que horas fecha o palácio?
a ki orash fesha oo palahsyoo

Is it open on Sundays?
Está aberto aos domingos?
ishtah abertoo owsh doomeeñgoosh

Can I/we visit the monastery?
Pode-se visitar o mosteiro?
pod-si veezeetahr oo mooshtayroo

Is it open to the public?
Está aberto ao público?
ishtah abertoo ow poobleekoo

Visiting places

One/Two, please
Um/Dois, por favor
ooñ/doysh poor favohr

Two adults and one child
Dois adultos e uma criança
doyz adooltoz ee ooma kreeañsa

Are there reductions for children?
Ha desconto para crianças?
ah dishkohñtoo para kreeañsash

For students
Para estudantes
para ishtoodañtish

For pensioners
Para reformados
para rrifoormahdoosh

For the disabled
Para deficientes
para difeesyayñtish

For groups
Para grupos
para groopoosh

Are there guided tours (in English)?
Há visitas guiadas (em inglês)?
ah veezeetash geeahdash (ayñ eeñglaysh)

Can I/we take photos?
Pode-se tirar fotografias?
pod-si teerahr footoografeeash

Would you mind taking a photo of me/us, please?
Podia-me/Podia-nos tirar uma fotografia, por favor?
poodeea-mi/poodeea-noosh teerahr ooma footoografeea poor favohr

When was this built?
Quando foi construído?
kwañdoo foy kohñshtrooeedoo

Who painted that picture?
Quem pintou esse quadro?
kayñ peeñtoh aysi kwahdroo

In what year?
Em que ano?
ayñ ki anoo

What time is mass?
A que horas é a missa?
a ki oraz e a meesa

Is there a priest who speaks English?
Há um padre que fale inglês?
ah ooñ pahdri ki fahli eeñglaysh

What is this flower called?
Como se chama esta flor?
kohmoo si shama eshta flohr

141

What is that bird called?
Como se chama aquele pássaro?
kohmoo si shama akayl pahsahroo

Is there a picnic area (in the park)?
Há uma zona de piquenique (no parque)?
ah ooma zohna di peekineek (noo pahrk)

Sightseeing excursions

What excursions are there?
Que excursões há?
ki ayshkoorsoyñsh ah

Are there any excursions to Óbidos?
Há excursões a Óbidos?
ah ayshkoorsoyñsh a obeedoosh

What time does it leave?
A que horas parte?
a ki orash pahrt

Where does it leave from?
De onde parte?
dohñd pahrt

How long does it last?
Quanto tempo dura?
kwañtoo taympoo doora

Does the guide speak English?
O/A guia fala inglês?
oo/a geea fahla eeñglaysh

What time does it get back?
A que horas regressa?
a ki orash rrigresa

How much is it?
Quanto é?
kwañtoo e

You may hear

O museu está aberto todos os dias, excepto às segundas
oo moozayoo ishtah abertoo tohdooz oosh deeash ayshsetoo ahs sigooñdash
The museum is open every day except Monday

É um quadro de Nuno Gonçalves
e ooñ kwahdroo di noonoo gohñsahlvish
Its a painting by Nuno Gonçalves

Está fechado às segundas
ishtah fishahdoo ahsh sigooñdash
It is closed on Mondays

Há excursões todas as terças e quintas
ah ayshkoorsoyñsh tohdaz ash tayrsaz ee keeñtash
There are excursions every Tuesday and Thursday

O castelo foi construído no século onze
oo kashteloo foy kohñshtrooeedoo noo sekooloo ohñz
The castle was built in the eleventh century

O autocarro sai às dez horas da Praça de Espanha
oo owtokahrroo siy ahsh dez orash da prahsa di ishpanya
The coach leaves at ten o'clock from the Praça de Espanha

ENTERTAINMENTS

● Portugal's most popular spectator sport is football. Most professional fixtures take place on Sundays.

● Bullfighting, which is quite different from the Spanish form, has a local following in the Lisbon area and in the Ribatejo, where the bulls are reared. When buying tickets for a bullfight, there'll be a choice of **sol** or **sombra** – seats in the sun or the shade. **Sombra** seats cost more.

● Evening performances at cinemas may start late – the final screening can be at midnight. Theatre performances and concerts often start at 9.30 p.m.

● Films are categorised as suitable for those over 6, 12, 16 or 18 years old (**maiores de 6/12/16/18 anos**). In newspaper listings, these categories are often abbreviated as **M/6**, etc.

Many American, British and other foreign films are shown in Portuguese cinemas. Most of them are subtitled (**com legendas**), but some are dubbed (**dobrados**).

● **Fado**, the traditional song of Lisbon, may be heard in certain cafés and restaurants in the Bairro Alto and Alfama districts of the city – it's best from about 11 p.m. onwards. Probably the best-known kind of **fado** is the sad, plaintive variety, telling of unhappy love (**fado** means fate, destiny), but the range is wider than that. Some **fados** express happiness and fulfilment, others are songs of social protest. Coimbra students have their own separate **fado** tradition.

You may see

Balcão	Balcony, circle
Bancadas	(Grand)stand
Barreiras	Ringside seats (*at bullring*)
Bengaleiro	Cloakroom
Bilhetes para hoje	Tickets for today
Camarotes	Boxes
Cineclube	Film club
Cinema	Cinema
Circo	Circus
Discoteca	Disco
Esgotado	Sold out
Estádio	Stadium
Fila	Row
Hipódromo	Racecourse
Interdito a menores de 18 anos	Under-18s not allowed
Lugar	Seat
Maiores de 16/18 anos	Over 16s/18s only
Matinée	Matinée
Não aconselhável a menores de 16/18 anos	Not recommended for under-16s/18s
Ópera	Opera (house)
Orquestra	Orchestra
Palco	Stage
Para todos	For general viewing
Plateia	Stalls
Poltronas	Front stalls
Porta	Door
Reserva de bilhetes	Advance booking
Sala de concertos	Concert hall
Salão de baile	Dance hall
Sanitários	Toilets
Sem intervalo	There is no interval

Sessão contínua	Continuous performance
Soirée	Evening performance
Teatro	Theatre
Versão original com legendas	Original language version with subtitles
Vestiário	Cloakroom

You may want to say

What's on

(*see* Time, *page 192*)

What is there to do in the evenings?
O que se pode fazer à noite?
oo ki si pod fazayr ah noyt

Is there a disco around here?
Há uma discoteca por aqui?
ah ooma deeshkooteka poor akee

Where can I/we hear fado?
Onde se pode ouvir fado?
ohñd si pod ohveer fahdoo

Is there any entertainment for children?
Há distracções para crianças?
ah deeshtrahsoyñsh para kreeañsash

What's on tonight?
O que há esta noite?
oo ki ah eshta noyt

What's on tomorrow?
O que há amanhã?
oo ki ah ahmanyañ

At the cinema
No cinema
noo seenayma

At the theatre
No teatro
noo teeahtroo

Who is playing? (*music*)
Quem toca?
kayñ toka

Who is singing?
Quem canta?
kayñ kañta

Who is dancing?
Quem dança?
kayñ dañsa

Does the film have subtitles?
O filme tem legendas?
oo feelm tayñ lijayñdash

Is there a football match on Sunday?
Há um desafio de futebol no domingo?
ah ooñ dizafeeoo di footbol noo doomeeñgoo

Who are playing? (*sport*)
Quem joga?
kayñ joga

What time does the show start?
A que horas começa o espectáculo?
a ki orash koomesa oo ishpetahkooloo

What time does the concert start?
A que horas começa o concerto?
a ki orash koomesa oo kohñsayrtoo

How long does the performance last?
Quanto tempo dura o espectáculo?
kwañtoo tayñpoo doora oo ishpetahkooloo

When does it end?
A que horas termina?
a ki orash tirmeena

Tickets

Where can I/we get tickets?
Onde se pode comprar bilhetes?
ohñd si pod kohñprahr beelyaytish

Could you get me tickets for the football match?
Podia-me arranjar bilhetes para o desafio de futebol?
poodeea-mi arrañjahr beelyaytish para oo dizafeeoo di footbol

For the bullfight
Para a tourada
para a tohrahda

For the theatre
Para o teatro
para oo teeahtroo

Two, please
Dois, por favor
doysh poor favohr

Two for tonight, please
Dois para esta noite, por favor
doysh para eshta noyt poor favohr

Two for the midnight screening, please
Dois para a sessão da meia-noite, por favor
doysh para a sisowñ da maya-noyt poor favohr

Are there any seats left for
  Saturday?
Ainda há lugares para sábado?
*aeeñda ah loogahrish para
  sahbadoo*

I'd like to book a box for
  four people
**Queria reservar um camarote
  para quatro pessoas**
*kireea rrizirvahr oom kamarot
  para kwahtroo pisohash*

I'd like to book two seats
Queria reservar dois lugares
*kireea rrizirvahr doysh
  loogahrish*

For Friday
Para sexta
para sayshta

In the stalls
Para a plateia
para a plataya

In the balcony
Para o balcão
para oo bahlkowñ

In the shade
À sombra
ah sohmbra

In the sun
Ao sol
ow sol

How much is a ticket?
Quanto é o bilhete?
kwañtoo e oo beelyayt

Do you have anything cheaper?
Tem algo mais barato?
taym ahlgoo miysh barahtoo

That's fine
Está bem
ishtah baym

At the show/game

Where is this, please?
  (*showing your ticket*)
Onde é, por favor?
ohñdee e poor favohr

Where is the cloakroom?
Onde é o bengaleiro?
ohñdee e o bayñgalayroo

Where is the bar?
Onde é o bar?
ohñdee e oo bahr

Where is the toilet?
Onde é a casa de banho?
ohñdee e a kahza di banyoo

A programme, please
Um programa, por favor
oom proograma poor favohr

Where can I/we get a programme?

Onde se pode arranjar um programa?

ohñd si pod arrañjahr ooṁ proograma

Is there an interval?

Tem intervalo?

tayṁ eeñtirvahloo

You may hear

Pode comprar bilhetes aqui no hotel

pod kohṁprahr beelyaytish akee noo otel

You can buy tickets here in the hotel

Na praça de touros

na prahsa di tohroosh

At the bullring

No estádio

noo ishtahdyoo

At the stadium

Começa às nove horas

koomesa ahsh nov orash

It begins at nine o'clock

Dura duas horas e um quarto

doora dooaz oraz ee ooṁ kwahrtoo

It lasts two and a quarter hours

Acaba às onze e meia

akahba ahz ohñz ee maya

It ends at half past eleven

Há intervalo de quinze minutos

ah eeñtirvahloo di keeñz meenootoosh

There is a fifteen-minute interval

Para quando?

para kwañdoo

When for?

Ao sol ou à sombra?

ow sol oh ah sohṁbra

In the sun or in the shade?

Na plateia, no balcão?

na plataya noo bahlkowñ

In the stalls, in the balcony?

Há dois aqui, na plateia

ah doyz akee na plataya

There are two here, in the stalls (*indicating on seating plan*)

Lamento, está esgotado

lamayñtoo ishtah ishgootahdoo

I'm sorry, we're sold out

Posso ver o seu bilhete?

posoo vayr oo sayoo beelyayt

May I see your ticket?

SPORTS AND ACTIVITIES

● There are excellent facilities in Portugal for golf, tennis, riding, shooting, fishing and watersports – information about locations is obtainable from the Portuguese National Tourist Office or travel agents.

● The beaches close to Lisbon are badly polluted. The best beaches are in the Algarve, and along the western, Atlantic coast. In many places, however, the Atlantic rollers hitting the open, straight coastline produce conditions that need to be treated with respect.

● At the beach, a red flag flying means swimming is prohibited. A yellow flag means swimming is not recommended, and a green flag means it is safe. A chequered flag means the beach is not being supervised – for example, during the lifeguard's lunch hour. Apart from flags, other signs that you may see at the beach are **praia sem assistência** or **praia não vigiada** (beach without guard), and **zona perigosa** (danger zone). **Área concessionada** indicates an area of the beach with a lifeguard; **zona de chapéus (de sol)** is an area where you can hire a beach umbrella, or use your own, sometimes for a small charge.

● River fishing is most common in the north of Portugal, but in many areas you can also go deep-sea and underwater fishing. In all cases, you need a permit. For information on how to obtain these, contact a tourist office, or the **Federação Portuguesa de Pescas** (address, page 207).

You may see

Aluguer de . . .	. . . for hire
Aluguer de barcos	Boat hire
Campo de futebol	Football pitch

Campo de golfe	Golf course
Campo de ténis	Tennis court
Centro desportivo	Sports centre
Court de ténis	Tennis court
Perigo	Danger
Piscina (coberta)	(Indoor) swimming pool
Praia	Beach
Pranchas de wind-surf	Sailboards
Proibido caçar	No shooting
Proibido nadar	No swimming
Proibido pescar	No fishing
Reserva de caça	Game reserve

You may want to say

General phrases

Can I/we . . . ?
Pode-se . . . ?
pod-si . . .

Where can I/we play tennis?
Onde se pode jogar ténis?
ohñd si pod joogahr teneesh

Can I/we hire bikes?
Pode-se alugar bicicletas?
pod-si aloogahr beeseekletash

Where can I/we go jogging?
Onde se pode ir fazer jogging?
ohñd si pod eer fazayr jogeeñg

Can I/we go fishing?
Pode-se ir pescar?
pod-si eer pishkahr

I don't know how to . . .
Não sei . . .
nowñ say . . .

Can I/we go horse-riding?
Pode-se ir montar a cavalo?
pod-si eer mohñtahr a kavahloo

I don't know how to water-ski
Não sei fazer esqui aquático
nowñ say fazayr ishkee akwateekoo

Where can I/we . . . ?
Onde se pode . . . ?
ohñd si pod . . .

Do you give lessons?
Dá lições?
dah leesoyñsh

I'm a beginner
Sou principiante
soh preeñseepyañt

I'm quite experienced
Tenho prática
taynyoo prahteeka

How much is it per hour?
Quanto é por hora?
kwañtoo e poor ora

How much is it for the whole day?
Quanto é pelo dia todo?
kwañtoo e payloo deea tohdoo

How much is it per game?
Quanto é por jogo
kwañtoo e poor johgoo

Is there a reduction for children?
Há desconto para crianças?
ah dishkohñtoo para kreeañsash

Can I/we hire equipment?
Pode-se alugar equipamento?
pod-si aloogahr ikeepamayñtoo

Can I/we hire rackets?
Pode-se alugar raquetes?
pod-si aloogahr rraketish

Can I/we hire clubs?
Pode-se alugar tacos
pod-si aloogahr tahkoosh

Do I/we need a licence?
É preciso licença?
e priseezoo leesayñsa

Where can I/we get one?
Onde se pode arranjar uma?
ohñd si pod arrañjahr ooma

Is it necessary to be a member?
É preciso ser sócio/a?
e priseezoo sayr sosyoo/a

Beach and pool

Can I/we swim here?
Pode-se nadar aqui?
pod-si nadahr akee

Can I/we swim in the river?
Pode-se nadar no rio?
pod-si nadahr noo rreeoo

Is it dangerous?
É perigoso?
e pireegohzoo

Is it safe for children?
É seguro para as crianças?
e sigooroo para ash kreeañsash

When is high tide?
Quando é a maré alta?
kwañdoo e a mare ahlta

You may hear

É principiante?
e preeñseepyañt
Are you a beginner?

Sabe fazer esqui aquático?
sahb fazayr ishkee akwateekoo
Do you know how to water-ski?

Sabe fazer wind-surf?
sahb fazayr weend-sarf?
Do you know how to windsurf?

São . . . escudos por hora
sowñ . . . ishkoodoosh poor ora
It's . . . escudos per hour

Tem de deixar um depósito de . . . escudos
tayñ di dayshahr ooñ dipozeetoo di . . . ishkoodoosh
You have to pay a deposit of . . . escudos

Lamento, está esgotado
lamayñtoo ishtah ishgootahdoo
I'm sorry, we're booked up

Tem de voltar mais tarde
tayñ di vohltahr miysh tahrd
You'll have to come back later

Qual é o seu número?
kwahl e oo sayoo noomiroo
What size are you?

Que tipo de prancha quer?
ki teepoo di prañsha ker
What type of board do you want?

É preciso uma fotografia
e priseezoo ooma footoografeea
You need a photo

152

HEALTH

Medical details - to show to a doctor

(Tick boxes or fill in details)	Self Eu	Other members of family/party		
Blood group **Grupo sanguíneo**				
Asthmatic **Asmático/a**				
Blind **Cego/a**				
Deaf **Surdo/a**				
Diabetic **Diabético/a**				
Epileptic **Epiléptico/a**				
Handicapped **Deficiente**				
Heart condition **Cardíaco/a**				
High blood pressure **Tensão alta**				
Pregnant **Grávida**				

Allergic to **Alérgico/a a:**				
Antibiotics **Antibióticos**				
Penicillin **Penicilina**				
Cortisone **Cortisona**				

Medicines **Medicamentos**

Self **Eu** _____

Others **Outros** _____

● Your local Department of Health office can provide information about medical care abroad. Within the EC, you can obtain the local equivalent of NHS treatment by producing the required form – you may have to pay first and reclaim the payment when you return to Britain.

Treatment at first aid posts is free.

● Chemists can often give medical advice and first aid, and provide medicines without a prescription.

● If you need an ambulance, call the emergency phone number, 115.

● To indicate where the pain is simply point and say 'it hurts here' (dói-me aqui). Otherwise, you can look up the Portuguese for the appropriate part of the body (see page 163).

Notice that in Portuguese you refer to 'the head', 'the stomach', etc. (a cabeça, o estômago) rather than '*my* head', '*my* stomach'.

You may see

Agitar antes de usar	Shake before use
Banco	Casualty department
Clínica	Clinic, hospital
Dentista	Dentist
Horas de consulta	Surgery hours
Hospital	Hospital
Médico	Doctor
Modo de usar	Instructions for use
Para uso externo apenas	For external use only
Posologia	Dosage
Posto de primeiros socorros	First aid post
Primeiros socorros	First aid post; casualty hospital
Serviços de emergência	Emergency services
Veneno!	Poison!

You may want to say

At the doctor's

I need a doctor
Preciso dum médico
priseezoo dooṁ medeekoo

Please call a doctor
Por favor, chame um médico
poor favohr shami ooṁ medeekoo

Quickly
Depressa
dipresa

Is there anyone who speaks English?
Há alguém que fale inglês?
ah ahlgayṁ ki fahli eeñglaysh

Can I make an appointment?
Posso marcar uma consulta?
posoo markahr ooma kohñsoolta

It's my husband
É o meu marido
e oo mayoo mareedoo

It's my wife
É a minha mulher
e a meenya moolyer

It's my friend
É o meu amigo/a minha amiga
e oo mayoo ameegoo/ a meenya ameega

It's my son
É o meu filho
e oo mayoo feelyoo

It's my daughter
É a minha filha
e a meenya feelya

How much will it cost?
Quanto custa?
kwañtoo kooshta

Your symptoms

I feel unwell
Sinto-me mal
seeñtoo-mi mahl

Someone else's symptoms

He/She feels unwell
Sente-se mal
sayñti-si mahl

He/She is unconscious
Está inconsciente
ishtah eeñkohñshseeayñt

It hurts here
Dói-me aqui
doy-mi akee

It hurts here
Dói-lhe aqui
doy-lyi akee

My . . . hurts
Dói-me o/a . . .
doy-mi oo/a . . .

His/Her . . . hurts
Dói-lhe o/a . . .
doy-lyi oo/a . . .

My stomach hurts
Dói-me o estômago
doy-mi oo ishtohmagoo

His/Her stomach hurts
Dói-lhe o estômago
doy-lyi oo ishtohmagoo

My hand hurts
Dói-me a mão
doy-mi a mowñ

His/Her hand hurts
Dói-lhe a mão
doy-lyi a mowñ

I have a sore throat
Dói-me a garganta
doy-mi a gargañta

He/She has a sore throat
Dói-lhe a garganta
doy-lyi a gargañta

My . . . hurt
Dóem-me os/as . . .
doaym-mi oosh/ash . . .

His/Her . . . hurt
Dóem-lhe os/as . . .
doaym-lyi oosh/ash . . .

My feet hurt
Dóem-me os pés
doaym-mi oosh pesh

His/Her feet hurt
Dóem-lhe os pés
doaym-lyi oosh pesh

My legs hurt
Dóem-me as pernas
doaym-mi ash pernash

His/Her legs hurt
Dóem-lhe as pernas
doaym-lyi ash pernash

I have a temperature
Tenho febre
taynyoo febri

He/She has a temperature
Tem febre
taym febri

I have diarrhoea
Tenho diarreia
taynyoo deearraya

He/She has diarrhoea
Tem diarreia
taym deearraya

I feel dizzy/sick
Sinto tonturas/enjôo
seeñtoo tohñtoorash/ayñjohoo

He/She feels dizzy/sick
Sente tonturas/enjôo
sayñt tohñtoorash/ayñjohoo

I have been sick
Vomitei
voomeetay

He/She has been sick
Vomitou
voomeetoh

I can't sleep
Não consigo dormir
nowñ kohñseegoo doormeer

He/She can't sleep
Não consegue dormir
nowñ kohñseg doormeer

I can't breathe
Não consigo respirar
nowñ kohñseegoo rrishpeerahr

He/She can't breathe
Não consegue respirar
nowñ kohñseg rrishpeerahr

I can't move my . . .
Não consigo mexer o/a . . .
nowñ kohñseegoo mishayr oo/a...

He/She can't move his *or* her . . .
Não consegue mexer o/a . . .
nowñ kohñseg mishayr oo/a...

157

My . . . is bleeding
O meu . . ./A minha . . .
  sangra
oo mayoo . . ./a meenya . . .
  sañgra

He/She is bleeding
Está a sangrar
istah a sañgrahr

It's my . . .
É o/a . . .
e oo/a . . .

It's his *or* her . . .
É o/a . . .
e oo/a . . .

It's my arm
É o braço
e oo brahsoo

It's his *or* her ankle
É o tornozelo
e oo toornoozayloo

It's my leg
É a perna
e a perna

It's his *or* her leg
É a perna
e a perna

I think that . . .
Acho que . . .
ashoo ki . . .

It's broken
Está partido/a
ishtah parteedoo/a

I've sprained it
Tenho uma entorse
taynyoo ooma ayñtorsi

He/She has sprained it
Tem uma entorse
taym ooma ayñtorsi

I have cut myself
Cortei-me
koortay-mi

He/She has cut himself/
herself
Cortou-se
koortoh-si

I have burnt myself
Queimei-me
kaymay-mi

He/She has burnt himself/
herself
Queimou-se
kaymoh-si

I have been stung by an
insect
**Fui mordido/a por um
insecto**
*fwee moordeedoo/a poor ooṁ
eeñsetoo*

He/She has been stung by
an insect
**Foi mordido/a por um
insecto**
*foy moordeedoo/a poor ooṁ
eeñsetoo*

I have been bitten by a dog
Fui mordido/a por um cão
*fwee moordeedoo/a poor ooṁ
kowñ*

He/She has been bitten by a
dog
Foi mordido/a por um cão
*foy moordeedoo/a poor ooṁ
kowñ*

You may hear

Qual é o problema?
kwahl e oo prooblayma
What is the matter?

Onde lhe dói?
ohñd lyi doy
Where does it hurt?

Dói-lhe aqui?
doy-lyi akee
Does it hurt here?

Muito? Pouco?
mweeñtoo pohkoo
A lot? A little?

Há quanto tempo se sente assim?
ah kwañtoo tayñpoo si sayñt aseeñ
How long have you been feeling like this?

Que idade tem?
ki eedahd tayñ
How old are you?/How old is he/she?

Abra a boca, por favor
ahbra a bohka poor favohr
Open your mouth, please

Dispa-se, por favor
deeshpa-si poor favohr
Get undressed, please

Deite-se ali, por favor
dayti-si alee poor favohr
Lie down over there, please

Está a tomar algum medicamento?
ishtah a toomahr ahlgooñ mideekamayñtoo
Are you taking any medicines?

É alérgico/a a algum medicamento?
e alerjeekoo/a a ahlgooñ mideekamayñtoo
Are you allergic to any medicines?

159

Foi vacinado/a contra o tétano?
foy vaseenahdoo/a kohñtra oo tetanoo
Have you been vaccinated against tetanus?

O que comeu (hoje)?
oo ki koomayoo (ohj)
What have you eaten (today)?

Tem uma infecção/Está infectado
taym̃ ooma eeñfesowñ/ishtah eeñfetahdoo
There's an infection/It's infected

Tem uma intoxicação alimentar
taym̃ ooma eeñtokseekasowñ aleemayñtahr
You have food poisoning

É um ataque cardíaco
e oom̃ atahk kardeeakoo
It's a heart attack

Tenho de lhe dar uma injecção
taynyoo di lyi dahr ooma eeñjesowñ
I have to give you an injection

Tem de levar alguns pontos
taym̃ di livahr ahlgooñsh pohñtoosh
You'll have to have some stitches

É preciso fazer um raio-X
e priseezoo fazayr oom̃ rriyoo-sheesh
It is necessary to do an X-ray

Preciso duma análise ao sangue/à urina
priseezoo dooma anahleez ow sañgi/ah ooreena
I need a blood/urine sample

Vou-lhe passar uma receita
voh-lyi pasahr ooma rrisayta
I'm going to give you a prescription

Tome um comprimido três vezes ao dia
tohmi oom̃ kohm̃preemeedoo traysh vayzish ow deea
Take one tablet three times a day

Antes/Depois das refeições
añtish/dipoysh dash rrifaysoyñsh
Before/After meals

Ao deitar
ow daytahr
At bedtime

Tem de descansar
taym̃ di dishkañsahr
You must rest

Tem de ficar na cama durante três dias
taym̃ di feekahr na kama doorañt traysh deeash
You must stay in bed for three days

160

Volte daqui a cinco dias
volti dakee a seeñkoo deeash
Come back in five days' time

Tem de beber muitos líquidos
taym di bibayr mweeñtoosh leekeedoosh
You must drink plenty of liquids

Deve fazer jejum
dev fazayr jijoom
You should eat nothing

Tem de ir para o hospital
taym di eer para oo ohshpeetahl
You have to go to hospital

Não é nada grave
nowñ e nahda grahv
It's nothing serious

Não tem nada
nowñ taym nahda
There is nothing wrong with you

Pode-se vestir
pod-si vishteer
You can get dressed

You may want to say

At the dentist's

I need a dentist
Preciso dum dentista
priseezoo doom dayñteeshta

I have a toothache
Tenho uma dor de dentes
taynyoo ooma dohr di dayñtish

This tooth hurts
Dói-me este dente
doy-mi aysht dayñt

He/She has toothache
Tem uma dor de dentes
taym ooma dohr di dayñtish

I have broken a tooth
Parti um dente
partee oom dayñt

I have lost a filling
Caíu-me um chumbo
kaeeoo-mi oom shoomboo

I have lost a crown
Caíu-me uma coroa
kaeeoo-mi ooma kooroha

He/She has broken a tooth
Partiu um dente
parteeoo oom daynt

He/She has lost a filling
Caíu-lhe um chumbo
kaeeoo-lyi oom shoomboo

He/She has lost a crown
Caíu-lhe uma coroa
kaeeoo-lyi ooma kooroha

Could you fix it temporarily?
**Podia arranjá-lo
provisoriamente?**
*poodeea arranjah-loo
prooveezoryamaynt*

Could you give me an
injection?
Podia-me dar uma injecção?
*poodeea-mi dahr ooma
eenjesown*

Could you give him/her an
injection?
Podia-lhe dar uma injecção?
*poodeea-lyi dahr ooma
eenjesown*

This denture is broken
Esta dentadura está partida
*eshta dayntadoora ishtah
parteeda*

Could you repair it?
Podia repará-la?
poodeea rriparah-la

How much will it cost?
Quanto custa?
kwantoo kooshta

You may hear

Abra a boca, por favor
ahbra a bohka poor favohr
Open your mouth, please

Precisa duma obturação/dum chumbo
priseeza dooma ohbtoorasowñ/ dooṁ shooṁboo
You need a filling

Tenho de lho tirar
taynyoo di lyoo teerahr
I have to extract it

Vou-lhe dar uma injecção
voh-lyi dahr ooma eeñjesowñ
I'm going to give you an injection

Parts of the body

ankle	o tornozelo	*toornoozayloo*
appendix	o apêndice	*apayñdeesi*
arm	o braço	*brahsoo*
back	as costas	*koshtash*
bladder	a bexiga	*bisheega*
blood	o sangue	*sañgi*
body	o corpo	*kohrpoo*
bone	o osso	*ohsoo*
bottom	o rabo	*rahboo*
bowels	os intestinos	*eeñtishteenoosh*
breast	o seio	*sayoo*
buttock	a nádega	*nahdiga*
cartilage	a cartilagem	*karteelahjayṁ*
chest	o peito	*paytoo*
chin	o queixo	*kayshoo*
ear	o ouvido	*ohveedoo*
elbow	o cotovelo	*kotovayloo*
eye	o olho	*ohlyoo*
face	a cara	*kahra*
finger	o dedo	*daydoo*
foot	o pé	*pe*

genitals	os genitais	*jineetiysh*
gland	a glândula	*glañdoola*
hair	o cabelo	*kabayloo*
hand	a mão	*mowñ*
head	a cabeça	*kabaysa*
heart	o coração	*koorasowñ*
heel	o calcanhar	*kahlkanyahr*
hip	a anca	*añka*
jaw	o maxilar	*mahkseelahr*
joint	a articulação	*arteekoolasowñ*
kidney	o rim	*rreeñ*
knee	o joelho	*jooaylyoo*
leg	a perna	*perna*
ligament	o ligamento	*leegamayñtoo*
lip	o lábio	*lahbyoo*
liver	o fígado	*feegadoo*
lung	o pulmão	*poolmowñ*
mouth	a boca	*bohka*
muscle	o músculo	*mooshkooloo*
nail	a unha	*oonya*
neck	o pescoço	*pishkohsoo*
nerve	o nervo	*nayrvoo*
nose	o nariz	*nareesh*
penis	o pénis	*peneesh*
private parts	as partes íntimas	*pahrtiz eeñteemash*
rectum	o recto	*rretoo*
rib	a costela	*kooshtela*
shoulder	o ombro	*ohñbroo*
skin	a pele	*pel*
spine	a coluna	*kooloona*
stomach	o estômago	*ishtohmagoo*
tendon	o tendão	*tayñdowñ*
testicles	os testículos	*tishteekooloosh*
thigh	a coxa	*kohsha*
throat	a garganta	*gargañta*

thumb	o polegar	*pooligahr*
toe	o dedo do pé	*daydoo doo pe*
tongue	a língua	*leeñgwa*
tonsils	as amígdalas	*ameegdalash*
tooth	o dente	*dayñt*
vagina	a vagina	*vajeena*
wrist	o pulso	*poolsoo*

PROBLEMS AND COMPLAINTS

(For car breakdowns, see page 42; see also Emergencies, *page 283)*

● There are several types of police in Portugal, all of them armed. They are:

A Polícia de Segurança Pública (PSP) – they are responsible for law and order in towns and cities, including traffic control. They wear dark blue uniforms. More serious crime may be investigated by the plainclothes **Polícia Judiciária**.

A Guarda Nacional Republicana (GNR) – they are responsible for law and order in rural areas, and also for traffic control on main roads. You may see the words **Brigada de Trânsito** (Traffic Brigade) on their patrol cars. They wear grey uniforms.

A Guarda Fiscal – they serve as customs officers and coastguards and, in small coastal communities, may have wider police functions.

● If your car is towed away, contact the **PSP**, who will tell you where to go to collect it.

● In a hotel or restaurant, if all else fails and you can't get a complaint sorted out to your satisfaction, you can ask for the complaints book (**o livro de reclamações**). Hotels are required by law to have one – you give your name, write down your complaint, and it will be dealt with by the Ministry of Tourism, the **Direcção-Geral do Turismo**. Alternatively you can make your complaint to an official tourist office (**Posto de Turismo**) or direct to the Ministry (address, page 206).

You may see

Avariado	Out of order
Esquadra (da polícia)	Police station
Livro de reclamações	Complaints book

You may want to say

General phrases

Could you help me?
Podia-me ajudar?
poodeea-mi ajoodahr

Could you fix it
  (immediately)?
Podia consertá-lo (já)?
poodeea kohñsirtah-loo (jah)

When can you fix it?
Quando pode consertá-lo?
kwañdoo pod kohñsirtah-loo

Can I speak to the manager?
Posso falar com o gerente?
posoo falahr kohñ oo jirayñt

There's a problem with ...
Há um problema com ...
ah ooñ prooblayma kohñ ...

There isn't/aren't any ...
Não há ...
nowñ ah ...

I need ...
Preciso de ...
priseezoo di ...

The ... doesn't work
O/A ... não funciona
oo/a ... nowñ fooñsyona

The ... is broken
O/A ... está partido/a
oo/a ... ishtah parteedoo/a

I can't ...
Não consigo ...
nowñ kohñseegoo ...

It wasn't my fault
Não tive culpa
nowñ teev koolpa

I have forgotten my ...
**Esqueci-me do meu .../da
  minha ...**
*ishkesee-mi doo mayoo .../da
  meenya ...*

I have lost my ...
Perdi o meu .../a minha ...
*pirdee oo mayoo .../
  a meenya ...*

167

We have lost our . . .
**Perdemos o nosso . . ./a
nossa . . .**
*pirdaymoosh oo nosoo . . ./a
nosa. . .*

My . . . isn't here
**O meu . . ./A minha . . . não
está aqui**
*oo mayoo . . ./a meenya . . .
nowñ ishtah akee*

Someone has stolen my . . .
Roubaram-me o . . ./a . . .
rrohbahrowñ-mi oo . . ./a . . .

Something is missing
Falta alguma coisa
fahlta ahlgooma koyza

My . . . has disappeared
**O meu . . ./A minha . . .
desapareceu**
*oo mayoo . . ./a meenya . . .
dizaparisayoo*

The . . . is missing
Falta o/a . . .
fahlta oo/a . . .

This isn't mine
Isto não é meu
eeshtoo nowñ e mayoo

Where you're staying

There isn't any (hot) water
Não há água (quente)
nowñ ah ahgwa (kayñt)

I need another blanket
Preciso doutro cobertor
priseezoo dohtroo koobirtohr

There isn't any toilet paper
Não há papel higiénico
nowñ ah papel eejyeneekoo

I need a light bulb
Preciso duma lâmpada
priseezoo dooma lañpada

There isn't any electricity
Não há electricidade
nowñ ah iletreeseedahd

There's no light
Não há luz
nowñ ah loosh

There aren't any towels
Não há toalhas
nowñ ah tooahlyash

The shower doesn't work
O chuveiro não funciona
oo shoovayroo nowñ fooñsyona

I need another pillow
Preciso doutra almofada
priseezoo dohtra ahlmoofahda

The lock is broken
A fechadura está partida
a fishadoora ishtah parteeda

The switch on the lamp is broken
O interruptor da lâmpada está partido
oo eeñtirrooptohr da lampada ishtah parteedoo

I can't open the window
Não consigo abrir a janela
nowñ kohñseegoo abreer a janela

I can't turn the tap off
Não consigo fechar a torneira
nowñ kohñseegoo fishahr a toornayra

The toilet doesn't flush
O autoclismo não descarrega
oo owtohkleeshmoo nowñ dishkarrega

The wash-basin is blocked
O lavatório está entupido
oo lavatoryoo ishtah ayñtoopeedoo

The wash-basin is dirty
O lavatório está sujo
oo lavatoryoo ishtah soojoo

The room is . . .
O quarto é . . .
oo kwahrtoo e . . .

The room is too dark
O quarto é muito escuro
oo kwahrtoo e mweeñtoo ishkooroo

The room is too small
O quarto é muito pequeno
oo kwahrtoo e mweeñtoo pikaynoo

It's too hot in the room
Está muito calor no quarto
ishtah mweeñtoo kalohr noo kwahrtoo

The bed is very uncomfortable
A cama é muito desconfortável
a kama e mweeñtoo dishkohñfoortahvel

There's a lot of noise
Há muito barulho
ah mweeñtoo baroolyoo

There's a smell of gas
Há um cheiro a gás
ah ooñ shayroo a gahsh

169

In bars and restaurants

This is undercooked
Isto está cru
eeshtoo ishtah kroo

This is burnt
Isto está queimado
eeshtoo ishtah kaymahdoo

This is cold
Isto está frio
eeshtoo ishtah freeoo

I didn't order this
Não pedi isto
nowñ pidee eeshtoo

This glass is cracked
Este copo está rachado
aysht kopoo ishtah rrashahdoo

This is dirty
Isto está sujo
eeshtoo ishtah soojoo

This smells bad
Isto cheira mal
eeshtoo shayra mahl

This tastes strange
Isto tem um sabor estranho
eeshtoo taym oom sabohr ishtranyoo

There is a mistake on the bill
Há um erro na conta
ah oom ayrroo na kohñta

In shops

I bought this here (yesterday)
Comprei isto aqui (ontem)
kohmpray eeshtoo akee (ohñtaym)

Could you change this for me?
Podia-mo trocar?
poodeea-moo trookahr

I want to return this
Quero devolver isto
keroo divohlvayr eeshtoo

Could you refund me the money?
Podia-me devolver o dinheiro?
poodeea-mi divohlvayr oo deenyayroo

Here is the receipt
Aqui está a factura
akee istah a fahtoora

It has a flaw
Tem um defeito
taym oom difaytoo

It has a hole
Tem um buraco
taym oom boorahkoo

There is a stain/mark
Tem uma mancha/nódoa
taym ooma mañsha/nodooa

This is off/rotten
Isto está estragado
eeshtoo ishtah ishtragahdoo

This isn't fresh	The lid is missing
Isto não é fresco	**Falta a tampa**
eeshtoo nowñ e frayshkoo	*fahlta a tañpa*

Forgetting and losing things and theft

I have forgotten my ticket
Esqueci-me do bilhete
ishkesee-mi doo beelyayt

I have forgotten the key
Esqueci-me da chave
ishkesee-mi da shahv

I have lost my wallet
Perdi a carteira
pirdee a kartayra

I have lost my driving licence
Perdi a carta de condução
pirdee a kahrta di kohñdoosowñ

We have lost our rucksacks
Perdemos as mochilas
pirdaymooz ash moosheelash

Where is the lost property office?
Onde é o serviço de perdidos e achados?
ohñdee e oo sirveesoo di pirdeedooz ee ashahdoosh

Where is the police station?
Onde é a esquadra?
ohñdee e a ishkwahdra

Someone has stolen my bag
Roubaram-me o saco
rrohbahrowñ-mi oo sahkoo

Someone has stolen my car
Roubaram-me o carro
rrohbahrowñ-mi oo kahrroo

Someone has stolen my money
Roubaram-me o dinheiro
rrohbahrowñ-mi oo deenyayroo

If someone is bothering you

Please leave me alone
Deixe-me em paz!
daysh-mi ayñ pahsh

Go away, or I'll call the police
Vá-se embora, ou eu chamo a polícia
vah-si ayñbora oh ayoo shamoo a pooleesya

There is someone bothering
me
Alguém me está a incomodar
*ahlgaym mi ishtah a
eeñkoomoodahr*

There is someone following
me
Alguém me anda a seguir
ahlgaym mi añda a sigeer

You may hear

Helpful and unhelpful replies

Um momento, por favor
ooñ moomayñtoo poor favohr
Just a moment, please

Com certeza
kohñ sirtayza
Of course

Aqui tem
akee taym
Here you are

Arranjo-lhe já outro
arrañjoo-lyi jah ohtroo
I'll bring you another one
immediately

Conserto-lho amanhã
kohñsertoo-lyoo ahmanyañ
I'll fix it for you tomorrow

Lamento, mas não é possível
*lamayñtoo mash nowñ e
pooseevel*
I'm sorry, but it's not possible

**Lamento, não há nada que eu
possa fazer**
*lamayñtoo nowñ ah nahda ki
ayoo posa fazayr*
I'm sorry, there's nothing I
can do

Não sou o/a responsável
nowñ soh oo/a rrishpohñsahvel
I am not the person
responsible

Não somos responsáveis
*nowñ sohmoosh
rrishpohñsahvaysh*
We are not responsible

Devia queixar-se à polícia
diveea kayshahr-si ah pooleesya
You should report it to the
police

O melhor seria . . .
oo milyor sireea . . .
The best thing would be . . .

Questions you may be asked

Quando o/a comprou?
kwañdoo oo/a kohrmproh
When did you buy it?

Tem a factura?
taym a fahtoora
Do you have the receipt?

Quando aconteceu?
kwañdoo akohñtisayoo
When did it happen?

Onde o/a perdeu?
ohñdi oo/a pirdayoo
Where did you lose it?

Onde lho/lha roubaram?
ohñd lyoo/lya rrohbahrowm
Where was it stolen?

Como é o seu saco?
kohmoo e oo sayoo sahkoo
What does your bag look like?

Como é o seu carro?
kohmoo e oo sayoo kahrroo
What does your car look like?

Qual é a marca?
kwahl e a mahrka
What make is it?

Qual é a matrícula do seu carro?
kwahl e a matreekoola doo sayoo kahrroo
What is the registration number of your car?

Como se chama?
kohmoo si shama
What's your name?

Qual é a sua morada?
kwahl e a sooa moorahda
What is your address?

Onde está instalado/a?
ohñd ishtah eeñshtalahdoo/a
Where are you staying?

Qual é o número do seu quarto?
kwahl e oo noomiroo doo sayoo kwahrtoo
What is your room number?

Qual é o número do seu apartamento?
kwahl e oo noomiroo doo sayoo apartamayñtoo
What is the number of your apartment?

Em que 'villa' está?
aym ki veela ishtah
What villa are you in?

Qual é o número do seu passaporte?
kwahl e oo noomiroo doo sayoo pahsaport
What is your passport number?

Tem seguro?
tayñ sigooroo
Are you insured?

Por favor, preencha este impresso
poor favohr priayñsha aysht eeñpresoo
Please fill in this form

BASIC GRAMMAR

Nouns

All Portuguese nouns have a gender – masculine or feminine.

Nouns for male people or animals are masculine; for females they are feminine. With other nouns you can often tell the gender from the word ending.

Most nouns ending in **-o** (but not necessarily **-ão**) are masculine. The few exceptions include **foto** (photo). Nouns ending in **-me** are also generally masculine.

Most nouns ending in **-a** are feminine. Exceptions include **dia** (day), **mapa** (map), and some words ending in **-ma** like **telegrama** (telegram) and **clima** (climate).

Nouns ending in **-ção, -são, -stão** and **-gião** are also feminine. So are nouns ending in **-gem, -ie, -dade** and **-tude**.

Nouns with other endings can be either gender – the Dictionary indicates which.

A masculine plural noun can refer to a mixture of masculine and feminine, e.g.:

irmãos	(brothers *or* brothers and sisters)
filhos	(sons *or* children, i.e. sons and daughters)
os portugueses	(Portuguese men *or* the Portuguese)

Plurals

Nouns are generally made plural by adding **-s** if they end in a vowel (other than **-ão**), or **-es** if they end in a consonant (except **-l** or **-m**), e.g.:

livro – livros   senhor – senhores   português – portugueses

Nouns ending in **-ão** usually change to **-ões**, e.g.: **região – regiões**

A few change to **-ães**, e.g.: **pão – pães**

And a few simply add **-s**, e.g.: **mão – mãos**

Nouns ending in **-al**, **-el**, and **-ol** change to **-ais**, **-éis**, and **-óis**, e.g.: **jornal – jornais   hotel – hotéis   lençol – lençóis**

Nouns ending in **-il** change to **-is** or **-eis**, e.g.:
barril – barris   têxtil – têxteis

Nouns ending in **-m** change to **-ns**, e.g.:
homem – homens   viagem – viagens

Adjectives are made plural in the same way as nouns, e.g.:
branco – brancos   melhor – melhores   azul – azuis
bom – bons

Articles ('a'/'an', 'the')

The Portuguese indefinite article (the equivalent of 'a' or 'an') has different forms: **um** is used with masculine nouns, **uma** with feminine ones, e.g.:
um carro   **uma estrada**

The definite article ('the') has different forms for masculine and feminine, and also for singular and plural:

	masculine	*feminine*
singular	**o**	**a**
plural	**os**	**as**

e.g.:	**o carro**	**a estrada**
	os carros	**as estradas**

In the Dictionary, nouns are given with the definite article to show their gender.

'A', 'de', 'em' and 'por'

When **de** or **em** are followed by the articles **um** or **uma**, they combine in speech as follows (though they are sometimes written as separate words):

with:	masculine	feminine	
de (of, from)	**dum**	**duma**	(of a, from a)
em (in, on)	**num**	**numa**	(in a, on a)

When **a**, **de**, **em** and **por** are followed by the articles **o**, **a**, **os** or **as**, they combine as follows:

with:		masculine	feminine	
a (to)	singular	ao	à	(to the)
	plural	aos	às	
de (of, from)	singular	do	da	(of/from the)
	plural	dos	das	
em (in, on)	singular	no	na	(in/on the)
	plural	nos	nas	
por (through,	singular	pelo	pela	(through, the, etc.)
for, because of)	plural	pelos	pelas	

When **de** or **em** are followed by the pronouns **ele**, **ela**, **eles** or **elas**, they combine as follows:
de + **ele** = **dele** (of him/it) **em** + **elas** = **nelas** (in them), etc.

This process of combination also happens with demonstratives (see below).

Adjectives

Adjectives 'agree' with the nouns they are describing – they have different endings for masculine and feminine, singular and plural. Plurals are formed as described earlier for nouns.

Many adjectives end in **-o** for masculine and **-a** for feminine, e.g.:

um carro branco   **uma casa branca**

Adjectives ending in **-es**, **-or** or **-u** usually add **-a** to form the feminine, e.g.:

inglês – inglesa　　　　　　**cru – crua**

Those ending in **-eu** change to **-eia**, e.g.: **europeu – europeia**
Those ending in **-ão** usually change to **-ã**, e.g.: **alemão – alemã**

Most adjectives with other endings have the same form in the masculine and feminine.

Position of adjectives

Most adjectives come after the noun, e.g.
vinho branco　　**as praias portuguesas**　　**uma camisa verde**

Some common adjectives normally come *before* the noun, including:

bom, boa (good)	**mau, má** (bad)
muito (much, many)	**pouco** (not much, few)
bastante (quite a lot)	**demasiado** (too much/many)
algum (any, some)	**outro** (other)
todo (every, all)	**cada** (each)
primeiro (first)	**último** (last)

e.g.:
uma boa ideia (a good idea)
todos os dias (every day)
a primeira vez (the first time)

Comparatives and superlatives ('more', 'the most')

'More' is **mais** and comes before the adjective – it also gives the equivalent of 'smaller', 'older', etc., e.g.:
mais interessante (more interesting)
mais pequeno (smaller)
mais velho (older)

'Less' is **menos**:
menos importante (less important)
menos complicado (less complicated)

The comparatives of 'good', 'bad' and 'big' are **melhor** (better), **pior** (worse) and **maior** (bigger).

'Than', as in 'more than' and 'less than', is **do que**, or just **que**, e.g.: **Este carro é maior do que aquele** (This car is bigger than that one).

To say 'the more/most' or 'the less/least', put the definite article **o** or **a** before **mais** or **menos**, e.g.:
o mais barato (the cheaper/cheapest)
a mais cara (the more/most expensive)

Possessives ('my', 'your', 'his', 'her', etc.)

Possessive adjectives are used with the definite article. Like other adjectives, they 'agree' with the nouns they are describing. The forms are:

	singular		*plural*	
	masculine	*feminine*	*masculine*	*feminine*
my	**o meu**	**a minha**	**os meus**	**as minhas**
our	**o nosso**	**a nossa**	**os nossos**	**as nossas**
your	**o teu**	**a tua**	**os teus**	**as tuas**
	o vosso	**a vossa**	**os vossos**	**as vossas**
his/her/				
your/their	**o seu**	**a sua**	**os seus**	**as suas**

e.g.
a minha mulher (my wife)
a nossa mesa (our table)

There is no Portuguese equivalent of the English -'s as in 'David's sister', 'my husband's passport', etc. Instead, the word **de** ('of') is used:

a irmã de David (David's sister)
o passaporte do meu marido (my husband's passport)

Since **o seu, a sua** and their plural forms can mean 'his', 'her', 'your' or 'their', an alternative form is used to avoid ambiguity. This alternative form is like saying 'the ... of him', 'the ... of you', etc., e.g.:
o quarto dele (his room)
a casa dela (her house)

Demonstratives ('this', 'that')

There is one way of saying 'this' and two of saying 'that' – one for things that are fairly close; one for things 'over there':

	singular		*plural*	
	masculine	*feminine*	*masculine*	*feminine*
this, these	**este**	**esta**	**estes**	**estas**
that, those	**esse**	**essa**	**esses**	**essas**
that, those (over there)	**aquele**	**aquela**	**aqueles**	**aquelas**

All of these words are also used as demonstrative pronouns ('this one', 'that one', etc.), e.g.: **Prefiro este** (I prefer this one).

There are also 'neuter' forms: **isto, isso, aquilo**. They are used when no specific noun is being referred to, e.g.: **Isto é impossível** (This is impossible).

When any of these demonstratives follow **de** or **em**, the words combine, e.g.:
de + este = deste	(of/from this one)
de + aquele = daquele	(of/from that one over there)
em + esse = nesse	(in/on that one)

When **aquele** follows **a**, the words combine as follows:
a + aquele = àquele	(to that one)
a + aquela = àquela	(to that one)
a + aquilo = àquilo	(to that)

Subject pronouns ('I', 'you', 'he', 'she', etc.)

1st person	I		**eu**
2nd person	you	*(informal)**	**tu**
	you		**você**
3rd person	you	*(formal)**	**o senhor** *(masculine)*
			a senhora *(feminine)*
	he		**ele**
	she		**ela**
1st person	we		**nós**
3rd person	you	*(informal)**	**vocês**
	you	*(formal)**	**os senhores** *(masculine)*
			as senhoras *(feminine)*
	they		**eles** *(masculine)*
			elas *(feminine)*

(**see 'You' below**)

These pronouns are used much less than their English equivalents – Portuguese verbs have different endings which show what the subject is (see **Verbs** below). However, the subject pronoun is often necessary to avoid confusion, or to give emphasis where in English you would stress the pronoun, e.g.: **Ele é inglês, ela é escocesa** (*He* is English, *she* is Scottish).

'You'

In English, there is only one way of addressing people using the word 'you'. In Portuguese, there are several ways, and you show different degrees of formality and politeness depending on the word you use for 'you'.

The most formal way uses the third person of the verb (singular or plural). The words for 'you' are **o senhor/os senhores** (talking to a man/to men) or **a senhora/as senhoras** (talking to a woman/to women).

Você (**vocês** in the plural) usually indicates greater familiarity, and is often used between colleagues at work, or when you feel on an equal footing with someone. It is not used in the north of Portugal. **Você/vocês** is also followed by the third person form of the verb.

The most informal way of saying 'you' implies intimacy. For example, it is used between brothers and sisters, and between close friends. It is also used, even on first acquaintance, between children and young people. The words for 'you' are **tu** (with the second person singular of the verb) or **vocês** (with the third person plural of the verb).

Object pronouns

These are the equivalent of 'me', 'him', 'it', 'us', etc. Portuguese has both direct object and indirect object pronouns. (Indirect objects are the equivalent of 'to/for me', 'to/for us', etc.)

The same words are used for both types, except in the third person. The full list is:

	singular	*plural*
	me	nos
	te	vos
direct	o, a	os, as
indirect	lhe	lhes

They normally come after the verb, joined to it by a hyphen, e.g.:
Prove-o (Try it)
Fica-lhe bem (It suits you)

But after **não**, and after words like **como, onde, que, quem, quando,** etc., the object pronoun comes before the verb, e.g.:
Não me fica bem (It doesn't suit me)
Onde o perdeu? (Where did you lose it?)

When the pronouns **o, a, os** or **as** come at the end of a word ending in **-r** or **-s**, the sound and spelling change, e.g.:
(provar + o)   **Posso prová-lo?** (May I try it?)
(queremos + o) **Queremo-lo** (We want it)

Portuguese object pronouns are complicated, but they are not always necessary, e.g.
Gosta? (Do you like it?)
Gosto (I do – i.e. I like it)

Verbs

Portuguese verbs have different endings according to (i) the subject of the verb, (ii) the tense. There are three main groups of verbs, with different sets of endings for each group.

In dictionaries, verbs are listed in the infinitive form which ends in **-ar**, **-er** or **-ir** (these are the three groups).

Below are the endings for the present tense of these three groups:

	-ar falar	-er comer	-ir partir
eu	falo	como	parto
tu	falas	comes	partes
você, o senhor, a senhora ele, ela	fala	come	parte
nós	falamos	comemos	partimos
vocês, os senhores, as senhoras, eles, elas	falam	comem	partem

Most uses of the Portuguese present tense are similar to English. It is used to say what is the case at the time of speaking, or to say what will happen in the future, e.g.:
Falo inglês (I speak English)
Parto amanhã (I'm leaving tomorrow)

To say what is happening at the moment, the present tense of **estar** is used, followed by **a** and the appropriate verb, e.g.:
Estou a ler (I'm reading)
Está a chover (it's raining)

Reflexives

Reflexive verbs are listed in dictionaries with the reflexive pronoun **se** on the end, e.g. **chamar-se** (to be called), **sentar-se** (to sit down).

The reflexive pronouns are:

me	**nos**
te	**vos**
se	**se**

e.g.: **Chamo-me John** (My name's John)
Sente-se (Sit down/Have a seat)

'To be'

There are two Portuguese verbs meaning 'to be': **ser** and **estar**.

Estar is used for temporary states, and to say where something is if you are referring to a person or to something that can be moved, e.g.:

Estou doente (I'm ill)
O carro está na rua (The car is in the street)
O dinheiro está no cofre (The money is in the safe)

Otherwise **ser** is used, e.g.:
Sou irlandês (I'm Irish)
Portugal é um país interessante (Portugal is an interesting country)
O hotel é na Rua Castilho (The hotel is in the Rua Castilho)

You may also come across the verb **ficar**, which can have several meanings depending on the context. Usually the meaning has to do with staying, or being situated. **Ficar** can be used instead of **ser** to say where something is, if you are referring to a place or to something that has a permanent location, e.g.:

O Museu Gulbenkian fica na Avenida de Berna (The Gulbenkian Museum is in the Avenida de Berna)
A estação fica longe (The station is a long way away)
Braga fica no norte (Braga is in the north)

Ser and **estar** are both irregular:

	ser	estar
eu	sou	estou
tu	és	estás
você, o senhor, a senhora ele, ela	é	está
nós	somos	estamos
vocês, os senhores, as senhoras eles, elas	são	estão

Other irregular verbs

Other common verbs that are also irregular include:

dar (to give)	ir (to go)	ter (to have)	ver (to see)	vir (to come)
dou	vou	tenho	vejo	venho
dás	vais	tens	vês	vens
dá	vai	tem	vê	vem
damos	vamos	temos	vemos	vimos
dão	vão	têm	vêem	vêm

Some common verbs are irregular mainly in the 'I . . .' form of the present tense: **dizer – digo** (I say), **fazer – faço** (I do), **poder – posso** (I can), **saber – sei** (I know), **trazer – trago** (I bring).

Parts of other irregular verbs are given in the Dictionary.

Other verb tenses

A few verbs in other tenses that you may find useful are:

ir (to go)	I went/have been	**fui**
	we went/have been	**fomos**
	I used to go	**ia**
	we used to go	**íamos**
ser (to be)	I was/used to be	**era**
	we were/used to be	**éramos**
estar (to be)	I was/have been	**estive**
	we were/have been	**estivemos**
ter (to have)	I had/used to have	**tinha**
	we had/used to have	**tínhamos**
vir (to come)	I came/have come	**vim**
	we came/have come	**viemos**
	I used to come	**vinha**
	we used to come	**vínhamos**

For talking about the future, you can often use the present tense, e.g.:

Amanhã jogo ténis (Tomorrow I am playing tennis)

Voltamos a Manchester no sábado (We return/are returning to Manchester on Saturday)

In a similar way to English, you can also say 'I'm going to . . .', using the verb **ir**, followed by an infinitive, e.g.:

Vou comprar estes postais (I'm going to buy these postcards)

Vai telefonar às oito horas (He/She is going to phone at 8.00)

Negatives

To make a verb negative, put **não** before it, e.g.:

Não tenho filhos (I don't have any children)

Não falo muito português (I don't speak much Portuguese)

O senhor Rodrigues não está (Mr Rodrigues isn't in)

Portuguese has double negatives, e.g.:
Não tenho nada (I don't have anything) (**nada** literally means 'nothing')

Questions

When a question does not begin with a question word ('where?', 'how?', 'why?', etc.), the word order is the same as it would be in an ordinary statement. The intonation of the voice changes to make it a question, e.g.:

Há um café na praça	There is a café in the square
Há um café na praça?	Is there a café in the square?

DAYS, MONTHS, DATES

Days

Portuguese names of days are not written with capital letters.

With the exception of Saturday and Sunday, the days of the week have numbers: 'second', 'third', etc. To remember which is which, it helps to think of the first day as Sunday.

Sunday	**o domingo**	*doomeeñgoo*
Monday	**a segunda-feira**	*sigooñda-fayra*
Tuesday	**a terça-feira**	*tayrsa-fayra*
Wednesday	**a quarta-feira**	*kwahrta-fayra*
Thursday	**a quinta-feira**	*keeñta-fayra*
Friday	**a sexta-feira**	*sayshta-fayra*
Saturday	**o sábado**	*sahbadoo*

People often leave off **feira** and just say **segunda, terça**, etc. In written notices and timetables, the names of the days are usually shortened by writing '2nd', etc. as a number, e.g. **2ª-feira**.

Months

January	**Janeiro**	*janayroo*
February	**Fevereiro**	*fivirayroo*
March	**Março**	*mahrsoo*
April	**Abril**	*abreel*
May	**Maio**	*miyoo*
June	**Junho**	*joonyoo*
July	**Julho**	*joolyoo*
August	**Agosto**	*agohshtoo*
September	**Setembro**	*sitaymbroo*
October	**Outubro**	*ohtoobroo*
November	**Novembro**	*noovaymbroo*
December	**Dezembro**	*dizaymbroo*

Seasons

spring	**a primavera**	*preemavera*
summer	**o verão**	*virowñ*
autumn	**o outono**	*ohtohnoo*
winter	**o inverno**	*eeñvernoo*

General phrases

day	**o dia**	*oo deea*
week	**a semana**	*a simana*
fortnight	**quinze dias**	*keeñz deeash*
month	**o mês**	*oo maysh*
year	**o ano**	*oo anoo*
today	**hoje**	*ohj*
tomorrow	**amanhã**	*ahmanyañ*
yesterday	**ontem**	*ohñtaym*
in the morning	**de manhã**	*di manyañ*
in the afternoon/ evening	**de tarde**	*di tahrd*
at night	**à noite**	*ah noyt*
this morning	**esta manhã**	*eshta manyañ*
this afternoon/ evening	**esta tarde**	*eshta tahrd*
tonight	**esta noite**	*eshta noyt*
tomorrow morning	**amanhã de manhã**	*ahmanyañ di manyañ*
tomorrow afternoon/ evening	**amanhã à tarde**	*ahmanyañ ah tahrd*
yesterday afternoon/ evening	**ontem à tarde**	*ohñtaym ah tahrd*
last night	**ontem à noite**	*ohñtaym ah noyt*

on Monday	**na segunda(-feira)**	*na sigooñda(-fayra)*
on Tuesdays	**às terças(-feiras)**	*ahsh tayrsash (-fayrash)*
every Wednesday	**todas as quartas (-feiras)**	*tohdaz ash kwahrtash (-fayrash)*
in August	**em Agosto**	*ayñ...*
in spring	**na primavera**	*na...*
at the beginning of March	**no princípio de Março**	*noo preeñseepyoo di...*
in the middle of June	**em meados de Junho**	*ayñ miahdoosh di...*
at the end of September	**no fim de Setembro**	*noo feeñ di...*
in six months' time	**daqui a seis meses**	*dakee a...*
during the summer	**durante o verão**	*doorañt...*
two years ago	**há dois anos**	*ah...*
in the '90s	**nos anos noventa**	*nooz anoosh...*
last...	**...passado/a**	*...pasahdoo/a*
last Monday	**na segunda-feira passada**	*na sigooñda-fayra pasahda*
last week	**na semana passada**	*na simana pasahda*
last month	**no mês passado**	*noo maysh pasahdoo*
last year	**no ano passado**	*noo ano pasahdoo*
next...	**próximo/a...**	*proseemoo/ proseema...*
or	**...que vem**	*...ki vayñ*
next Tuesday	**na próxima terça-feira**	*na proseema tayrsa-fayra*
next week	**na semana que vem**	*na simana ki vayñ*
next month	**no mês que vem**	*noo maysh ki vayñ*
next year	**no ano que vem**	*noo ano ki vayñ*

What day is it today?	**Que dia é hoje?** *ki deea e ohj*
What is the date today?	**Qual é a data de hoje?** *kwahl e a dahta di ohj*
When is your birthday?	**Quando é o seu aniversário?** *kwañdoo e oo sayoo aneevirsahryoo*
It's (on) the first of January	**É no dia um de Janeiro** *e noo deea oom di janayroo*
(on) Tuesday 10th May	**(na) terça-feira, dez de Maio** *(na) tayrsa-fayra desh di miyoo*
1992	**mil novecentos e noventa e dois** *meel novisayñtooz ee noovayñta ee doysh*
the 20th century	**o século vinte** *oo sekooloo veeñt*

TIME

one o'clock	**uma hora**	*ooma ora*
two o'clock	**duas horas**	*dooaz orash*
twelve o'clock	**doze horas**	*dohzi orash*
a quarter past eight	**oito e um quarto**	*oytoo ee ooṁ kwahrtoo*
half past...	**...e meia**	*...ee maya*
five past...	**...e cinco**	*...ee seeñkoo*
twenty-five past...	**...e vinte e cinco**	*...ee veeñt ee seeñkoo*
a quarter to...	**um quarto para...**	*ooṁ kwahrtoo para...*
or	**...menos um quarto**	*...maynooz ooṁ kwahrtoo*
ten to...	**dez para...**	*desh para...*
or	**...menos dez**	*...maynoosh desh*
twenty to...	**vinte para...**	*veeñt para...*
or	**...menos vinte**	*...maynoosh veeñt*
in the morning (a.m.)	**da manhã**	*da manyañ*
in the afternoon/ evening (p.m.)	**da tarde**	*da tahrd*
at night	**da noite**	*da noyt*
in the early morning	**da madrugada**	*da madroogahda*
noon/midday	**meio-dia**	*mayoo-deea*
midnight	**meia-noite**	*maya-noyt*
a quarter of an hour	**um quarto de hora**	*ooṁ kwahrtoo di ora*
three quarters of an hour	**três quartos de hora**	*traysh kwahrtoosh di ora*
half an hour	**meia hora**	*maya ora*

24-hour clock

0000	**zero (horas)**	*zeroo (orash)*
0900	**nove (horas)**	*nov (orash)*
1300	**treze (horas)**	*trayzi (orash)*
1430	**catorze e trinta**	*katohrz ee treeñta*
2149	**vinte e uma e quarenta e nove**	*veeñt ee ooma ee kwarayñta ee nov*
at...	**à.../às...**	*ah.../ahsh...*
exactly/precisely...	**...em ponto**	*...ayñ pohñtoo*
just after...	**...e picos**	*...ee peekoosh*
about...	**mais ou menos**	*...miyz oh maynoosh*
approximately...	**aproximadamente...**	*aproseemahdamayñt...*
nearly...	**quase...**	*kwahzi...*
soon	**daqui a pouco**	*dakee a pohkoo*
early	**cedo**	*saydoo*
late	**tarde**	*tahrd*
on time	**à hora**	*ah ora*
in time	**a tempo**	*a tayñpoo*
earlier on	**antes**	*añtish*
later on	**mais tarde**	*miysh tahrd*
half an hour ago	**há meia hora**	*ah maya ora*
in ten minutes' time	**daqui a dez minutos**	*dakee a desh meenootoosh*

What time is it? **Que horas são?**
ki orash sowñ

It's... **É.../São...**
e.../sowñ...

It's one o'clock **É uma hora**
e ooma ora

It's six o'clock **São seis horas**
sowñ sayz orash

It's a quarter past eight **São oito e um quarto**
sowñ oytoo ee ooñ kwahrtoo

(At) what time ...?	**A que horas ... ?**
	a ki orash ...
At ...	**À ... / Às ...**
	ah ... / ahsh ...
At half past one	**À uma e meia**
	*ah **ooma** ee **maya***
At a quarter to seven	**Às sete menos um quarto**
	*ahsh set **maynoosh** oom **kwahr**too*
At 2055	**Às vinte e cinquenta e cinco**
	*ahsh veent ee seeñ**kwayñ**ta ee*
	***seeñ**koo*

COUNTRIES AND NATIONALITIES

Languages are the same as the masculine adjective. Nationalities are written with a small letter.

The word for 'the' (**o** or **a**) is used before the names of most countries when they form part of a sentence, but not when they appear on their own (e.g. in the address on an envelope).

Country/Continent   Nationality

Country/Continent		Nationality (masculine, feminine)
Africa	**África**	**africano, africana**
Algeria	**a Argélia**	**argelino, argelina**
Angola	**Angola**	**angolano, angolana**
Asia	**a Ásia**	**asiático, asiática**
Australia	**a Austrália**	**australiano, australiana**
Austria	**a Áustria**	**austríaco, austríaca**
Azores	**os Açores**	**açoriano, açoriana**
Basque Country	**o País Basco**	**basco, basca**
Belgium	**a Bélgica**	**belga, belga**
Brazil	**o Brasil**	**brasileiro, brasileira**
Canada	**o Canadá**	**canadiano, canadiana**
Cape Verde	**Cabo Verde**	**cabo-verdiano, cabo-verdiana**
Catalonia	**a Catalunha**	**catalão, catalã**
China	**a China**	**chinês, chinesa**
Czechoslovakia	**a Checoslováquia**	**checoslovaco, checoslovaca**
Denmark	**a Dinamarca**	**dinamarquês, dinamarquesa**
England	**a Inglaterra**	**inglês, inglesa**

Europe	a Europa	europeu, europeia
France	a França	francês, francesa
Germany	a Alemanha	alemão, alemã
Great Britain	a Grã-Bretanha	britânico, britânica
Greece	a Grécia	grego, grega
Guinea Bissau	a Guiné	guineense, guineense
Hungary	a Hungria	húngaro, húngara
India	a Índia	indiano, indiana
Ireland	a Irlanda	irlandês, irlandesa
Italy	a Itália	italiano, italiana
Japan	o Japão	japonês, japonesa
Macao	Macau	macaense, macaense
Madeira	a Madeira	madeirense, madeirense
Morocco	Marrocos	marroquino, marroquina
Mozambique	Moçambique	moçambicano, moçambicana
Netherlands	os Países Baixos, a Holanda	holandês, holandesa
New Zealand	a Nova Zelândia	neo-zelandês, neo-zelandesa
North America	a América do Norte	norte-americano, norte-americana
Northern Ireland	a Irlanda do Norte	norte-irlandês, norte-irlandesa
Norway	a Noruega	norueguês, norueguesa
Poland	a Polónia	polaco, polaca
Portugal	Portugal	português, portuguesa
Russia	a Rússia	russo, russa
São Tomé and Príncipe	São Tomé e Príncipe	são-tomense, são-tomense
Scotland	a Escócia	escocês, escocesa
South America	a América do Sul	sul-americano, sul-americana
Soviet Union	a União Soviética	soviético, soviética
Spain	a Espanha	espanhol, espanhola
Sweden	a Suécia	sueco, sueca

Switzerland	a Suíça	suíço, suíça
Timor	Timor	timorense, timorense
Turkey	a Turquia	turco, turca
United Kingdom	o Reino Unido	
United States	os Estados Unidos	estadunidense, estadunidense
Wales	o País de Gales	galês, galesa
West Indies	as Antilhas	antilhano, antilhana
Yugoslavia	a Jugoslávia	jugoslavo, jugoslava

GENERAL SIGNS AND NOTICES

Aberto	Open
Água potável	Drinking water
Aluga-se	To let
Andar	Floor
Atenção	Caution, Beware
Atenção ao comboio	Mind the train
Atraso	Delay
Avariado/a	Out of order
Aviso	Notice
Bilheteira	Ticket office
Bilhetes	Tickets
Caixa	Cash desk, Cashier
Caixa automática	Cash dispenser
Casa de banho	Toilet
Cave	Basement
Chegadas	Arrivals
Completo	Full, No vacancies
Correio	Post (Office)
Cuidado	Caution, Take care
Cuidado com o cão	Beware of the dog
Direito de admissão reservado	The management reserves the right of admission
É favor (não)	Please (do not)
Elevador	Lift
Empurre	Push
Encerrado	Closed
Entrada	Entrance
Entrada proibida (a pessoas estranhas ao serviço)	No entry (to unauthorized persons)
Esgotado	Sold out
Fechado (para almoço/férias)	Closed (for lunch/holidays)

Frio	Cold
Fumadores	Smokers
Greve	Strike
Homens	Gentlemen
Horário de expediente	Office hours
Horário de visita	Visiting hours
Lavar à mão	Handwash
Limpar a seco	Dry-clean
Liquidação	Sale
Livre	Free, Vacant
Mantenha o acesso livre	Keep entrance clear
Manter num local fresco	Keep in a cool place
Miradouro	Vantage point (*for views*)
Modo de emprego	Instructions for use
Não distraia o motorista	Do not distract the driver's attention
Não fumadores	Non-smokers
Não fumar	No smoking
Não funciona	Out of order
Não mexer	Do not touch
Não pisar a relva	Keep off the grass
Ocupado	Occupied, Engaged
Pare, Escute, Olhe	Stop, Listen, Look (*at railway crossings*)
Perigo de incêndio	Fire hazard
Perigo (de morte)	Danger (of death)
Pintado de fresco	Wet paint
Piso	Floor
Privado	Private
Proibido fumar	No smoking
Proibido vazar lixo	No litter
Promoção	Special offers
Puxe	Pull
Quente	Hot
Rés-do-chão (R/C)	Ground floor

Reservado	Reserved
Saída (de emergência)	(Emergency) exit
Sala de espera	Waiting room
Saldos	Sale, Bargains
Senhoras	Ladies
Silêncio	Silence
Toque a campainha	Ring the bell
Usar antes de	Consume before
Venda de selos	Stamps sold
Vende-se	For sale

CONVERSION TABLES
(approximate equivalents)

Linear measurements

centimetres	**centímetros (cm)**
metres	**metros (m)**
kilometres	**quilómetros (km)**

10 cm = 4 inches	1 inch = 2.54 cm
50 cm = 19.6 inches	1 foot = 30 cm
1 metre = 39.37 inches	1 yard = 0.91 m
(just over 1 yard)	
100 metres = 110 yards	
1 km = 0.62 miles	1 mile = 1.61 km

To convert
km to miles: divide by 8 and multiply by 5
miles to km: divide by 5 and multiply by 8

Miles		Kilometres
0.6	1	1.6
1.2	2	3.2
1.9	3	4.8
2.5	4	6.4
3	5	8
6	10	16
12	20	32
19	30	48
25	40	64
31	50	80
62	100	161
68	110	177
75	120	193
81	130	209

Liquid measures

litre   **litro (l)**

1 litre = 1.8 pints   1 pint = 0.57 litre
5 litres = 1.1 gallons   1 gallon = 4.55 litres
'A litre of water's a pint and three quarters'

Gallons		Litres
0.2	1	4.5
0.4	2	9
0.7	3	13.6
0.9	4	18
1.1	5	23
2.2	10	45.5

Weights

gram   **grama (g)**
kilo   **quilo (kg)**

100 g = 3.5 oz   1 oz = 28 g
200 g = 7 oz   ¼ lb = 113 g
½ kilo = 1.1 lb   ½ lb = 227 g
1 kilo = 2.2 lb   1 lb = 454 g

Pounds		Kilos (Grams)
2.2	1	0.45 (450)
4.4	2	0.9 (900)
6.6	3	1.4 (1,400)
8.8	4	1.8 (1,800)
11	5	2.3 (2,300)
22	10	4.5 (4,500)

Area

hectare   **hectare (ha)**

1 hectare = 2.5 acres   1 acre = 0.4 hectares

To convert
hectares to acres: divide by 2 and multiply by 5
acres to hectares: divide by 5 and multiply by 2

Hectares		Acres
0.4	1	2.5
2.0	5	12
4	10	25
10	25	62
20	50	124
40.5	100	247

Clothing and shoe sizes

Women's dresses and suits

UK	10	12	14	16	18	20
Continent	36	38	40	42	44	46

Men's suits and coats

UK	36	38	40	42	44	46
Continent	46	48	50	52	54	56

Men's shirts

UK	14	14½	15	15½	16	16½	17
Continent	36	37	38	39	41	42	43

Shoes

UK	2	3	4	5	6	7	8	9	10	11
Continent	35	36	37	38	39	41	42	43	44	45

Waist and chest measurements

inches	28	30	32	34	36	38	40	42	44	46	48	50
centimetres	71	76	81	87	91	97	102	107	112	117	122	127

Tyre pressures

lb/sq in	15	18	20	22	24	26	28	30	33	35
kg/sq cm	1.1	1.3	1.4	1.5	1.7	1.8	2.0	2.1	2.3	2.5

NATIONAL HOLIDAYS

Ano Novo	New Year's Day	1 January
Terça-feira de Carnaval	Shrove Tuesday	
Sexta-feira Santa	Good Friday	
Dia da Liberdade	Freedom Day	25 April
Dia do Trabalhador	Labour Day	1 May
Corpo de Deus	Corpus Christi	
Dia de Portugal	National Day	10 June
Assunção de Nossa Senhora	Assumption	15 August
Implantação da República	Republic Day	5 October
Todos os Santos	All Saints' Day	1 November
Restauração da Independência	Restoration of Independence	1 December
Imaculada Conceição	Immaculate Conception	8 December
Natal	Christmas Day	25 December

USEFUL ADDRESSES

In the UK and Ireland

Portuguese National Tourist Office
1–5 New Bond Street
London W1Y 0NP
Tel: 071–493 3873

Portuguese Embassy
11 Belgrave Square
London SW1X 8PP
Tel: 071–235 5331

Portuguese Embassy
Knocksinna House
Knocksinna
Fox Rock
Dublin 18
Tel: 2893569

Portuguese Chamber of Commerce and Industry
1–5 New Bond Street
London W1Y 9PE
Tel: 071–493 9973

Portuguese Government Trade Office
1–5 New Bond Street
London W1Y 9PE
Tel: 071–493 0212

TAP Air Portugal
Gillingham House
38 Gillingham Street
London SW1V 1JW
Tel: 071–828 2521

In Portugal

Automóvel Club de Portugal
Rua Rosa Araújo, 24–26
1200 Lisboa
Tel: 563931

Instituto de Promoção Turística
R. Alexandre Herculano,
  51–2.º
1200 Lisboa
Tel: 681174

ENATUR (Empresa Nacional de Turismo)
Av. Stª Joana a Princesa, 10-A
1700 Lisboa
Tel: 8481221/8489078

Direcção-Geral do Turismo
Av. António Augusto de
  Aguiar, 86
1099 Lisboa
Tel: 571524

Federação Portuguesa de
Pescas
Rua Sociedade
Farmacêutica, 56–2.º
Lisboa
Tel: 539027/8

There are British consulates in: Oporto, Portimão, Funchal
(Madeira) and Ponta Delgada (Azores).

British Embassy
Rua S. Domingos à Lapa, 37
1200 Lisboa
Tel: 3961191

Irish Embassy
Rua Imprensa à Estrela, 1–4.º
Lisboa
Tel: 3961569

NUMBERS

0	**zero**	*zeroo*
1	**um/uma**	*ooñ/ooma*
2	**dois/duas**	*doysh/dooash*
3	**três**	*traysh*
4	**quatro**	*kwahtroo*
5	**cinco**	*seeñkoo*
6	**seis**	*saysh*
7	**sete**	*set*
8	**oito**	*oytoo*
9	**nove**	*nov*
10	**dez**	*desh*
11	**onze**	*ohñz*
12	**doze**	*dohz*
13	**treze**	*trayz*
14	**catorze**	*katohrz*
15	**quinze**	*keeñz*
16	**dezasseis**	*dizasaysh*
17	**dezassete**	*dizaset*
18	**dezoito**	*dizoytoo*
19	**dezanove**	*dizanov*
20	**vinte**	*veeñt*
21	**vinte e um/uma**	*veeñt ee ooñ/ooma*
22	**vinte e dois/duas**	*veeñt ee doysh/dooash*
23, etc.	**vinte e três**	*veeñt ee traysh*
30	**trinta**	*treeñta*
31	**trinta e um/uma**	*treeñta ee ooñ/ooma*
32	**trinta e dois/duas**	*treeñta ee doysh/dooash*
33, etc.	**trinta e três**	*treeñta ee traysh*
40	**quarenta**	*kwarayñta*
50	**cinquenta**	*seeñkwayñta*
60	**sessenta**	*sisayñta*
70	**setenta**	*sitayñta*
80	**oitenta**	*oytayñta*

90	**noventa**	*noovaynta*
100	**cem**	*sayñ*
101	**cento e um/uma**	*sayñtoo ee ooñ/ooma*
102	**cento e dois/duas**	*sayñtoo ee doysh/dooash*
103, etc.	**cento e três**	*sayñtoo ee traysh*
200	**duzentos, -as**	*doozayñtoosh, -ash*
300	**trezentos, -as**	*trizayñtoosh, -ash*
400	**quatrocentos, -as**	*kwahtroosayñtoosh, -ash*
500	**quinhentos, -as**	*keenyayñtoosh, -ash*
600	**seiscentos, -as**	*sayshsayñtoosh, -ash*
700	**setecentos, -as**	*setisayñtoosh, -ash*
800	**oitocentos, -as**	*oytoosayñtoosh, -ash*
900	**novecentos, -as**	*novisayñtoosh, -ash*
1,000	**mil**	*meel*
2,000, etc.	**dois mil**	*doysh meel*
1,000,000	**um milhão (de)**	*ooñ meelyowñ (di)*
2,000,000	**dois milhões (de)**	*doysh meelyoyñsh (di)*

● The words for 'one', 'two' and hundreds (like other adjectives) have different endings for masculine and feminine, e.g. **dois cafés** (two coffees), **duas cervejas** (two beers), **duzentos e vinte e um escudos** (221 escudos), **trezentas e quarenta e duas pessoas** (342 people).

● In numbers from 101 to 199, 201 to 299, etc., the hundred(s) word is followed by **e**, e.g. **cento e trinta** (130), **setecentos e cinquenta e cinco** (755).

● When **mil** is followed by hundreds, **e** is used after **mil** if the number ends in -00, e.g. **dois mil e quinhentos** (2,500), but **dois mil quinhentos e vinte** (2,520).

● For talking about millions of something, add **de**, e.g. **dois milhões de habitantes** (2,000,000 inhabitants).

● **Years**
1992 **mil novecentos e noventa e dois**
1500 **mil e quinhentos**

DICTIONARY

Portuguese nouns are given with the definite article ('the') to show their gender: **o** for masculine, **a** for feminine (**os** or **as** in the plural).

Adjectives which have different endings for masculine and feminine are shown like this: **branco/a** (i.e. **branco** for masculine, **branca** for feminine). See Basic grammar, page 175, for notes on gender, plurals, etc.

Portuguese–English

Words for food and drink are given in the Menu reader, page 108.

See also General signs and notices, page 198, and the 'You may see' lists in the individual sections.

A

a at, in, on, to; the; her, it
a . . . (quilómetros) . . . (kilometres) away
à = a+a to the
abaixo down; downstairs
aberto/a open
aborrecido/a bored, boring
o **abre-latas** tin opener
abrir to open
acabar to finish
acampar to camp
aceitar to accept
acender to light; to switch on
aceso/a switched on
achar to think

o **acidente** accident
o **aço** steel
acontecer to happen
a **actividade** activity
o **açúcar** sugar
a **adega** cellar (*wine*)
adeus goodbye
adiante forward
adiar to postpone
o **adulto, a adulta** adult
o **aeroporto** airport
afogado/a drowned
a **agência** agency
a **agência de viagens** travel agency
a **agenda** diary
o **agente imobiliário** estate agent
agora now

agradável pleasant
agradecido/a grateful
a **água** water
aguçado/a sharp (*edge*)
agudo/a sharp (*pain*)
a **agulha** needle
ainda still; yet
  ainda não not yet
ajudar to help
a **alcatifa** carpet
a **aldeia** village
além de beyond
  além disso besides
a **alfândega** customs
o **alfinete** pin
a **algibeira** pocket
algo something
o **algodão** cotton
  o **algodão (hidrófilo)** cotton wool
alguém someone
algum/a any, some
  alguma coisa something
  alguns, algumas some, a few
o **alho** garlic
ali there
o **almoço** lunch
  o **pequeno almoço** breakfast
a **almofada** pillow, cushion
o **alojamento** accommodation
a **alpercata** espadrille
alto/a tall, high; loud
alugar to rent, to hire
o **aluguer** rent(al)
amanhã tomorrow
amarelo/a yellow
amargo/a bitter
amável kind (*helpful*)

o **ambiente** atmosphere
ambos/as both
o **amigo, a amiga** friend
a **amostra** sample
andar to go
o **andar** floor, storey
o **anel** ring (*jewellery*)
o **aniversário** anniversary; birthday
o **ano** year
  antecedência: com antecedência in advance
a **antena** aerial
antes (de) before
o **anticongelante** antifreeze
a **antiguidade** antique
o **anúncio** advertisement
ao=a+o to the
apagar to switch/turn off
apanhar to pick up; to take/catch (*bus, etc.*)
o **apartamento** apartment, flat
o **apelido** surname
apenas just, only
apertado/a tight
aprender to learn
apresentar to introduce
o **aquecedor** heater
o **aquecimento** heating
aquele, aquela that, that one
aqueles, aquelas those
àquele/a=a+aquele/a to that, to that one
àqueles/as=a+aqueles/as to those, to those ones
aqui here
o **ar** air
  ao ar livre outdoors
o **ar condicionado** air conditioning

a **areia** sand
o **armário** cupboard
o **armazém** department store
o **arranhão** scratch (*on skin*)
os **arredores** suburbs
arrumado/a tidy
a **arte** art
o **artesanato** handicrafts
o **artigo** article
a **árvore** tree
áspero/a rough
assado/a roast
o **assento** seat
assim thus, like this/that
assinar to sign
a **assinatura** signature; season ticket
a **assoalhada** room (*in house*)
atacar to attack
atar to tie
até as far as, until; even
aterrar to land
atrás (de) behind
o **atraso** delay
atravessar to cross
o **atrelado** trailer
o **autocarro** bus
avariado/a broken down, out of order
o **avião** aeroplane
o **avô** grandfather
a **avó** grandmother
o **avogado** lawyer
azedo/a sour
o **azeite** olive oil
a **azeitona** olive
azul blue
azul marinho navy blue

B

a **bagagem** baggage, luggage
a **baía** bay
o **baile** dance
o **bairro** district, quarter
baixo/a low
baixo de below
o **balcão** counter (*shop*); balcony (*theatre, etc.*)
o **balde** bucket
o **banco** bank
o **banho** bath
    a **casa de banho** bathroom, toilet
barato/a cheap
a **barba** beard
o **barco** boat
o **barulho** noise
bastante quite, fairly; enough
a **bateria** car battery
o **baton** lipstick
bêbado/a drunk
o **bebé** baby
a **bebida** drink
o **beijo** kiss
o **beliche** berth
bem well
    bem educado/a polite
    está bem fine, right (*agreed*)
bem-vindo/a welcome
o **bengaleiro** cloakroom
a **berma** hard shoulder
o **biberão** baby's bottle
a **biblioteca** library
a **bicha** queue
a **bicicleta** bicycle
o **bigode** moustache

o **bilhete** ticket
a **bilheteira** ticket office
o **bloco** writing pad
a **blusa** blouse
o **blusão** jacket
boa (*see* **bom**)
boa noite goodnight
boa tarde good afternoon/
evening
a **boca** mouth
a **bola** ball
boleia: andar à boleia to
hitchhike
o **bolo** cake
a **bolsa** purse; stock
exchange
bom dia good morning
bom, boa good
a **bomba** bomb; pump
os **bombeiros** fire brigade
a **boneca** doll
bonito/a pretty, nice
a **borracha** rubber
a **bota** boot
o **botão** button
o **bracelete** bracelet;
watchstrap
o **braço** arm
branco/a white
bravo/a rough (*sea*)
breve: em breve soon
o **brinquedo** toy
o **buraco** hole
o **burro** donkey
buscar to look for

C

cabe: não cabe it doesn't
fit, it won't go in
a **cabeça** head

o **cabedal** leather
o **cabeleireiro, a cabeleireira**
hairdresser
o **cabelo** hair
a **cabra** goat
cada each, every
a **cadeia** chain
a **cadeira** chair
a **cadeira de lona** deckchair
a **cadeira de rodas**
wheelchair
o **café** café; coffee
o **cais** quay
a **caixa** box; cash desk, till
calado/a quiet (*person*)
as **calças** trousers
a **calculadora** calculator
o **caldo** soup
o **calor** heat
está calor it's hot
estar com calor to be
hot
a **cama** bed
a **câmara municipal** town
hall
cambiar to change
o **câmbio** exchange rate;
bureau de change
o **camião** lorry
o **caminho** track, path; way,
route
o **caminho de ferro** railway
a **camioneta** coach
a **camisa** shirt
a **camisola** jumper, sweater;
sweatshirt
a **campainha** bell
o **campismo** camping
o **campo** field; court (*tennis,
etc.*)
o **canal** channel

o **canalizador** plumber
a **canção** song
cancelar to cancel
o **candeeiro** lamp; street light
a **caneca** mug
a **caneta** pen
cansado/a tired
cantar to sing
o **cão** dog
a **cara** face
os **caramelos** sweets
a **carne** meat
caro/a expensive, dear
o **carrinho** trolley
o **carrinho de bebé** pram
o **carrinho de criança** push-chair
o **carro** car
a **carruagem** carriage (*railway*)
a **carta** letter
a **carta de condução** driving licence
o **cartão** card
a **carteira** wallet
o **carteiro** postman
o **carvão** coal
a **casa** house, home
a **casa de banho** bathroom, toilet
o **casaco** jacket
casado/a married
o **casal** couple
o **casamento** wedding
a **casca** shell (*egg, nut*)
caso: no caso de in case
castanho/a brown
o **castelo** castle
o **cavalo** horse
a **cave** basement

cedo early
cego/a blind
a **ceia** supper
o **centro** centre, middle
a **cerâmica** pottery
o **cesto, a cesta** basket
o **céu** sky; heaven
o **chá** tea
a **chaleira** kettle; teapot
a **chamada** call
chamar to call
  como se chama? what is your name?
o **champô** shampoo
o **chão** floor, ground
  o **rés-do-chão** ground floor
o **chapéu** hat
a **chave** key
a **chávena** cup
o **chefe** boss, head, chief
a **chegada** arrival
chegar (a) to arrive (at)
cheio/a full
cheira it smells
o **cheiro** smell
chorar to cry
chover: está a chover it's raining
o **chumbo** lead; (dental) filling
a **chuva** rain
o **chuveiro** shower
a **cidade** city
o **cigarro** cigarette
cima: em/por cima above, upstairs
o **cinto** belt
a **cintura** waist
o **cinzeiro** ashtray
cinzento/a grey

claro/a clear; light (-coloured)
claro! of course!
a **classe** class
o **clima** climate
o **cobertor** blanket
a **cobertura** cover
cobrar to cash (*cheque*); to charge
o **código** code
o **cofre** safe, strongbox
a **coisa** thing
coitado!, coitada! poor thing!
a **cola** glue
o **colarinho** collar
o **colchão** mattress
o **colete** waistcoat
o **colete salva-vidas** lifejacket
colher to pick
a **colher** spoon
a **colina** hill
com with
a **combinação** slip, petticoat
o **comboio** train
o **combustível** fuel
começar to begin
o **começo** beginning
comer to eat
a **comida** food
o **comissário de voo** air steward
como as, like
como? pardon?
como . . . ? how . . . ?
a **companhia** company
completamente completely
completo/a complete; full up

comprar to buy
as **compras** shopping
compreender to understand
comprido/a long
o **comprimento** length
o **comprimido** pill
comum common
concordar to agree
conduzir to drive
congelado/a frozen
o **congresso** conference
conhecer to know (*someone*)
o **conjunto** set, group
consertar to fix
a **Consoada** Christmas Eve
constipado/a: estar constipado/a to have a cold
a **consulta** appointment (*medical*)
a **conta** bill; account (*bank*)
o **contador** meter
contente pleased
o **conto** story
contra against
o **contraceptivo** contraceptive
a **contusão** bruise
convém: não me convém it doesn't suit me, it's not convenient
o **convés** deck
o **convidado, a convidada** guest
convidar to invite
o **convite** invitation
o **copo** glass
a **cor** colour
cor-de-rosa pink

o **coração** heart
a **corda** rope; string
o **cordeiro** lamb
a **coroa** crown
o **corpo** body
o **correio** post; post office
a **corrente** (electrical)
  power, current; draught
  (*of air*)
correr to run
a **correspondência**
  connection
a **corrida** race
a **corrida de touros** bullfight
cortar to cut, to cut off
a **cortiça** cork
a **cortina** curtain
coser to sew
a **costa** coast
a **costura** sewing

o **cozido** stew
cozido/a boiled (*cooked*)
a **cozinha** kitchen
cozinhar to cook
o **creme** cream, lotion
crer to believe; to think
  creio que sim/não I think
  so/I don't think so
a **criança** child
cru, crua raw
a **cruz** cross
o **cruzamento** crossroads,
  junction
o **cruzeiro** cruise
as **cuecas** pants, panties
cuidado: ter cuidado to
  take care
cuidar de to look after
cujo/a, cujos/as whose
culpado/a guilty
a **cunhada** sister-in-law

o **cunhado** brother-in-law
curto/a short
a **custa** cost

D

da=de+a of the
dançar to dance
daquele/a=de+aquele/a
  of that, of that one
daqueles/as=de+aqueles/as
  of those, of those ones
dar to give
a **data** date
de of; from
debaixo (de) under,
  underneath
decidir to decide
o **defeito** fault, defect
deficiente disabled
deitar to pour
deitar fora to throw away
deixar to leave (*message,
  etc.*)
dela hers
  o/a … dela her …
dele his
  o/a … dele his
delgado/a thin
demasiado/a too (much)
a **demora** delay
demorar to take (*time*)
o **dente** tooth
dentro (de) in, inside
depois after(wards), later
  on
o **desafio** game, match
desagradável unpleasant
descansar to rest
descer to come/go down
descrever to describe

desculpe! sorry!
desde from; since
o **desenho** drawing, design
desligar to turn/switch off
desmaiado/a faint, in a faint; pale (*colour*)
o **desporto** sport
desse/a=de+esse/a of that, of that one
desses/as=de+esses/as of those, of those ones
deste/a=de+este/a of this, of this one
destes/as=de+estes/as of these, of these ones
o **destino** destination
o **desvio** diversion (*traffic*)
devagar slowly
devolver to return, to give back
o **dia** day
o **dia útil** weekday
o **diapositivo** slide (*photo*)
diário/a daily
difícil difficult
o **dinheiro** money
a **direcção** direction
a **direita** right
os **direitos** rights; duty (*customs*)
o **disco** disc, record
a **discussão** discussion; argument
a **disquete** disc (*computer*)
dizer to say
quer dizer that is to say
do=de+o of the
do que than
o **doce** jam
doce sweet
a **doença** illness

doente ill
dói it hurts
dois, duas two
os dois, as duas both
a **dona, o dono** owner
a **dor** pain, ache
dormir to sleep
dorme he/she sleeps, you sleep
dou I give
duas vezes twice
o **duche** shower
dum, duma=de+um, uma of a
duplo/a double
durante during
durar to last
duro/a hard; tough
durmo I sleep

E

e and
é he/she/it is; you are
o **écran** screen (*TV, cinema, etc.*)
o **edifício** building
ela she; her
elas they; them
ele he; him
o **eléctrico** tram
eles they; them
o **elevador** lift
em in, on
a **embaixada** embassy
o **embarque** boarding
embora although
embrulhar to wrap (up)
o **embrulho** parcel
a **ementa** menu
a **ementa turística** set menu

a **emissora de rádio** radio station
emocionante exciting
empinado/a steep
a **empregada** waitress; shop assistant; employee
o **empregado** waiter; shop assistant; employee
empregar to use; to employ
o **emprego** job
a **empresa** firm, business
empurrar to push
encher to fill (up); to pump up (*tyre*)
encoberto/a overcast (*weather*)
encontrar to find
o **encontro** appointment
o **endereço** address

o **engarrafamento** traffic jam
enquanto while
ensinar to teach
então then
entender to understand
a **entrada** admission
a **entrada** entrance, way in; admission; ticket; starter (*food*)
entrar (em) to enter, go in; to get on (*bus, etc.*)
entre among
entretanto meanwhile
a **entrevista** interview; appointment
entupido/a blocked (*pipe*)
enviar to send
a **equipa** team
o **equipamento** equipment
a **erva** herb

esbelto/a slim
a **escada** stairs; ladder
escocês, escocesa Scottish
a **escola** school
escolher to choose
a **escova** brush
escrever to write
o **escritório** office
esgotado/a sold out
o **esmalte** enamel
o **espaço** space
a **Espanha** Spain
espanhol, espanhola Spanish
especial special
a **especiaria** spice
o **espectáculo** show
o **espelho** mirror
esperar to wait (for), to expect; to hope (for)
espesso/a thick
a **esplanada** terrace
a **espuma** foam
a **esquadra da polícia** police station
esquecer to forget
o **esquentador** water-heater
a **esquerda** left
o **esqui aquático** water-skiing
a **esquina** corner
esquisito/a strange, odd
esse/a that, that one
esses/as those, those ones
está he/she/it is; you are
a **estação** station; season
o **estacionamento** parking
o **estádio** stadium
o **estado** state
estar to be
o **este** east
este/a this, this one

estes/as these, these ones
o estômago stomach
estou I am
a estrada road
estragado/a damaged
estrangeiro: no estrangeiro abroad
estrangeiro/a foreign
estranho/a strange, odd
estreito/a narrow
a estrela star
eu I
o exemplar copy
o exemplo example
o êxito success
explicar to explain
a exposição exhibition

F

a fábrica factory
a faca knife
fácil easy
faço I do/make
falar to speak, to talk
falso/a false, fake
a família family
a fatia slice
o fato suit
o fato de banho bathing costume, swimsuit
faz he/she/it does/makes; you do/make
faz favor please
fazer to do, to make
a febre fever; (high) temperature
fechado/a shut
a fechadura lock
fechar to close; to turn off (*tap*)

o feijão bean
feio/a ugly
a feira fair
feito/a done, made
feliz happy
o feriado public holiday
as férias holiday(s)
ferido/a injured
o ferro iron
fervido/a boiled (*liquid*)
a festa festival; party
o fiambre (boiled) ham
a fila row (*of seats*); queue
a filha daughter
o filho son
o filial branch (*of bank, etc.*)
o fim end
o fino glass of draught beer
a fita tape; ribbon
a flor flower
o fogão cooker
o fogo fire
a folha leaf; sheet of paper
o folheto leaflet
a fome hunger
   ter fome to be hungry
a fonte fountain
fora (de) out (of), outside
a força strength, power
a forma form, shape
o forno oven
os fósforos matches
as fraldas nappies
o frango chicken
o frasco pot, jar
a frase phrase; sentence
frente: em frente de opposite
   (sempre) em frente straight on
fresco/a cool; fresh

a **frigideira** frying pan
o **frigorífico** refrigerator
frio/a cold
   está frio it's cold
   ter frio to be cold
frito/a fried
a **fronha** pillowcase
fumar to smoke
funcionar to work, to function
o **furgão** van

G

a **gabardina** raincoat
Gales Wales
galês, galesa Welsh
ganhar to earn; to win
o **garfo** fork
a **garganta** throat
a **garrafa** bottle
gás: com/sem gás fizzy/still (*water*)
a **gasolina** petrol
gastar to spend
o **gato** cat
a **gaveta** drawer
o **gelado** ice-cream
o **gelo** ice
o **genro** son-in-law
a **gente** people
geral general
o **gerente** manager
gordo/a fat (*person, etc.*)
a **gorjeta** tip
gosta de . . . ? do you like . . . ?
gosto de . . . I like . . .
o **governo** government
a **Grã-Bretanha** Great Britain
grande big, large; great

grátis free
o **grau** degree (*of temperature*)
gravar to record
grave serious
grávida pregnant
a **graxa** polish (*shoe, etc.*)
a **greve** strike
a **gripe** flu
o **grito** shout
a **gruta** cave
o **guarda-chuva** umbrella
o **guardanapo** napkin, serviette
guardar to keep
a **guerra** war
o **guia** guide; guidebook
a **guitarra** (Portuguese) guitar

H

há there is/are
   há . . . (anos) . . . (years) ago
a **herdade** estate (*country*)
hoje today
o **homem** man
a **hora** hour
a **hora de ponta** rush hour
o **horário** timetable
o **hóspede** guest; host
a **hospedeira** air stewardess
húmido/a damp

I

idade: que idade tem? how old are you?, how old is he/she?

a igreja church
igual equal
a ilha island
a imperial glass of draught beer
impermeável waterproof
o impermeável raincoat
importa: não importa it doesn't matter
imprescindível essential
impressionante impressive
o impresso form (*document*)
incluído/a included
inclusive including
incómodo/a uncomfortable
indisposto/a unwell
o inferno hell
a informática computer science/studies
a Inglaterra England
inglês, inglesa English
íngreme steep
a insolação sunstroke
o interruptor switch
inútil (*pl.* **inúteis**) useless
o inverno winter
ir to go
a Irlanda Ireland
irlandês, irlandesa Irish
a irmã sister
o irmão brother
o isqueiro cigarette lighter
o IVA VAT

J

já already; immediately
a janela window
o jantar dinner
o jardim garden
o jarro jug
jogar to play (*sport*)
o jogo game; gambling
o jornal newspaper
o/a jornalista journalist
jovem young
juntos/as together
a juventude youth

L

lá there
a lã wool
a ladeira hill
o lado side
  ao lado de beside, next to
o lago lake
a lâmina de barbear razor blade
a lâmpada light bulb
o lápis pencil
a laranja orange
o largo square
largo/a broad, wide
a lata tin
a lavagem washing
a lavandaria laundry
lavar to wash
o lavatório wash-basin
a lei law
o leite milk
a leitura reading
a lembrança souvenir
o lenço handkerchief
o lençol (*pl.* **os lençóis**) sheet
a lente lens
lento/a slow
ler to read
levar to carry

lhe (to) her; (to) him; (to) you
lhes (to) them; (to) you
a **libra (esterlina)** pound (sterling)
a **licença** licence, permit
  com licença! excuse me!
a **ligação** connection
ligar to switch on
ligeiro/a light
a **lima** file
limpar to clean
limpo/a clean
a **língua** tongue; language
a **linha** line
a **lista** list; menu
a **livraria** bookshop
livre free, unoccupied, vacant; for hire
o **livro** book
o **lixo** rubbish
a **loção** lotion
a **loja** shop
Londres London
longe far (away)
a **loteria** lottery
louco/a mad
louro/a fair, blond(e)
a **lua** moon
o **lugar** place
a **luva** glove
a **luz** light

M

má (see **mau**)
macio/a soft
a **madeira** wood (*material*)
maduro/a mature, ripe
a **mãe** mother

maior bigger; elder; main
a **maior parte** most, the majority
mais more
  mais alguma coisa? anything else?
mal badly
a **mala** suitcase; car boot
a **mancha** stain
a **maneira** way, manner
a **manga** sleeve
a **manhã** morning
a **manifestação** demonstration (*protest*)
a **mão** hand
a **maquilhagem** make-up
a **máquina** machine
a **máquina de escrever** typewriter
a **máquina fotográfica/de filmar** camera
o **mar** sea
a **marca** make, brand
marcar to dial
o **marco de correio** postbox, letterbox
o **marido** husband
o **marisco** shellfish, seafood
o **martelo** hammer
mas but
a **massa** dough, pastry; pasta
a **mata** wood (*trees*)
matar to kill
a **matrícula** registration number
mau, má bad
me (to) me
o **médico** doctor
a **medida** measurement; size
médio/a medium

medo: ter medo to be afraid
a meia-noite midnight
as meias stockings
o meio environment
meio/a half
o meio-dia midday
melhor better; best
o membro member
a menina girl, miss
menos less
   pelo menos at least
o mercado market
a mercearia grocer's
o mês month
a mesa table
mesmo really; very
mesmo/a same
a metade half
o meu (*pl.* **os meus**) my; mine
mexer to move
mim me
a minha (*pl.* **as minhas**) my; mine
a missa mass (*ceremony*)
misto/a mixed
a mochila rucksack
a moda fashion
a moeda coin
o moinho mill
mole soft, flabby
molhado/a wet
o molhe pier
o molho sauce
a montanha mountain
a montra shop window
a morada address
morar to live (*reside*)
morder to bite
moreno/a dark (*hair/skin*)

morto/a dead
a mosca fly
mostrar to show
a motorizada motorbike
os móveis furniture
mover to move
mudar to change; to move
muito very (much), a lot
muito/a a lot (of)
muitos/as many, lots (of)
a mulher woman; wife
a multa fine (*penalty*)
o mundo world
as muralhas walls (*city*)

N

nada nothing
   de nada not at all, don't mention it
   mais nada/nada mais nothing else
nadar to swim
a namorada girlfriend, fiancée
o namorado boyfriend, fiancé
não no; not
o nariz nose
a natação swimming
o Natal Christmas
necessitar to need
os negócios business
nem nor
   nem . . . nem . . . neither . . . nor . . .
   nenhum, nenhuma no, not any; none
a neta granddaughter
o neto grandson
a neve snow

o **nevoeiro** fog
ninguém nobody
a **noite** night
a **noiva** bride; fiancée
o **noivo** bridegroom; fiancé
o **nome** name
a **nora** daughter-in-law
o **norte** north
nos us
nós we
o **nosso, a nossa** our; ours
a **nota** note; banknote
as **notícias** news
novo/a new
a **noz** nut; walnut
nu, nua naked
nublado/a cloudy
num, numa = em + um, uma
in a
o **número** number; size
(*shoe, etc.*)
nunca never

O

o **the**; him; it
a **obra** work; play (*at
theatre*)
obrigado/a thank you
os **óculos** glasses, spectacles
ocupado/a occupied,
taken; engaged; busy
o **oeste** west
a **oferta** offer; special offer
olá hello
a **olaria** pottery
o **óleo** oil
olhar (para) look (at)
o **olho** eye
a **onda** wave
onde where

ontem yesterday
óptimo! great!
o **ordenado** salary, wages
a **orelha** ear
os the; them
o **osso** bone
ou or
ou . . . ou . . . either . . .
or . . .
o **ouro** gold
o **outono** autumn
outra vez again
outro/a another, other
ouvir to listen; to hear
a **ovelha** sheep
o **ovo** egg

P

a **padaria** baker's
o **padre** priest
pagar to pay (for)
a **página** page
o **pai** father
os **pais** parents
o **país** country
a **paisagem** countryside,
scenery
a **palavra** word
pálido/a pale
a **panela** saucepan
o **pano** cloth
o **pão** bread, loaf
o **papel** paper
para to; towards; for
o **parafuso** screw
a **paragem** stop (*bus, etc.*)
parar to stop
parecer to seem
a **parede** wall
o **parque** park

a **parte** part
a **partida** departure; game, match
o **partido** (political) party
partido/a broken
partir to depart, to leave; to break
passado/a past; last
   mal/bem passado rare/well done (*steak*)
o **passageiro** passenger
a **passagem de nível** level crossing
passar to pass; to spend (*time*)
o **pássaro** bird
o **passatempo** hobby
o **passeio** walk; pavement
a **pasta** briefcase
a **pasta de dentes** toothpaste
o **pastel** cake, pastry
a **pastilha elástica** chewing gum
os **patins** skates
o **pau** stick
a **paz** peace
o **pé** foot
   ao pé de beside, next to
o **peão** (*pl.* **peões**) pedestrian
a **peça (de teatro)** play (*at theatre*)
o **pedaço** piece
pedir to ask (for), to order
a **pedra** stone
o **peixe** fish
a **pele** skin; fur; leather
pendurar to hang (up)
o **penico** potty (*child's*)
a **pensão** pension; guest house

pensar to think
o **penso adesivo** sticking plaster
pequeno/a small, little
perder to lose; to miss
o **perigo** danger
o **perito** expert
permitido/a allowed
a **perna** leg
a **persiana** blind (*Venetian*); shutter
perto (de) close (to), near
pesado/a heavy
a **pesca** fishing
o **peso** weight
a **pessoa** person
as **peúgas** socks
a **piada** joke
picante hot, spicy
picar to sting, to bite
a **pilha** battery
a **pílula** pill
a **pimenta** pepper
pintar to paint
a **pintura** painting
pior worse
o **pires** saucer
a **piscina** swimming pool
o **piso** floor, storey
a **pista** track, course
a **planta** plant
a **plateia** stalls (*theatre*)
o **pó** dust; powder
pobre poor
poder to be able
   pode he/she/it can; you can
podre rotten
põe he/she/it puts; you put
pois é that's right
a **polícia** police

a política politics
a poluição pollution
ponho I put
a ponte bridge
por by; for; per; through; via
por favor please
pôr to put; to place; to put down
o porco pig; pork
porque because
porquê? why?
a porta door
a portagem toll
o porto port, harbour, docks
posso I can, I may
posso? can I?, may I?
o postal postcard
um pouco a bit, a little
pouco/a little, not much
poucos/as few, not many
a pousada luxury hotel
a pousada de juventude youth hostel
o povo people
a praça square
a praça de táxis taxi rank
a praça de touros bullring
a prancha sailboard; diving board
a prata silver
o prato plate; dish, course
precisar to need
o preço price
o prédio building
preferir to prefer
o prego nail; steak sandwich
preguiçoso/a lazy
o prémio prize

preocupado/a worried
preparar to prepare, to get ready
o preservativo condom
pressa: estar com pressa/ ter pressa to be in a hurry
o presunto cured ham
preto/a black
primeiro/a first
o primo, a prima cousin
o/a principiante beginner
a prisão prison
privado/a private
o problema problem
procurar to look for
o professor, a professora teacher
profundo/a deep
proibido/a prohibited, forbidden
pronto/a ready
o proprietário, a proprietária owner
próximo/a next
público/a public
o pulgar thumb
o punho cuff
puxar to pull

Q

o quadro painting, picture
qual? (*pl.* **quais?**) which?
a qualidade quality
qualquer (*pl.* **quaisquer**) any, whichever
qualquer coisa anything; something
quando? when?
a quantidade amount

quanto/a? how much?
  quanto tempo? how long? (*time*)
  quanto antes as soon as possible
quantos/as? how many?
  quantos anos tem? how old is he/she?, how old are you?
  quantas vezes? how often?, how many times?
o quarto bedroom; quarter
quase nearly
que that, which, who; than
  do que than
  que?/o que? what?, which?
o queijo cheese
queimar to burn
a queixa complaint
quem? who?
quente hot
quer dizer it means
querer to want
  queria I would like
o quilo kilo(gram)
o quilómetro kilometre
a quinta farm, estate

R

a rainha queen
o ramo branch
a rapariga girl
o rapaz boy
raro/a rare
rasgado/a torn
a razão reason
  tem razão you are right

real royal
rebocar to tow
o recado message
a recarga refill
a receita prescription; recipe
o recibo receipt
a reclamação complaint
a recolha collection (*post, rubbish*)
a rede net; network
redondo/a round
ao redor de around
o reembolso refund
a refeição meal
a reforma reform; retirement; pension
reformado/a retired
a região region, area
a régua ruler (*measuring*)
o rei king
o relatório report (*business, etc.*)
o relógio clock; watch
a relva grass, lawn
o remédio remedy, cure
reparar to repair
repente: de repente suddenly
repetir to repeat
a reportagem report (*newspaper*)
a representação performance
o rés-do-chão ground floor
a reserva reservation, booking
reservar to reserve, to book
a resposta answer, reply
o resultado result

revelar to show; to develop (*film*)
a **revista** magazine
o **ribeiro** stream
rico/a rich
rígido/a stiff
o **rio** river
riscado/a striped
o **riso** laugh
a **roda** wheel
rodeado/a (de) surrounded (by)
a **rolha** cork
o **rolo** (roll of) film
a **rosa** rose
roubar to rob, to steal
a **roupa** clothes
a **roupa interior** underwear
a **rua** street
o **ruído** noise
a **ruína** ruin

S

S = São, Santo Saint
SA = Sociedade Anónima Limited, PLC
saber to know; to know how to
o **sabonete** soap
o **sabor** taste; flavour
o **saca-rolhas** corkscrew
o **saco** bag
a **saia** skirt
a **saída** exit, way out
sair (de) to come/go out; to leave; to get off
o **sal** salt
a **sala** room
a **sala de concertos** concert hall

salgado/a salty
saltar to jump
salvar to rescue, to save
a **sandes** sandwich
o **sangue** blood
santo/a holy; saint
são, sã healthy
o **sapato** shoe
a **saúde** health
saúde! cheers!
se if; him/her/itself; yourself; themselves
a **sé** cathedral
secar to dry
seco/a dry
o **século** century
a **seda** silk
a **sede** thirst
tenho sede I am thirsty
ter sede to be thirsty
seguinte following, next
segundo according to, depending on
segundo/a second
o **seguro** insurance
seguro/a sure, certain; safe
sei, não sei I know, I don't know
o **selo** stamp
selvagem wild
sem without
os **semáforos** traffic lights
a **semana** week
semelhante (a) similar (to)
sempre always
o **senhor** gentleman; Mr; you
a **senhora** lady; Mrs/Miss; you
a **senhoria** landlady
o **senhorio** landlord

sensato/a sensible
sentado/a sitting (down)
sentir to feel
o **sentido** sense; direction
ser to be
sério/a serious
o **serviço** service; service charge
servir to serve
a **sessão** session; performance, screening (*cinema*)
o **seu** (*pl.* **os seus**) his/her/ its; their; your
o **SIDA** AIDS
silencioso/a silent
sim yes
simpático/a nice, charming, pleasant
simples simple; single (*ticket*)
o **sinal** sign; signal
sinto I feel
só alone; only
   um só only one
sobre on, upon; about
a **sobremesa** sweet, dessert
sobretudo especially
a **sobrinha** niece
o **sobrinho** nephew
sóbrio/a sober
o **sócio, a sócia** member; partner
a **sogra** mother-in-law
o **sogro** father-in-law
o **sol** sun
solteiro/a single, unmarried
solto/a loose
a **sombra** shade
a **sopa** soup

o **sorriso** smile
a **sorte** luck
   ter sorte to be lucky
   boa sorte! good luck!
sou I am
o **soutien** bra
sozinho/a (all) alone
a **sua** (*pl.* **as suas**) his/her/ its; their; your
suave gentle, mild
subir to come/go up; to rise; to raise
sujo/a dirty
o **sul** south
o **sumo** juice
o **supositório** suppository
surdo/a deaf
a **surpresa** surprise
o **susto** fright, scare

T

o **tabaco** tobacco
tal such
o **talho** butcher's
talvez perhaps
o **tamanho** size
também also, as well, too
a **tampa** lid; plug (*bath, etc.*)
tanto/a so much
tantos/as so many
tão so
tarde late
a **tarde** afternoon; evening
o **teatro** theatre
o **tecido** fabric, material
o **tecto** ceiling; roof
o **telefone** telephone
o **telefonema** phone call
tem he/she/it has; you have

tem de/que . . . he/she/it must/has to . . . ; you must/have to . . .

o **tempo** time; weather

a **tenda** tent

tenho I have
tenho que . . . I must, I have to . . .

tentar to try

ter to have

terceiro/a third

a **terra** earth; land; ground

o **terraço** terrace

o **terremoto** earthquake

a **tesoura** scissors

o **teu** (*pl.* **os teus**) your; yours

a **tia** aunt

tinto: o vinho tinto red wine

o **tio** uncle

o **tipo** type, sort, kind

tirar to remove, to take off; to take away

a **toalha** towel

tocar to touch; to play (*instrument*)

todo/a, todos/as all, every

a **tomada** plug; socket

tomar to take; to have (*drink*)

torcido/a twisted; sprained

a **torneira** tap

as **torradas** toast

a **torre** tower

a **tosse** cough

o **touro** bull

trabalhar to work

o **trabalho** work

a **tradução** translation

traduzir to translate

tranquilo/a calm, quiet

o **trânsito** traffic

as **traseiras** back, rear (*of house*)

o **traseiro** rear, bottom (*person's*)

trazer to bring

triste sad

trocar to change (*money*)

os **trocos** change

tu you (*informal*)

a **tua** (*pl.* **as tuas**) your; yours

tudo everything

U

último/a last

um a/an; one

uma a/an; one

a **unha** nail (*finger/toe*)

o **uso** use

útil (*pl.* **úteis**) useful

utilizar to use

V

a **vaca** cow

vai he/she/it goes/is going; you go/are going

o **vale** valley

vale a pena it's worth it

valente brave

o **vapor** steam

vários/as several, some

a **vassoura** broom

vazio/a empty

vejo I see

a **vela** candle; sail, sailing

velho/a old

a **velocidade** speed
vem he/she/it comes/is coming; you come/are coming
a **venda** sale
o **vendedor, a vendedora** salesman, saleswoman
vender to sell
o **veneno** poison
venho I come/am coming
o **vento** wind
ver to see
o **verão** summer
a **verdade** truth
é verdade it's true
verde green
verificar to check
vermelho/a red
o **vestido** dress
a **vez** time
às vezes sometimes
em vez de instead of
outra vez again
uma vez once
a **viagem** journey, trip
viajar to travel
a **vida** life
o **vidro** glass
a **vila** town
a **vinha** vineyard
o **vinho** wine
o **vinho branco** white wine

o **vinho tinto** red wine
o **vinho verde** green/young wine
a **viola** (Spanish) guitar
violar to rape
vir to come
virar to turn
visitar to visit
a **vista** view
a **viúva** widow
o **viúvo** widower
viver to live
vivo/a live, alive; vivid, bright
o **vizinho, a vizinha** neighbour
você, vocês you
a **volta** turn; return
voltar to turn; to return
o **voo** flight
vou I go/am going
a **voz** voice
vulgar ordinary

X

o **xadrez** chess

Z

zangado/a angry

There is a list of car parts on page 46, and parts of the body on page 163. See also the lists on pages 188–197.

A

a/an **um, uma**
abbey **a abadia**
about (*on the subject of*) **sobre, de**
(*approximately*) **mais ou menos**
above (*upstairs, etc.*) **em cima**
(*on top of*) **por cima de**
abroad **no estrangeiro**
to go abroad **ir ao estrangeiro**
abscess **o abcesso**
to accept **aceitar**
accident **o acidente**
accommodation **o alojamento**
according to **segundo**
account (*bank*) **a conta**
accountant **o/a contabilista**
ache **a dor**
acid **o ácido**
across (*on the other side of*) **do outro lado de**
acrylic **o acrílico**
to act **actuar**
activity **a actividade**
actor **o actor**
actress **a actriz**
adaptor (*voltage*) **o adaptador**
(*multiple plug*) **a ficha múltipla**

adhesive tape **a fita adesiva**
address **a morada**
admission **a entrada**
adopted **adoptivo/a**
adult **o adulto, a adulta**
advance: in advance **com antecedência**
advanced (*level*) **avançado/a**
advertisement **o anúncio**
advertising **a publicidade**
aerial **a antena**
aeroplane **o avião**
afford: I can't afford it **é muito caro**
afraid: to be afraid **ter medo** (**ter**, *see page 185*)
after **depois de**
afterwards **depois**
afternoon **a tarde**
aftershave **o aftershave**
again **outra vez**
against **contra**
age **a idade**
agency **a agência**
ago: . . . ago **há . . .**
to agree **concordar**
AIDS **o SIDA**
air **o ar**
by air **por avião**
air conditioning **o ar condicionado**
air force **a força aérea**
airline **a linha aérea**

air mattress **o colchão de ar**
airport **o aeroporto**
aisle **o corredor**
  (*church*) **a nave lateral**
alarm **o alarme**
  alarm clock **o despertador**
alcohol **o álcool**
alcoholic **alcoólico/a**
alive **vivo/a**
all **todo/a, todos/as**
allergic to **alérgico/a a**
to allow **permitir**
  allowed **permitido/a**
all right (*agreed*) **está bem**
almond **a amêndoa**
alone **só, sozinho/a**
along **por**
already **já**
also **também**
although **embora**
always **sempre**
am (*see* to be)
ambition **a ambição**
ambulance **a ambulância**
among **entre**
amount **a quantidade**
amusement park **a feira popular**
anaesthetic **o anestésico**
and **e**
angry **zangado/a**
animal **o animal**
anniversary **o aniversário**
annoyed **irritado/a**
anorak **o anorak**
another **outro/a**
to answer **responder**
answer **a resposta**
antibiotic **o antibiótico**

antifreeze **o anticongelante**
antique **a antiguidade**
antiseptic **o anti-séptico**
any **algum/a**
anyone **alguém**
anything (*something*) **qualquer coisa**
  anything else? **mais alguma coisa?**
anyway **de qualquer maneira**
anywhere **em qualquer parte**
apart from **para além de**
aperitif **o aperitivo**
apartment **o apartamento**
appendicitis **a apendicite**
apple **a maçã**
appointment (*interview*) **a entrevista**
  (*medical*) **a consulta**
approximately **aproximadamente, mais ou menos**
apricot **o alperce**
arch **o arco**
archaeology **a arqueologia**
architect **o arquitecto**
architecture **a arquitectura**
are (*see* to be)
area (*surface*) **a área**
  (*region*) **a região**
argument **a discussão**
arm **o braço**
armbands (*swimming*) **as braçadeiras**
army **o exército**
around **ao redor de**
  around the corner **ao virar da esquina**

233

to arrange **organizar**
arrest: under arrest **preso/a**
arrival **a chegada**
to arrive **chegar**
art **a arte**
  art gallery **a galeria de arte**
  fine arts **as belas artes**
arthritis **a artrite**
artichoke **a alcachofra**
article **o artigo**
artificial **artificial**
artist **o/a artista**
as **como**
  as far as **até**
ash **a cinza**
ashtray **o cinzeiro**
to ask **perguntar**
to ask for **pedir**
asparagus **o espargo**
aspirin **a aspirina**
assistant **o/a assistente**
  (*shop*) **o empregado, a empregada**
asthma **a asma**
at **a, em**
athletics **o atletismo**
Atlantic **o Atlântico**
atmosphere **o ambiente**
to attack **atacar**
attractive **atraente**
aubergine **a beringela**
auction **o leilão**
aunt **a tia**
author **o autor, a autora**
automatic **automático/a**
autumn **o outono**
avocado **o abacate**
to avoid **evitar**
away: ... (kilometres)

away **a . . . (quilómetros)**
awful **terrível**

B

baby **o bebé**
baby cereal **a farinha de bebé**
baby food **a comida de bebé**
baby's bottle **o biberão**
babysitter **a ama**
back (*rear*) **a traseira**
  at the back **atrás**
  on the back **no dorso**
backwards **para trás**
bacon **o toucinho fumado**
bad **mau, má**
badly **mal**
bag **o saco**
baggage **a bagagem**
baker **o padeiro**
baker's **a padaria**
balcony **a varanda**
  (*theatre, etc.*) **o balcão**
bald **careca**
ball (*football, tennis, etc.*) **a bola**
ballet **o ballet**
ballpoint pen **a esferográfica**
banana **a banana**
band (*music*) **a banda**
bandage **o penso**
bank **o banco**
barber **o barbeiro**
basement **a cave**
basket **o cesto, a cesta**
basketball **o basquetebol**
bath **o banho**

to have a bath **tomar banho**
bathing costume **o fato de banho**
bathroom **a casa de banho**
battery (*torch, radio, etc.*) **a pilha**
(*car*) **a bateria**
bay **a baía**
to be **ser; estar** (*see page 184*)
I am **sou; estou**
we are **somos; estamos**
he/she/it is, you are **é; está**
beach **a praia**
bean **o feijão**
beard **a barba**
beautiful **lindo/a**
because **porque**
bed **a cama**
bedroom **o quarto**
bee **a abelha**
beef **a carne de vaca**
beer **a cerveja**
beetroot **a beterraba**
before **antes (de)**
to begin **começar**
beginner **o/a principiante**
beginning **o começo**
behind **atrás (de)**
beige **bege**
to believe **crer**
I believe so/not **creio que sim/não**
bell (*church*) **o sino**
(*door*) **a campainha**
to belong to **pertencer a**
(*to be a member of*) **ser sócio/a de** (ser, *see page 184*)
below **em baixo**

(*beneath*) **debaixo de**
belt **o cinto**
bend **a curva**
bent **torcido/a**
berry **a baga**
berth **o beliche**
beside (*next to*) **ao lado de**
besides **além disso**
best **(o/a) melhor**
better **melhor**
between **entre**
beyond **além de**
bib (*baby's*) **o babete**
Bible **a Bíblia**
bicycle **a bicicleta**
big **grande**
bigger **maior**
bill **a conta**
bin (*rubbish*) **o caixote do lixo**
binoculars **os binóculos**
biology **a biologia**
bird (*small*) **o pássaro**
(*large*) **a ave**
birthday **o aniversário**
biscuit **a bolacha, o biscoito**
bishop **o bispo**
a bit **um pouco**
to bite **morder**
bitter **amargo/a**
black **preto/a**
black and white (film) **(o filme) a preto e branco**
blackberry **a amora**
black coffee **o café**
blackcurrant **a groselha preta**
blanket **o cobertor**
bleach **a lixívia**
to bleed **sangrar**

blind **cego/a**
blind (*Venetian*) **a persiana**
blister **a bolha**
blocked (*passage*) **impedido/a**
(*pipe*) **entupido/a**
blond(e) **louro/a**
blood **a sangue**
blouse **a blusa**
to blow **soprar**
blow-dry **a secagem**
blue **azul**
boarding **o embarque**
boarding card **o cartão de embarque**
boat **o barco**
by boat **de barco**
body **o corpo**
boiled (*liquid*) **fervido/a**
(*cooked*) **cozido/a**

boiled egg **o ovo cozido**
boiler **a caldeira**
boiling **a ferver**
bomb **a bomba**
bone **o osso**
book **o livro**
to book **reservar**
booking **a reserva**
booking office **a bilheteira**
bookshop **a livraria**
boot **a bota**
(*car*) **a mala**
border (*edge*) **a margem**
(*frontier*) **a fronteira**
bored, boring **aborrecido/a**
both **ambos/as; os dois, as duas**
bottle **a garrafa**
bottle opener **o abre-garrafas**

bottom **o fundo**
(*person's*) **o traseiro**
bow (*ship*) **a proa**
bow (*knot*) **o nó**
bowl **a bacia**
bowls (*game*) **o boliche**
box **a caixa**
(*theatre*) **o camarote**
box office **a bilheteira**
boy **o rapaz**
boyfriend **o namorado**
bra **o soutien**
bracelet **o bracelete**
braces **os suspensórios**
brain **o cérebro**
branch **o ramo**
(*bank, etc.*) **o filial**
brand **a marca**
brandy **o brande**
brass **o latão**
brave **valente**
bread **o pão**
to break **partir**
I have broken **parti**
breakdown truck **o reboque**
breakfast **o pequeno almoço**
to breathe **respirar**
brick **o tijolo**
bricklayer **o pedreiro**
bride **a noiva**
bridegroom **o noivo**
bridge **a ponte**
briefcase **a pasta**
bright (*colour, light*) **claro/a**
to bring **trazer**
can you bring me . . . ? **podia-me trazer . . . ?**
British **britânico/a**

broad **largo/a**
broad bean **a fava**
brochure **a brochura**
broken **partido/a**
broken down **avariado/a**
bronchitis **a bronquite**
bronze **o bronze**
brooch **o broche**
broom **a vassoura**
brother **o irmão**
brother-in-law **o cunhado**
brown **castanho/a**
bruise **a contusão**
brush **a escova**
bucket **o balde**
budgerigar **o periquito**
buffet car **a carruagem-restaurante**
to build **construir**
building **o edifício**
bulb (*light*) **a lâmpada**
bull **o touro**
bullfight **a corrida de touros**
bullfighter **o toureiro**
bullring **a praça de touros**
bumper **o para-choques**
burn **a queimadura**
to burn **queimar**
burnt **queimado/a**
bus **o autocarro**
  bus station **a estação de autocarros**
  bus stop **a paragem de autocarros**
  by bus **de autocarro**
bush **o arbusto**
business **os negócios**
  business studies **os estudos de gestão**

business trip **a viagem de negócios**
businessman **o homem de negócios**
businesswoman **a mulher de negócios**
busy **ocupado/a**
but **mas**
butane gas **o gás butano**
butcher's **o talho**
butter **a manteiga**
butterfly **a borboleta**
button **o botão**
to buy **comprar**
by **por**

C

cabbage **a couve**
cabin **a cabine**
café **o café**
cake **o bolo**
  (*pastry*) **o pastel**
cake shop **a pastelaria**
calculator **a calculadora**
call (*phone*) **a chamada**
to call **chamar**
to be called **chamar-se**
  I am called **chamo-me**
  he/she/it is called **chama-se**
  what is he/she/it called? **como se chama?**
calm **tranquilo/a**
camera **a máquina fotográfica**
camomile tea **o chá de camomila**
to camp **acampar**
  campbed **a cama de campanha**

camping **o campismo**
campsite **o parque de campismo**
can (*to be able*) **poder**
  I can **posso**
  can you . . . ? **pode . . . ?**
  could you . . . ? **podia . . . ?**
  (*to know how to*) . . . **saber . . .**; I (don't) know how to . . . **(não) sei . . .**
can (*tin*) **a lata**
  can opener **o abre-latas**
to cancel **cancelar**
cancer **o cancro**
candle **a vela**
canoe **a canoa**
capital (*city*) **a capital**
captain **o capitão**
car **o carro, o automóvel**
  by car **de carro**

  car park **o parque de estacionamento**
  car wash **a lavagem automática**
carafe **a jarra**
caravan **a caravana**
caravan site **o parque de campismo**
care: to take care **ter cuidado** (**ter**, *see page 185*)
  I don't care **não me importa**
careful **cuidadoso/a**
cardigan **o blusão**
careless **descuidado/a**
carpenter **o carpinteiro**
carpet **a alcatifa**
carriage (*railway*) **a carruagem**

carrier bag **o saco de compras**
carrot **a cenoura**
to carry **levar**
to carry on **continuar**
case: just in case **no caso de**
cash: to pay cash **pagar a dinheiro**
to cash (*cheque*) **cobrar**
cash desk **a caixa**
cassette **a cassete**
cassette player **o gravador de cassetes**
castle **o castelo**
cat **o gato**
catalogue **o catálogo**
to catch (*train, bus, etc.*) **apanhar**
cathedral **a sé**
Catholic **católico/a**
cauliflower **a couve-flor**
to cause **causar**
cave **a gruta**
ceiling **o tecto**
celery **o aipo**
cellar **a cave**
  (*wine*) **a adega**
cemetery **o cemitério**
centimetre **o centímetro**
central **central**
central heating **o aquecimento central**
centre **o centro**
century **o século**
cereal **os cereais**
certain **seguro/a**
certainly (*why not?*) **certamente**
certificate **o certificado**
chain **a cadeia**

chair **a cadeira**

chalet **o chalé**

champagne **o champanhe**

change (*small coins*) **os trocos**

to change (*money*) **cambiar** (*clothes*) **mudar**
   I have to change **tenho de me mudar**

changing room **o vestiário**

channel **o canal**
   English Channel **o Canal da Mancha**

chapel **a capela**

charcoal **o carvão vegetal**

charge **o preço**

charter flight **o voo charter**

cheap **barato/a**

check (*pattern*) **axadrezado/a**

to check (*inspect*) **controlar**

check-in (desk) **o (balcão de) check-in**

to check in **fazer o check-in**

cheek **a bochecha**

cheeky **descarado/a**

cheers! **saúde!**

cheese **o queijo**

chef **o chefe**

chemist`s **a farmácia**

chemistry **a química**

cheque **o cheque**

cherry **a cereja**

chess **o xadrez**

chestnut **a castanha**

chewing gum **a pastilha elástica**

chicken **o frango**

chickenpox **a varicela**

child **a criança**

children **as crianças** (*sons and daughters*) **os filhos**

chimney **a chaminé**

china **a porcelana**

chips **as batatas fritas**

chocolate **o chocolate**

chocolates **os bombons**

to choose **escolher**

chop **a costeleta**

Christian **cristão/cristã**

Christian name **o nome**

Christmas **o Natal**

Christmas Eve **a Consoada**

church **a igreja**

cigar **o charuto**

cigarette **o cigarro**

cigarette lighter **o isqueiro**

cinema **o cinema**

cinnamon **a canela**

circle **o círculo** (*theatre*) **o balcão**

circus **o circo**

city **a cidade**

civil servant **o funcionário público, a funcionária pública**

class **a classe**

classical music **a música clássica**

clean **limpo/a**

to clean **limpar**

cleansing cream **o creme de limpeza**

clear **claro/a**

clerk **o funcionário, a funcionária**

clever **inteligente**

cliff **o rochedo**

climate **o clima**

to climb (up) **subir**
climber **o alpinista**
climbing **o alpinismo**
clinic **a clínica**
cloakroom **o bengaleiro**
clock **o relógio**
close (by) **perto**
close to **perto de**
to close **fechar**
closed **fechado/a**
cloth (*for cleaning*) **o pano**
clothes **a roupa**
clothes peg **a mola para a roupa**
cloud **a nuvem**
cloudy **nublado/a**
club **o clube**
  (*golf*) **o taco (de golfe)**
coach **o autocarro, a camioneta**
  (*railway*) **a carruagem**

240

coal **o carvão**
coarse (*texture, skin*) **áspero/a**
coast **a costa**
coat **o casaco**
coat-hanger **o cabide**
cocktail **o cocktail**
coffee **o café**
coin **a moeda**
cold **frio/a**
  I'm cold **tenho frio** (ter, *see page 185*)
  it's cold (*weather*) **está frio** (estar, *see page 184*)
cold: to have a cold **estar constipado/a**
collar (*shirt, jacket*) **o colarinho**
  (*jerseys, etc.*) **a gola**

(*dog's, etc.*) **a coleira**
colleague **o/a colega**
to collect (*rubbish, etc.*) **recolher**
collection (*stamps, etc.*) **a colecção**
  (*post, rubbish*) **a recolha**
college **o colégio**
colour **a cor**
  (*in colour*) **a cores**
colour-blind **daltónico/a**
comb **o pente**
to come **vir** (*see page 185*)
  are you coming? **vem?**
to come back **voltar**
to come down **descer**
comedy **a comédia**
to come in **entrar**
  come in! **entre!**
to come out **sair**
comfortable **confortável**
comic (*magazine*) **a revista de banda desenhada**
commercial **comercial**
common **comum**
communion **a comunhão**
communism **o comunismo**
communist **comunista**
compact disc **o disco compacto**
company **a companhia**
compared with **comparado/a com**
compartment **o compartimento**
compass **a bússola**
to complain (*make a complaint*) **reclamar**
complaint **a reclamação**
completely **completamente**

complicated **complicado/a**

compulsory **obrigatório/a**

composer **o compositor**

computer **o computador**

computer science/studies **a informática**

concert **o concerto**

concert hall **a sala de concertos**

concussion **a concussão**

condition **a condição**

conditioner (*hair*) **o amaciador**

condom **o preservativo**

conference **o congresso**

to confirm **confirmar**

connection (*travel*) **a ligação**

conscious **consciente**

conservation **a conservação**

conservative **conservador/ora**

constipation **a prisão de ventre**

consulate **o consulado**

to contact **contactar**

I want to contact ... **quero contactar ...**

contact lens **a lente de contacto**

contact lens cleaner **o soro de limpeza para lentes de contacto**

continent **o continente**

contraceptive **o contraceptivo**

contract **o contrato**

convenient **conveniente**

it's (not) convenient for me **convém-me/não me convém**

convent **o convento**

cook **o cozinheiro, a cozinheira**

to cook **cozinhar**

cooker **o fogão**

cool **fresco/a**

cool box **a geleira**

copper **o cobre**

copy **a cópia** (*of book*) **o exemplar**

cork **a cortiça** (*in bottle*) **a rolha**

corkscrew **o saca-rolhas**

corner (*street*) **a esquina** (*room*) **o canto**

correct **correcto/a**

corridor **o corredor**

cosmetics **os cosméticos**

cost **o preço**

how much does it cost? **quanto custa?**

cot **o berço**

cottage **a casa de campo**

cotton (*material*) **o algodão** (*thread*) **a linha**

cotton wool **o algodão (hidrófilo)**

couchette **a couchette**

cough **a tosse**

cough medicine **o xarope para a tosse**

to count **contar**

counter (*shop*) **o balcão**

country (*nation*) **o país**

countryside **o campo**

couple (*things*) **o par** (*people*) **o casal**

course (*of lessons*) **o curso** (*of meal*) **o prato**

court (*law*) **o tribunal** (*tennis, etc.*) **o campo**

cousin o primo, a prima
cover a cobertura
cover charge o serviço
cow a vaca
cramp (*medical*) a cãibra
crash (*car*) o acidente
crayon o lápis para desenho
crazy louco/a
cream (*food*) as natas (*lotion*) o creme
credit card o cartão de crédito
crisps as batatas fritas
cross a cruz
  Red Cross a Cruz Vermelha
to cross (*road, etc.*) atravessar
crossing (*sea*) a travessia
crossroads o cruzamento
crowded cheio/a
crown a coroa
cruise o cruzeiro
crutch a muleta
to cry chorar
crystal o cristal
cucumber o pepino
cuff o punho
cup a chávena
cupboard o armário
cure (*remedy*) o remédio
to cure curar
curly encaracolado/a
current (*electrical*) a corrente
curtain a cortina
curve a curva
cushion a almofada
customs a alfândega
cut o corte

to cut, to cut off cortar
cutlery os talheres
cycling o ciclismo
cyclist o/a ciclista
cystitis a cistite

D

daily diário/a
damaged estragado/a
damp húmido/a
dance o baile
to dance dançar
danger o perigo
dangerous perigoso/a
dark escuro/a
  (*hair/skin*) moreno/a
darling querido/a
darts os dardos
data (*information*) os dados
date (*day*) a data
  (*fruit*) a tâmara
daughter a filha
daughter-in-law a nora
day o dia
  day after tomorrow depois de amanhã
  day before yesterday anteontem
  day after/before o dia seguinte/anterior
dead morto/a
deaf surdo/a
dealer o negociante
dear (*loved*) querido/a
  (*expensive*) caro/a
death a morte
debt a dívida
decaffeinated descafeinado/a

deck o convés
deckchair a cadeira de lona
to decide decidir
to declare declarar
deep profundo/a
deep freeze o congelador
deer o veado
defect o defeito
definitely! absolutamente!
to defrost descongelar
degree (*of temperature*) o grau
(*university*) a licenciatura
delay a demora
(*late arrival/departure*) o atraso
delicate delicado/a
delicious delicioso/a
demonstration a demonstração
(*protest*) a manifestação
dentist o/a dentista
dentures as dentaduras
deodorant o desodorizante
to depart partir
department o departamento
department store os armazéns
departure a partida
departure lounge a sala de embarque
deposit o depósito
to describe descrever
description a descrição
desert o deserto
design o desenho
to design desenhar
designer o/a desenhista

dessert a sobremesa
destination o destino
detail o pormenor
detergent o detergente
to develop (*film*) revelar
diabetes o diabetes
to dial marcar
dialling code o indicativo
dialling tone o sinal de marcar
diamond o diamante
diarrhoea a diarreia
diary a agenda
dice o dado
dictionary o dicionário
to die morrer
he/she died morreu
diesel o gasóleo
diet a dieta
to be on a diet estar a dieta (estar, *see page 184*)
different diferente
difficult difícil
dining-room a sala de jantar
dinner o jantar
dinner jacket o smoking
diplomat o/a diplomata
direct directo/a
direction a direcção
director o director, a directora
directory (*telephone*) a lista telefónica
dirty sujo/a
disabled deficiente
disappointed desiludido/a
disc o disco
(*computer*) a disquete
disco a discoteca

discount o **desconto**
dish (*course*) o **prato**
dishwasher a **máquina de lavar loiça**
disinfectant o **desinfectante**
dislocated **deslocado/a**
disposable nappies as **fraldas descartáveis**
distance a **distância**
distilled water a **água destilada**
district a **zona** (*city*) o **bairro**
to dive **mergulhar**
diversion (*traffic*) o **desvio**
diving board a **prancha**
divorced **divorciado/a**
dizzy **tonto/a**
to do **fazer**
  I do **faço**
  he/she/it does; you do **faz**
  we do **fazemos**
docks as **docas**
doctor o **médico**
document o **documento**
dog o **cão**
doll a **boneca**
dollar o **dólar**
dome a **cúpula**
dominoes o **dominó**
donkey o **burro**
door a **porta**
double **duplo/a**
double bed a **cama de casal**
dough a **massa**
down(stairs) **abaixo**
drain o **esgoto**
drama o **drama**

draught (*of air*) a **corrente**
draught beer a **cerveja de barril**
  glass of draught beer **uma imperial**, (*northern Portugal*) um **fino**
to draw **desenhar**
drawer a **gaveta**
drawing o **desenho**
drawing-pin o **percevejo**
dreadful **terrível**
dress o **vestido**
dressing (*medical*) o **penso** (*salad*) o **tempero**
drink a **bebida**
to drip **pingar**
to drive **conduzir**
driver o/a **motorista**
driving licence a **carta de condução**
drowned **afogado/a**
drug a **droga**
drug addict o/a **viciado/a em drogas**
drum o **tambor**
drunk **bêbado/a**
dry **seco/a**
dry-cleaner's a **limpeza a seco**
dubbed **dobrado/a**
duck o **pato**
Dublin **Dublim**
dull (*weather*) **nublado/a**
dumb **mudo/a**
dummy (*baby's*) a **chucha**
during **durante**
dust o **pó**
dustbin o **caixote do lixo**
dusty **poeirento/a**
duty (*customs*) os **direitos**

duty-free **livre de direitos**
duvet **o edredão**

E

each **cada**
ear **a orelha**
earache **a dor de ouvido**
earlier (*before*) **antes**
early **cedo**
to earn **ganhar**
earring **o brinco**
earth **a terra**
earthquake **o terremoto**
east **o este**
eastern **oriental**
Easter **a Páscoa**
easy **fácil**
to eat **comer**
economical **económico/a**
economy, economics **a economia**
Edinburgh **Edimburgo**
egg **o ovo**
either . . . or . . . **ou . . . ou . . .**
elastic band **o elástico**
election **a eleição**
electric **eléctrico/a**
electrician **o/a electricista**
electricity **a electricidade, a luz**
electronic **electrónico/a**
else: everything else **o resto**
embarrassing **embaraçoso/a**
embassy **a embaixada**
emergency **a emergência**
empty **vazio/a**
  (*house, etc.*) **desocupado/a**

to empty **esvaziar**
enamel **o esmalte**
end **o fim**
to end **terminar**
energetic **energético/a**
energy **a energia**
engaged (*to be married*) **comprometido/a**
  (*occupied*) **ocupado/a**
engine **o motor**
engineer **o engenheiro**
engineering **a engenharia**
England **Inglaterra**
English **inglês, inglesa**
enough **bastante**
to enter **entrar (em)**
entertainment **a diversão**
enthusiastic **entusiasta**
entrance **a entrada**
envelope **o envelope**
environment **o ambiente**
equal **igual**
equipment **o equipamento**
-er (*e.g. smaller, cheaper*) **mais . . .**
escalator **a escada rolante**
espadrille **a alpercata**
especially **especialmente, sobretudo**
essential **essencial**
estate (*country*) **a herdade**
estate agent **o agente imobiliário**
evaporated milk **o leite evaporado**
even (*including*) **até**
  (*not odd*) **par**
evening **a tarde**
evening dress **o vestido de noite**

every (*each*) **cada**
  (*all*) **todos/as**
everyone **todos**
everything **tudo**
everywhere **em todo o
  lado**
exactly **exactamente**
examination (*school, etc.*)
  o exame
example **o exemplo**
  for example **por
  exemplo**
excellent **excelente**
except **excepto**
excess luggage **o excesso
  de bagagem**
exchange **cambiar**
exchange rate **o câmbio**
excited **excitado/a**
exciting **emocionante**
excursion **a excursão**
excuse me! (*I'm sorry*)
  desculpe!
  (*may I?*) **com licença!**
executive **o executivo, a
  executiva**
exercise **o exercício**
exhibition **a exposição**
exit **a saída**
to expect **esperar**
expensive **caro/a**
experience **a experiência**
expert **o perito**
to explain **explicar**
explosion **a explosão**
export **a exportação**
to export **exportar**
extension (*telephone*) **a
  extensão**
external **externo/a**
extra (*in addition*) **extra**

eye **o olho**
eyebrow **a sobrancelha**
eyebrow pencil **o lápis
  para as sobrancelhas**
eyelash **a pestana**
eyeliner **o lápis para os
  olhos**
eyeshadow **a sombra para
  os olhos**

F

fabric **o tecido**
face **a cara**
face cream **o creme facial**
face powder **o pó-de-arroz**
facilities **as facilidades**
fact **o facto**
  in fact **de facto**
factory **a fábrica**
to fail (*exam/test*) **reprovar**
failure **o fracasso**
faint: fainted, in a faint
  desmaiado/a
fair (*hair*) **louro/a**
fair **a feira**
  trade fair **a feira de
  indústrias**
fairly (*quite*) **bastante**
faith **a fé**
faithful **fiel**
fake **falso/a**
to fall **cair**
  he/she fell down **caiu**
false **falso/a**
false teeth/eye **a prótese
  dentária/ocular**
family **a família**
famous **famoso/a**
fan **o leque**
  (*electric*) **a ventoinha**

(*supporter*) o adepto
fantastic fantástico/a
far (*away*) longe
  is it far? fica longe?
fare o preço do bilhete
farm a quinta
farmer o agricultor, a
  agricultora
fashion a moda
fashionable/in fashion na
  moda
fast rápido/a
fat a gordura
fat (*person, etc.*) gordo/a
father o pai
father-in-law o sogro
fault (*defect*) o defeito
faulty defeituoso/a
favourite favorito/a
feather a pena
fed up farto/a
to feed dar de comer a
  (*baby*) dar de mamar a
to feel sentir
  I feel well/unwell sinto-
  me bem/mal
  he/she feels, you feel
  sente-se
felt-tip pen a caneta de
  feltro
female, feminine
  feminino/a
feminist feminista
fence a vedação
ferry o ferry-boat
festival (*village, etc.*) a festa
  (*film, etc.*) o festival
fever a febre
few poucos/as
  a few (*some*) alguns/
  algumas

fiancé(e) o noivo, a noiva
fibre a fibra
field o campo
fig o figo
fight a luta
file o ficheiro
  (*nail, DIY*) a lima
to fill (up) encher
filling (*dental*) o chumbo,
  a obturação
film (*cinema*) o filme
  (*camera*) o rolo
film star a estrela de
  cinema
filter o filtro
finance as finanças
find encontrar
fine (*weather*) bom/boa
  (*OK*) está bem
fine (*penalty*) a multa
finish acabar
fire o fogo
fire brigade os bombeiros
fire extinguisher o
  extintor
firewood a lenha
fireworks o fogo de
  artifício
firm (*company*) a
  empresa, a firma
first primeiro/a
first aid os primeiros
  socorros
first aid box/kit a caixa de
  primeiros socorros
fish o peixe
to fish/go fishing pescar
fishing a pesca
fishing rod a cana de
  pesca
fishmonger's a peixaria

fit (*healthy*) **em forma**
to fit: it fits/it doesn`t fit
  serve/não serve
fitting room **a sala de
provas**
to fix **reparar, consertar**
fizzy **com gás**
flag **a bandeira**
flat (*apartment*) **o
apartamento**
flat (*level*) **plano/a**
  (*battery*) **em baixo**
flavour **o sabor**
flaw **o defeito**
flea **a pulga**
flight **o voo**
flight bag **o saco de
viagem**
flippers **as barbatanas**
flood **a inundação**
floor **o chão**
floor (*storey*) **o andar**
  ground floor **o res-do-
chão**
flour **a farinha**
flower **a flor**
flu **a gripe**
fluid **o líquido**
fly **a mosca**
fly sheet **a duplo-tecto**
foam **a espuma**
fog **o nevoeiro**
foggy: it`s foggy **está
nevoeiro**
foil **a folha de alumínio**
folding (*chair, etc.*)
  dobradiço/a
following (*next*) **seguinte**
food **a comida**
food poisoning **a
intoxicação alimentar**

foot **o pé**
  on foot **a pé**
football **o futebol**
footpath **o caminho**
for **para; por**
forbidden **proibido/a**
foreign **estrangeiro/a**
forest **a floresta**
to forget **esquecer**
to forgive **perdoar**
fork **o garfo**
form (*document*) **o
impresso**
fortnight **quinze dias**
forward **adiante**
foundation (*make-up*) **a
base**
fountain **a fonte**
foyer **o hall**
fracture **a fractura**
fragile **frágil**
frankly **francamente**
freckle **a barda**
free **grátis**
  (*available, unoccupied*)
  livre
freedom **a liberdade**
to freeze **congelar**
freezer **a arca congeladora**
frequent **frequente**
fresh **fresco/a**
fridge **o frigorífico**
fried **frito/a**
friend **o amigo, a amiga**
frightened **assustado/a**
fringe (*of hair*) **a franja**
frog **a rã**
from **de, desde**
front: in front (of) **em
frente (de)**
front door **a porta principal**

frontier a **fronteira**
frost a **geada**
frozen **congelado/a**
fruit a **fruta**
fruiterer's a **frutaria**
frying pan a **frigideira**
fuel o **combustível**
full **cheio/a**
full board a **pensão completa**
full up (*hotel, etc.*) **completo/a**
funeral o **enterro**
funfair a **feira popular**
funny (*amusing*) **engraçado/a** (*peculiar*) **esquisito/a**
fur a **pele**
furniture os **móveis**
further on **mais adiante**
fuse o **fusível**

G

gallery a **galeria**
gambling a **jogo**
game o **jogo** (*match*) a **partida** (*in hunting*) a **caça**
garage a **garagem**
garden o **jardim**
gardener o **jardineiro**
garlic o **alho**
gas o **gás**
gas bottle/cylinder a **garrafa de gás**
gas refill a **recarga de gás**
gastritis a **gastrite**
gate o **portão**
general **geral**
general (*military*) o **general**

generous **generoso/a**
gentle **suave**
gentleman o **senhor**
genuine **autêntico/a**
geography a **geografia**
to get (*obtain*) **obter**
to get off (*bus, etc.*) **sair**
to get on (*bus, etc.*) **entrar (em)**
gift o **presente**
gin o **gin**
gin and tonic o **gin tónico**
girl a **rapariga**
girlfriend a **namorada**
to give **dar**
I give **dou**
can you give me . . . ? **podia-me dar . . . ?**
glass (*container*) o **copo** (*material*) o **vidro**
glasses os **óculos**
glove a **luva**
glue a **cola**
to go **ir** (*see page 185*)
I go/am going (to) **vou**
let's go **vamos**
to go down **descer**
to go in **entrar (em)**
to go out **sair**
I go/am going out **saio**
to go up **subir**
goal (*in sport*) o **golo**
goat a **cabra**
God **Deus**
goggles (*diving*) os **óculos de mergulho**
gold o **ouro** (*made of*) **de ouro**
golf o **golfe**
golf clubs os **tacos de golfe**
golf course o **campo de golfe**

good **bom/boa**
good afternoon/evening
  boa tarde
good morning **bom dia**
goodnight **boa noite**
goodbye **adeus**
government **o governo**
gram **o grama**
grammar **a gramática**
grandchildren **os netos**
granddaughter **a neta**
grandfather **o avô**
grandmother **a avó**
grandparents **os avós**
grandson **o neto**
grandstand **as
  bancadas**
grape **a uva**
grapefruit **a toranja**
grass (*lawn*) **a relva**
grateful **agradecido/a**
greasy **gorduroso/a**
great **grande**
  great! **óptimo!**
Great Britain **a Grã-Bretanha**
green **verde**
green card **a carta verde**
greengrocer's **a frutaria**
greet **saudar**
grey **cinzento/a**
grilled **grelhado/a**
grocer's **a mercearia**
ground **o chão**
ground floor **o rés-do-chão**
groundsheet **o chão da tenda**
group **o grupo**
to grow (*cultivate*) **cultivar**
guarantee **a garantia**
guest **o convidado, a convidada**
  (*hotel*) **o hóspede**
guest house **a pensão**

guide **o/a guia**
guidebook **o guia (turístico)**
guided tour **a visita com guia**
guilty **culpado/a**
guitar (*Spanish*) **a viola**
  (*Portuguese*) **a guitarra**
gun **a arma**
  (*shotgun*) **a espingarda**
guy rope **a espia**
gymnastics **a ginástica**

H

habit (*custom*) **o costume**
haemorrhoids **as
  hemorróidas**
hail **o granizo**
hair **o cabelo**
hairbrush **a escova para
  cabelo**
haircut **o corte de cabelo**
hairdresser's **o
  cabeleireiro,
  a cabeleireira**
hair dryer **o secador de
  cabelo**
hairgrip **o gancho**
hairspray **a laca**
half **a metade**
half **meio/a**
  half an hour **meia hora**
  half board **a meia
  pensão**
  half past (*see* Time, *page
  192*)
  half price/fare **o meio
  bilhete**
hall (*in house*) **o hall**
  (*concert*) **a sala**
ham (*cured*) **o presunto**
  (*boiled*) **o fiambre**

hamburger o hamburguer
hammer o martelo
hand a mão
handbag o saco
hand cream o creme para as mãos
handicapped deficiente
handkerchief o lenço
handle a asa
(door) o manípulo
hand luggage a bagagem de mão
hand-made feito/a a mão
hangover a ressaca
to hang (up) pendurar
to happen acontecer
what has happened? que aconteceu?
happy feliz
harbour o porto
hard duro/a
(difficult) difícil
hard shoulder a berma
hat o chapéu
to hate odiar
to have ter (see page 185)
do you have ...? tem ...?
hay fever a febre dos fenos
hazelnut a avelã
he ele
head a cabeça
(boss) o chefe
headache a dor de cabeça
headphones os auscultadores
to heal curar
health a saúde
healthy são/sã
to hear ouvir
hearing aid o aparelho de surdez

heart a coração
heart attack o ataque cardíaco
heat o calor
heater (water) o esquentador
heating o aquecimento
heaven o céu
heavy pesado/a
hedge a sebe
heel o calcanhar
(of shoe) o salto
height a altura
helicopter o helicóptero
hell o inferno
hello olá
help a ajuda
help! socorro!
to help ajudar
her a, lhe; ela
her (of her) o/a ... dela;
(pl.) os/as ... dela (see page 179)
herb a erva
herbal tea o chá de ervas
here aqui
hiccups: to have hiccups ter soluços (ter, see page 185)
high alto/a
high chair a cadeira de bebé
to hijack sequestrar
hill a colina
(slope) a ladeira
hill-walking o montanhismo
him o, lhe; ele
to hire alugar
his o/a ... dele; (pl.) os/as ... dele (see page 179)
history a história

to hit **bater**
to hitchhike **andar à boleia**
hobby **o passatempo**
hole **o buraco**
holiday(s) **as férias**
  on holiday **em férias**
  public holiday **o feriado**
holy **santo/a**
  Holy Week **a Semana Santa**
home **a casa**
  at home **em casa**
  to go home **ir para casa**
home address **a morada**
homosexual **homosexual**
honesto **honesto/a**
honeymoon **a lua de mel**
to hope **esperar**
  I hope so/not **espero que sim/não**
horrible **horrível**
horse **o cavalo**
horse-riding **a equitação**
hose **a mangueira**
hospital **o hospital**
hot **quente**
  I'm hot **estou com calor**
  it's hot (*weather*) **está calor**
hot (*spicy*) **picante**
hotel **o hotel**
hour **a hora**
house **a casa**
housewife **a dona de casa**
housework **o trabalho doméstico**
hovercraft **o hovercraft**
how? **como?**
  how are you? **como está?**
how long? **quanto tempo?**

how many? **quantos/as?**
how much? **quanto/a?**
how much is it? **quanto é?**
human **humano/a**
hungry: to be hungry **ter fome (ter,** *see page 185*)
to hunt **caçar**
hunting **a caça**
hurry: to be in a hurry **ter pressa (ter,** *see page 185*)
hurt: my . . . hurts **dói-me o/a . . .** (*see page 154*)
husband **o marido**
hut **a cabana**
hypermarket **o hipermercado**

I

I **eu**
ice **o gelo**
ice-cream **o gelado**
ice rink **o ringue de patinagem**
icy **gelado/a**
idea **a ideia**
if **se**
ill **doente**
illness **a doença**
to imagine **imaginar**
imagination **a imaginação**
immediately **imediatamente, já**
immersion heater **o aquecedor de imersão**
impatient **impaciente**
important **importante**
impossible **impossível**
impressive **impressionante**
in **em; dentro (de)**
included **incluído/a**

income o **rendimento**
independent **independente**
indigestion a **indigestão**
indoors **dentro**
industrial **industrial**
industry a **indústria**
infected **infectado/a**
infection a **infecção**
infectious **contagioso/a**
inflamed **inflamado/a**
inflammation
  a **inflamação**
influenza a **gripe**
informal **informal**
information a **informação**
information office o **posto
  de informação**
injection a **injecção**
injured **ferido/a**
injury a **ferida**
ink a **tinta**
inner **interno/a**
innocent **inocente**
insect o **insecto**
insect bite a **mordedura de
  insecto**
insecticide o **insecticida**
insect repellent o
  repelente de insectos
inside **dentro (de)**
instant coffee o **café
  instantâneo**
instead of **em lugar de**
instructor o **instrutor**
to insist **insistir**
insulin a **insulina**
insult o **insulto**
insurance o **seguro**
insurance certificate o
  certificado de seguro
intelligent **inteligente**

interested: I'm (not)
  interested in ...
    ... **interessa-me/ ...
    não me interessa**
interesting **interessante**
interior **interior**
international
  internacional
interpreter o/a **intérprete**
internal **interno/a**
interval (*in theatre, etc.*) o
  intervalo
interview a **entrevista**
into **em**
to introduce **apresentar**
to invite **convidar**
invitation o **convite**
iodine o **iodo**
Ireland **Irlanda**
Irish **irlandês, irlandesa**
iron (*metal*) o **ferro**
  (*for clothes*) o **ferro (de
  engomar)**
to iron **passar a ferro**
ironmonger's a **loja de
  ferragens**
is (*see* to be)
  is there ... ? **há ... ?**
island a **ilha**
it **o/a**
itch a **comichão**

J

jacket o **casaco**
jam a **compota**
jar o **frasco**
jazz o **jazz**
jeans os **jeans**
Jesus, Jesus Christ **Jesus,
  Jesus Cristo**

jelly (*jam*) a geleia
(*gelatine*) a gelatina
jellyfish a medusa
jeweller's a joalharia
Jewish judeu, judia
job o emprego
jogging: to go jogging
fazer jogging
I go jogging faço
jogging
joke a piada
journalist o/a jornalista
journey a viagem
judge o juiz
jug o jarro
juice o sumo
to jump saltar
jump leads os cabos de
emergência
jumper a camisola
junction o cruzamento
just (*only*) só

K

to keep guardar
kettle a chaleira
key a chave
key ring o porta-chaves
kidney o rim
to kill matar
kilo(gram) o quilo
kilometre o quilómetro
kind (*sort*) o tipo
kind (*helpful*) amável
king o rei
kiss o beijo
to kiss beijar
kitchen a cozinha
knickers (*women's*) as
cuecas de mulher

knife a faca
to knit tricotar
to knock bater em/a
knot o nó
to know (*someone*) conhecer
I don't know him/her
não o/a conheço
(*something*) saber
I (don't) know (não)
sei
to know how to . . . saber . . .
I (don't) know how to . . .
(não) sei . . .

L

label a etiqueta
lace (*cloth*) a renda
(*shoe*) o atacador
ladder a escada
lady a senhora
ladies and gentlemen
senhoras e senhores
lager a cerveja
lake o lago
lamb o cordeiro
lamp o candeeiro
lamp post o candeeiro
land a terra
to land aterrar
landlady a senhoria
landlord o senhorio
lane (*country road*) o
caminho
language a língua
large grande
last último/a
(*week, etc.*) passado/a
(*see page 190*)
to last durar
late tarde

later **mais tarde**
laugh **o riso**
to laugh **rir**
launderette **a lavandaria
automática**
laundry **a lavandaria**
(*dirty clothes*) **a roupa
para lavar**
law **a lei**
(*subject*) **o direito**
lawn **a relva**
lawyer **o avogado**
laxative **o laxativo**
lazy **preguiçoso/a**
lead **o chumbo**
lead-free **sem chumbo**
leaf **a folha**
leaflet **o folheto**
to learn **aprender**
learner **o aprendiz**
least: at least **pelo menos**
leather **a pele, o cabedal**
to leave (*message, etc.*) **deixar**
(*depart*) **partir**
left **a esquerda**
on/to the left **à esquerda**
on the left-hand side **do
lado esquerdo**
left-luggage (office) **o
depósito de bagagem**
left-hand **esquerdo/a**
left-handed **canhoto/a**
leg **a perna**
legal **legal**
lemon **o limão**
lemonade **a limonada**
to lend **emprestar**
length **o comprimento**
(*duration*) **a duração**
lens **a lente**
less **menos**

lesson **a lição**
to let (*allow*) **permitir**
(*rent*) **alugar**
letter **a carta**
(*of alphabet*) **a letra**
letterbox **o marco de
correio**
lettuce **o alface**
level (*height, standard*) **o
nível**
level (*flat*) **nivelado/a**
level crossing **a passagem
de nível**
library **a biblioteca**
licence (*driving*) **a carta de
condução**
(*fishing, etc.*) **a licença**
lid **a tampa**
life **a vida**
lifebelt **o cinto salva-vidas**
lifeboat **o bote salva-vidas**
lifeguard **o nadador-
salvador**
lifejacket **o colete salva-
vidas**
lift **o elevador**
light **a luz**
light (*in colour*) **claro/a**
(*in weight*) **ligeiro/a**
to light (*fire, etc.*) **acender**
light bulb **a lâmpada**
lighter (*cigarette*) **o
isqueiro**
lightning **o relâmpago**
like (*similar to*) **como,
semelhante a**
like this/that **assim**
what is . . . like? **como
é . . . ?**
what are . . . like? **como
são . . . ?**

like: I like ... **gosto de ...**
(*see page 21*)
do you like ...? **gosta
de ...?**
likely **provável**
limited **limitado/a**
line a **linha**
lion o **leão**
lipstick o **baton**
liqueur o **licor**
liquid o **líquido**
Lisbon **Lisboa**
list a **lista**
to listen **ouvir**
I listen **ouço**
he/she/it listens, you
listen **ouve**
litre o **litro**
litter o **lixo**
little (*small*) **pequeno/a**
a little **um pouco (de)**
to live **viver**
(*reside*) **morar**
where do you live? **onde
mora?**
liver o **fígado**
living room a **sala de
estar**
loaf o **pão**
local **local**
lock a **fechadura**
to lock **fechar à chave**
London **Londres**
lonely **sozinho/a**
long **comprido/a**
to look (at) **olhar (para)**
to look after **cuidar de**
to look for **procurar**
to look like **parecer**
loose **solto/a**
(*clothes*) **largo/a**

lorry o **camião**
lorry-driver o **camionista**
to lose **perder**
lost property office o
**posto de perdidos e
achados**
a lot (of) **muito/a**
lotion a **loção**
lottery a **loteria**
loud **alto/a**
lounge a **sala de estar**
love o **amor**
to love **amar**
lovely **lindo/a**
low **baixo/a**
lower **inferior**
lozenge a **pastilha**
LP o **LP**
lucky: to be lucky **ter
sorte (ter, *see page 185*)**
luggage a **bagagem**
lump (*swelling*) o **inchaço**
lump of sugar o **cubo de
açúcar**
lunch o **almoço**

M

machine a **máquina**
machinist o **maquinista**
mad **louco/a**
madam **senhora**
magazine a **revista**
main **principal**
make (*brand*) a **marca**
to make **fazer**
I make **faço**
he/she/it makes, you
make **faz**
make-up a **maquilhagem**
male **masculino/a**

man **o homem**
manager **o gerente**
managing director **o director gerente**
many **muitos/as**
not many **poucos/as**
map **o mapa**
marble **o mármore**
margarine **a margarina**
market **o mercado**
married **casado/a**
mascara **o rímel**
masculine **masculino/a**
mask **a máscara**
mass (*ceremony*) **a missa**
match (*game*) **a partida**
matches **os fósforos**
material (*cloth*) **o tecido**
mathematics **a matemática**
matter: it doesn't matter **não importa**
what's the matter? **o que é?**
mattress **o colchão**
mature **maduro/a**
mayonnaise **a maionese**
me **me; mim**
meadow **o prado**
meal **a refeição**
mean: what does it mean? **que quer dizer?**
meanwhile **entretanto**
measles **o sarampo**
German measles **a rubéola**
to measure **medir**
measurement **a medida**
meat **a carne**
cold meats **as carnes frias**

mechanic **o mecânico**
medical **médico/a**
medicine (*subject*) **a medicina**
(*drug*) **o medicamento**
Mediterranean **o Mediterrâneo**
medium **médio/a**
medium dry (*wine*) **meio-seco**
meeting **a reunião**
melon **o melão**
water melon **a melancia**
member **o membro**
to mend **reparar**
menu **a ementa, a lista**
set menu **a ementa turística**
message **o recado**
metal **o metal**
meter **o contador**
metre **o metro**
microwave (*oven*) **o (forno) micro-ondas**
midday **o meio-dia**
middle **o centro**
middle-aged **de meia idade**
midnight **a meia-noite**
migraine **a enxaqueca**
mild (*taste*) **suave**
(*temperature*) **ameno/a**
mile **a milha**
milk **o leite**
milkshake **o batido**
mill **o moinho**
mince **a carne picada**
mind: do you mind if . . . ? **importa-se que . . . ?**
I don't mind **não me importa**

mine (*of me*) o meu, a minha

minister o ministro

minute o minuto

mirror o espelho

Miss (a) senhora

to miss (*bus, etc.*) perder

mist o nevoeiro

mistake o erro

mistaken enganado/a

mixed misto/a

mixture a mistura

model o modelo

moderno moderno/a

moisturiser o creme hidratante

monastery o mosteiro

money o dinheiro

month o mês

monument o monumento

moon a lua

moped a motocicleta

more mais

morning a manhã

mortgage a hipoteca

mosque a mesquita

mosquito o mosquito

mosquito net o mosquiteiro

most (of) a maior parte (de)

mother a mãe

mother-in-law a sogra

motor o motor

motorbike a motorizada

motorboat o barco a motor

motor racing o automobilismo

motorway a auto-estrada

mountain a montanha

mountaineering o alpinismo

moustache o bigode

mouth a boca

to move mover

to move house mudar de casa

movement o movimento

Mr (o) senhor

Mrs (a) senhora

much muito/a

not much pouco/a

mug a caneca

to murder assassinar

museum o museu

mushroom o cogumelo

music a música

musical musical

musician o músico, a música

must: you must . . . tem de . . .

mustard a mustarda

my o meu, a minha; (*pl.*) os meus, as minhas

N

nail o prego

(*finger/toe*) a unha

nail file a lima para as unhas

nail polish o verniz

nail polish remover o tira-verniz

naked nu, nua

name o nome

my name is . . . o meu nome é . . . ; chamo-me . . .

what is your name? **qual é o seu nome?; como se chama?**
napkin **o guardanapo**
　paper napkin **o guardanapo de papel**
nappy **a fralda**
　disposable nappies **as fraldas descartáveis**
　nappy liner **a gaze**
narrow **estreito/a**
national **nacional**
nationality **a nacionalidade**
natural **natural**
naturally **naturalmente**
naughty **travesso/a**
navy **a marinha**
　navy blue **azul marinho**
near (to) **perto (de)**
nearly **quase**
necessary **necessário/a**
necklace **o colar**
to need **precisar**
needle **a agulha**
negative (*of photo*) **o negativo**
neighbour **o vizinho, a vizinha**
neither . . . nor . . . **nem . . . nem . . .**
nephew **o sobrinho**
nervous **nervoso/a**
net **a rede**
never **nunca**
new **novo/a**
　New Year **o Ano Novo**
news **as notícias**
newspaper **o jornal**
newspaper kiosk **o quiosque**

next **próximo/a**
　week/month/year (*see page 190*)
nice (*person*) **simpático/a** (*place, thing*) **bonito/a**
niece **a sobrinha**
night **a noite**
nightclub **a boite**
nightdress **o vestido de noite**
no **não**
nobody **ninguém**
noise **o barulho**
noisy **barulhento/a**
non-alcoholic **sem álcool**
none **nenhum, nenhuma**
non-smoking **não-fumador**
normal **normal**
north **o norte**
northern **do norte**
nose **o nariz**
nosebleed **a hemorragia nasal**
not **não**
note (*bank*) **a nota**
notepad **o bloco para notas**
nothing **nada**
nothing else **mais nada**
now **agora**
nowhere **em parte nenhuma**
nuclear **nuclear**
nuclear energy **a energia nuclear**
number **o número**
nurse **o enfermeiro, a enfermeira**

(*see page 190*)

nut **a noz**
  (*for bolt*) **a porca**
nylon **o nylon**

O

oar **o remo**
object **o objecto**
obvious **óbvio/a**
occasionally **às vezes**
occupied (*seat*) **ocupado/a**
odd **estranho/a**
  (*not even*) **impar**
of **de**
of course **claro**
off (*switched off*)
  desligado/a
offended **ofendido/a**
office **o escritório**
official **oficial**
official **o funcionário**
often **muitas vezes**
  how often? **quantas**
    vezes?
oil **o óleo**
  olive oil **o azeite**
OK **está bem**
old **velho/a**
  how old are you?; how
    old is he/she? **quantos**
    anos tem?
  I am . . . years old **tenho**
    . . . anos
old-fashioned **antiquado/a**
olive **a azeitona**
olive oil **o azeite**
on **em**
  (*switched on*) **aceso/a**
once **uma vez**
onion **a cebola**
only **só**

open **aberto/a**
to open **abrir**
opera **a ópera**
operation **a operação**
opinion **a opinião**
  in my opinion **na minha**
    opinião
Oporto **(o) Porto**
opposite (*contrary*)
  contrário/a
opposite (to) **em frente**
  (de)
optician **o óptico**
or **ou**
orange (*fruit*) **a laranja**
  (*colour*) **cor-de-laranja**
order **a ordem**
to order (*in restaurant*) **pedir**
ordinary **vulgar**
to organise **organizar**
original **original**
other **outro/a, outros/as**
others **outros/as**
our; ours **o nosso, a nossa;**
  (*pl.*) **os nossos, as nossas**
out (of) **fora (de)**
  he/she is out **não está**
outdoors **ao ar livre**
outside **fora**
over (*above*) **sobre**
overcast (*sky*) **encoberto/a**
overcoat **o sobretudo**
to overtake **ultrapassar**
owner **o proprietário, a**
  proprietária

P

package tour **a excursão**
  organizada
packet **o embrulho**

padlock o cadeado
page a página
pain a dor
painful doloroso/a
painkiller o analgésico
paint a tinta
to paint pintar
painter o pintor, a pintora
painting (picture) o
  quadro
  (art) a pintura
pair o par
palace o palácio
pale pálido/a
  (colour) desmaiado/a
panties (women's) as
  calcinhas (de mulher)
pants (men's) as cuecas
paper o papel
paper clip o clipe
paraffin a parafina
parcel o embrulho
pardon? como?
parents os pais
park o parque
to park estacionar
parking o estacionamento
parking meter o
  parquímetro
parliament o parlamento
part a parte
parting (in hair) o risco do
  cabelo
partly em parte
partner (business) o sócio,
  a sócia
party (celebration) a festa
to pass (salt, etc., exam)
  passar
passenger o passageiro
passport o passaporte

past o passado
past (time, see page 192)
pasta a massa
pastille a pastilha
pastry o pastel
  (dough) a massa de bolos
path o caminho
patient (hospital) o/a
  doente
pattern o padrão
pavement o passeio
to pay pagar
to pay cash pagar a dinheiro
pea a ervilha
peace a paz
peach o pêssego
peanut o amendoim
pear a pera
pedal o pedal
pedestrian o peão
pedestrian crossing a
  passagem para peões
to peel descascar
peg o grampo
  (clothes) a mola para a
  roupa
pen a caneta
pencil o lápis
pencil sharpener o apara-
  lápis
penfriend o/a
  correspondente
penknife o canivete
pension a pensão
  (retirement) a reforma
pensioner o/a pensionista
people as pessoas
  (nation) o povo
pepper a pimenta
  green/red o pimento
  verde/encarnado

peppermint (*herb*) a **hortelã-pimenta**
(*sweet*) **o rebuçado de mentol**
per **por**
perfect **perfeito/a**
performance a **representação**
(*cinema*) **a sessão**
perfume **o perfume**
perhaps **talvez**
period (*menstrual*) a **menstruação**
period pains **as dores menstruais**
perm **o permanente**
permit **a licença**
to permit **permitir**
person **a pessoa**
personal **pessoal**
personal stereo **o walkman**

petrol **a gasolina**
petrol can **a lata de gasolina**
petrol station **a estação de serviço**
petticoat **o saiote, a combinação**
philosophy **a filosofia**
photocopy **a fotocópia**
to photocopy **fotocopiar**
photo(graph) a **foto(grafia)**
photographer **o fotógrafo**
photography **a fotografia**
phrase book **o guia de conversação**
physics **a física**
piano **o piano**
to pick (*choose*) **escolher**
(*flowers, etc.*) **colher**

to pick up **apanhar**
picnic **o piquenique**
picture **o quadro**
piece **o pedaço**
pier **o molhe**
pig **o porco**
pill **o comprimido**
(*contraceptive*) a **pílula**
pillow **a almofada**
pillowcase **a fronha**
pilot **o piloto**
pin **o alfinete**
pineapple **o ananás**
pink **cor-de-rosa**
pipe (*for smoking*) o **cachimbo**
(*drain, etc.*) **o cano**
place **o lugar**
plan (*of town*) **o mapa**
plant **a planta**
plaster (*sticking*) **o penso adesivo**
plastic **o plástico**
plastic bag **o saco de plástico**
plate **o prato**
platform (*station*) **a linha, a plataforma**
play (*at theatre*) **a obra, a peça (de teatro)**
to play (*instrument, record*) **tocar**
(*sport*) **jogar**
pleasant **agradável**
please **por favor; faz favor**
pleased **contente**
plenty (of) **bastante**
pliers **o alicate**
plimsolls **os sapatos de ténis**
plug (*bath, etc.*) **a tampa**
(*electrical*) **a tomada**

plumber o canalizador
pneumonia a pneumonia
pocket a algibeira
point o ponto
poison o veneno
poisonous venenoso/a
police a polícia
police car o carro da polícia
police station a esquadra (da polícia)
polish (*shoe, etc.*) a graxa
polite bem educado/a
political político/a
politician o político
politics a política
polluted poluído/a
pollution a poluição
pool (*swimming*) a piscina
poor pobre
  poor thing! coitado!, coitada!
pop (*music*) a música pop
Pope o Papa
popular popular
pork (a carne de) porco
port (*harbour*) o porto
  (*wine*) o vinho do Porto
portable portátil
porter o porteiro
porthole a vigia
portrait o retrato
possible possível
  as . . . as possible o mais . . . possível
  if possible se possível
possibly possivelmente
post (*mail*) o correio
postbox o marco de correio
postcard o postal

postcode o código postal
postman o carteiro
post office o correio
to postpone adiar
pot o frasco
potato a batata
pottery a cerâmica, a olaria
potty (*child's*) o penico
pound (sterling) a libra (esterlina)
to pour deitar
powder o pó
power a força
  (*electrical*) a corrente
power cut o corte de energia
pram o carrinho de bebé
to prefer preferir
  I prefer prefiro
pregnant grávida
to prepare preparar
prescription a receita
present (*gift*) o presente
pretty bonito/a
price o preço
priest o padre
prime minister o primeiro ministro, a primeira ministra
prince o príncipe
princess a princesa
print (*photo*) a fotografia
  (*picture*) a gravura
prison a prisão
private privado/a
prize o prémio
probable provável
probably provavelmente
problem o problema
producer (*radio/TV*) o chefe de produção

profession **a profissão**
professor **o professor
(catedrático), a
professora
(catedrática)**
profit **o lucro**
program (*computer*) **o
programa**
programme **o programa**
prohibited **proibido/a**
to promise **prometer**
promise **a promessa**
to pronounce **pronunciar**
properly **correctamente**
property **a propriedade**
protestant **protestante**
province **a província**
public **o público**
public holiday **o feriado**
to pull **puxar**
to pump up (*tyre, etc.*) **encher**
puncture **o furo**
pure **puro/a**
purple **púrpura**
purse **a bolsa**
to push **empurrar**
push-chair **o carrinho de
criança**
to put, put down **pôr**
  I put **ponho**
  he/she/it puts, you put
  põe
pyjamas **o pijama**

Q

quality **a qualidade**
quarter **o quarto**
  (*of town*) **o bairro**
quay **o cais**
queen **a rainha**

question **a pergunta**
queue **a bicha, a fila**
quick **rápido/a**
quickly **rapidamente**
quiet (*person*) **calado/a**
  (*place*) **tranquilo/a**
quite (*fairly*) **bastante**
  (*completely*)
  completamente

R

rabbi **o rabino**
rabbit **o coelho**
rabies **a raiva**
race **a corrida**
racecourse/track **a pista**
  (*for horses*) **o hipódromo**
racing **as corridas**
racket **o raquete**
radio **a rádio**
radioactive **radioactivo/a**
radio station **a emissora
de rádio**
raft **a jangada**
railway **o caminho de
ferro**
railway station **a estação
de caminho de ferro**
rain **a chuva**
to rain **chover**
  it's raining **está a chover**
raincoat **a gabardina**
rainy **chuvoso/a**
to rape **violar**
rare **raro/a**
  (*steak*) **mal passado/a**
rash **a erupção cutânea**
raspberry **a framboesa**
rate (*speed*) **a velocidade**
  (*tariff*) **a tarifa**

rather (*quite*) **bastante**
raw **cru, crua**
razor **a gilete**
razor blade **a lâmina de barbear**
to reach (*arrive at*) **chegar a**
to read **ler**
reading **a leitura**
ready **pronto/a**
real (*authentic*) **autêntico/a**
really (*very*) **mesmo**
really? **sim?**
rear (*of house*) **as traseiras** (*of vehicle*) **a retaguarda**
reason **a razão**
the reason why **o porquê**
receipt **o recibo**
receiver (*telephone*) **o auscultador**
reception **a recepção**
receptionist **o/a recepcionista**
recipe **a receita**
to recognise **reconhecer**
I recognise **reconheço**
to recommend **recomendar**
record **o disco**
to record **gravar**
record player **o gira-discos**
red **vermelho/a**
Red Cross **a Cruz Vermelha**
red wine **o vinho tinto**
reduction **a redução** (*discount*) **o desconto**
refill **a recarga** (*pen*) **a carga**
refrigerator **o frigorífico**
refund **o reembolso**

region **a região**
to register (*letter*) **registar**
registration number **a matrícula**
relation (*family*) **o familiar**
religion **a religião**
to remain **ficar**
to remember **lembrar-se**
I remember **lembro-me**
to remove **tirar**
to rent **alugar**
rent(al) **o aluguer**
to repair **reparar**
to repeat **repetir**
reply **a resposta**
report (*business, etc.*) **o relatório** (*newspaper*) **a reportagem**
to report (*crime, etc.*) **dar parte (de)**
to rescue **salvar**
reservation **a reserva**
to reserve **reservar**
reserved **reservado/a**
responsible **responsável**
to rest **descansar**
restaurant **o restaurante**
restaurant car **a carruagem-restaurante**
result **o resultado**
retired **reformado/a**
return **a volta** (*ticket*) **ida e volta**
to return **voltar** (*give back*) **devolver**
reverse charge call **a chamada a pagar pelo destinatário**
rheumatism **o reumatismo**
ribbon **o laço**

rice o arroz
rich rico/a
ride: to go for a ride dar uma volta
to ride (a bike/in a car) andar de (bicicleta/ carro)
to ride a horse andar a cavalo
right a direita
on/to the right à direita
on the right-hand side do lado direito
right: you are (not) right (não) tem razão
that's right pois é; é isso
right-hand direito/a
rights (human, etc.) os direitos
ring (jewellery) o anel
ripe maduro/a
river o rio
road a estrada
roadworks as obras
roast assado/a
to rob roubar
I've been robbed fui roubado/a
robbery o roubo
roll (bread) o pãozinho
roof o tecto
roof rack o tejadilho, o porta-bagagem
room (in house) a assoalhada
(hotel) o quarto
(space) o espaço
rope a corda
rose a rosa
rosé rosé
rotten podre

rough (surface) áspero/a
(sea) bravo/a
round redondo/a
roundabout (traffic) a rotunda
(funfair) o carrossel
row (of seats) a fila
to row remar
rowing boat o barco a remos
royal real
rubber (material, eraser) a borracha
rubber band o elástico
rubbish o lixo
rubbish! disparate!
rucksack a mochila
rude mal educado/a
ruins as ruínas
ruler (measuring) a régua
rum o rum
to run correr
rush hour a hora de ponta
rusty ferrugento/a

S

sad triste
safe (strongbox) o cofre
safe seguro/a
safety pin o alfinete-de-ama
sail a vela
sailboard a prancha
sailing a vela
sailing boat o barco a vela
sailor o marinheiro
saint o santo, a santa
salad a salada
salami o salame
sale a venda
(reduced prices) os saldos

266

sales representative o **vendedor viajante, a vendedora viajante**
salesman o **vendedor**
saleswoman a **vendedora**
salmon o **salmão**
salt o **sal**
salty **salgado/a**
same **mesmo/a**
sample a **amostra**
sand a **areia**
sandal a **sandália**
sandwich a **sanduíche, a sandes**
    toasted sandwich a **tosta**
sanitary towel o **penso higiénico**
sauce o **molho**
saucepan a **panela**
saucer o **pires**
sauna a **sauna**
sausage a **salsicha**
to save (*rescue*) **salvar** (*money*) **poupar**
to say **dizer**
    I say **digo**
    he/she says, you say **diz**
    how do you say it? **como se diz?**
    people say that ... **dizem que ...**
    that is to say **quer dizer**
scales a **balança**
scarf o **cachecol**
scene (*in play*) a **cena** (*view*) o **panorama**
scenery (*countryside*) a **paisagem**
scent o **perfume**
school a **escola**

science a **ciência**
scientist o/a **cientista**
scientific **científico/a**
scissors a **tesoura**
score: what's the score? a **quantos estão?**
    final score o **resultado final**
Scotland **Escócia**
Scottish **escocês, escocesa**
scrambled eggs os **ovos mexidos**
scratch (*on skin*) o **arranhão**
screen (*TV, cinema, etc.*) o **écran** (*partition*) o **biombo**
screw o **parafuso**
screwdriver a **chave de parafusos**
sculpture a **escultura**
sea o **mar**
seafood o **marisco**
seasick **enjoado/a**
season (*of year*) a **estação**
season ticket a **assinatura**
seat o **assento** (*chair*) a **cadeira**
seatbelt o **cinto de segurança**
second **segundo/a** (*time*) o **segundo**
secret o **secreto**
secret **secreto/a**
secretary o **secretário, a secretária**
section a **secção**
to see **ver**
    I see (*understand*) **estou a ver**
    I (can't) see ... **(não) vejo ...**

to seem **parecer**
    it seems that . . . **parece que . . .**
self-service o **self-service**
to sell **vender**
to send **enviar**
senior citizen o **reformado, a reformada**
sensible **sensato/a**
sentence a **frase**
    (*prison*) a **sentença**
separate, separated **separado/a**
serious **sério/a**
    (*important*) **grave**
to serve **servir**
service (*church*) a **cerimónia religiosa**
service (*charge*) o **serviço**
set (*group*) o **conjunto**
    (*series*) a **série**
    (*for hair*) a **mise**
setting lotion o **fixador**
several **vários/as**
to sew **coser**
sewing a **costura**
sex (*gender*) o **sexo**
    (*intercourse*) as **relações sexuais**
shade (*colour*) o **tom**
shadow a **sombra**
shampoo o **champô**
shampoo and set a **lavagem e mise**
shampoo and blow-dry a **lavagem e o brushing**
sharp (*edge*) **aguçado/a**
    (*pain*) **agudo/a**
to shave **fazer a barba**
shaver a **máquina de barbear**

shaving cream/foam o **creme de barbear**
she **ela**
sheep a **ovelha**
sheet o **lençol** (*pl.* os **lençóis**)
shelf a **prateleira**
shell (*egg, nut*) a **casca**
    (*sea*) a **concha**
shellfish o **marisco**
shelter o **refúgio**
shiny **lustroso/a**
ship o **navio**
shirt a **camisa**
shock (*fright*) o **susto**
shoe o **sapato**
shoelace o **atacador**
shoe polish a **graxa**
shoe shop a **sapataria**
shop a **loja**
shop assistant o **empregado, a empregada**
shopping: to go shopping **ir às compras** (ir, *see page 185*)
shopping centre o **centro comercial**
short **curto/a**
shorts os **calções**
to shout **gritar**
show o **espectáculo**
to show **mostrar**
shower (*bathroom fitting*) o **chuveiro**
shower: to have a shower **tomar um duche**
to shrink **encolher**
shut **fechado/a**
shutter a **persiana**
    (*camera*) o **obturador**
sick (*ill*) **doente**

to be sick **vomitar**
to feel sick **sentir-se mal**
I feel sick **sinto-me mal**
side **o lado**
sieve **a peneira**
sight (*vision*) **a visão**
sights (*tourist*) **os locais de interesse**
sightseeing **o turismo**
sign **o sinal**
to sign **assinar**
signal **o sinal**
signature **a assinatura**
silent **silencioso/a**
silk **a seda**
silver **a prata**
similar (to) **semelhante (a)**
simple **simples**
since **desde**
to sing **cantar**
single (*room, bed*) **individual**
(*ticket*) **simples**
(*unmarried*) **solteiro/a**
sink **o lava-louça**
sir **senhor**
sister **a irmã**
sister-in-law **a cunhada**
to sit (down) **sentar-se**
sit down **sente-se**
sitting (down) **sentado/a**
size (*dimension*) **o tamanho**
(*clothes*) **a medida**
(*shoe, etc.*) **o número**
skates **os patins**
to skate **patinar**
ski, skiing **o esqui**
skimmed milk **o leite desnatado**
skin **a pele**

skindiving **o mergulho**
skirt **a saia**
sky **o céu**
to sleep **dormir**
I sleep **durmo**
he/she/it sleeps, you sleep **dorme**
sleeper/sleeping car **a carruagem-cama**
sleeping bag **o saco de dormir**
sleeve **a manga**
slice **a fatia**
sliced **às fatias**
slide (*film*) **o slide**
slim **esbelto/a**
slip (*petticoat*) **a combinação**
slippery **escorregadio/a**
slow **lento/a**
slowly **devagar**
small **pequeno/a**
smell **o cheiro**
smell: it smells bad/good **cheira mal/bem**
it smells of ... **cheira a ...**
smile **o sorriso**
smoke **o fumo**
to smoke **fumar**
smoked **fumado/a**
smooth **polido/a**
snake **a cobra**
to sneeze **espirrar**
snorkel **o tubo de ar**
snow **a neve**
to snow **nevar**
so **tão**
(*thus*) **assim**
soap **o sabonete**
sober **sóbrio/a**
socialism **o socialismo**

socialist **socialista**
social worker **o/a assistente social**
sociology **a sociologia**
sock **a peúga**
socket (*electrical*) **a tomada**
soda (water) **a soda**
soft **macio/a** (*flabby*) **mole**
soft drink **a bebida não alcoólica**
sold out **esgotado/a**
soldier **o soldado**
solid **sólido/a**
some **alguns, algumas**
somehow **de alguma maneira**
someone **alguém**
something **algo, alguma coisa**
sometimes **às vezes**
somewhere **algures**
so many **tantos/as**
so much **tanto/a**
son **o filho**
song **a canção**
son-in-law **o genro**
soon **em breve**
  as soon as possible **quanto antes**
sore throat **a dor de garganta**
sorry! **desculpe!**
sort (*type*) **o tipo**
sound **o som**
soup **a sopa** (*broth*) **o caldo**
sour **azedo/a, ácido/a**
south **o sul**
southern **do sul**

souvenir **a lembrança**
space **o espaço**
spade **a pá**
Spain **Espanha**
Spanish **espanhol, espanhola**
spanner **a chave de porcas**
spare (*available*) **disponível** (*left over*) **restante**
spare time **o tempo livre**
spare wheel **a roda sobresselente**
sparkling (*wine*) **espumante**
to speak **falar**
special **especial**
  special offer **a oferta**
specialist **o/a especialista**
speciality **a especialidade**
spectacles **os óculos**
speed **a velocidade**
speed limit **o limite de velocidade**
to spend (*money*) **gastar** (*time*) **passar**
spice **a especiaria**
spicy **picante**
spinach **o espinafre**
spirits **os licores**
splinter **a lasca**
to spoil **estragar**
sponge (*bath*) **a esponja** (*cake*) **o pão-de-ló**
spoon **a colher**
sport **o desporto**
spot **a pinta** (*place*) **o sítio**
to sprain **torcer**
spring (*season*) **a primavera**

square **a praça**
square (*shape*) **quadrado/a**
stadium **o estádio**
stain **a nódoa**
stainless steel **o aço inoxidável**
stairs **a escada**
stalls (*theatre*) **a plateia**
stamp **o selo**
stand (*stadium*) **as bancadas**
standing (up) **de pé**
staple **o agrafo**
stapler **o agrafador**
star **a estrela**
start (*beginning*) **o começo**
to start **começar**
   I start **começo**
starter (*food*) **a entrada**
state **o estado**
station **a estação**
station master **o chefe de estação**
stationer's **a papelaria**
statue **a estátua**
stay **a estadia**
stay: I'm staying at . . . **estou em . . .**
steak **o bife**
to steal **roubar**
steam **o vapor**
steel **o aço**
steep **íngreme**
step **o passo**
   (*stair*) **o degrau**
step-children **os enteados**
step-daughter **a enteada**
step-father **o padrasto**
step-mother **a madrasta**
step-son **o enteado**
stereo **o stéreo**

sterling: pound sterling **a libra esterlina**
steward (*air*) **o comissário de voo**
stewardess (*air*) **a hospedeira**
stick **o pau**
   (*walking*) **a bengala**
to stick **colar**
sticking plaster **o penso adesivo**
sticky **pegajoso/a**
sticky tape **a fita gomada**
stiff **rígido/a**
still **ainda**
still (*non-fizzy*) **sem gás**
sting **a picada**
to sting **picar**
stock exchange **a bolsa**
stockings **as meias**
stolen: my . . . has been stolen **roubaram-me o/a . . .** (*see page 171*)
stomach **o estômago**
stomach ache **a dor de estômago**
stomach upset **a perturbação gástrica**
stone **a pedra**
stop (*bus, etc.*) **a paragem**
to stop **parar**
   stop! **pare!**
stopcock **a torneira de segurança**
storey **o andar**
story **o conto**
stove (*cooker*) **o forno**
straight **direito/a**
straight on **(sempre) em frente**
strange **estranho/a**

271

strap **a correia**
straw (*drinking*) **a palhinha**
strawberry **o morango**
stream **o ribeiro**
street **a rua**
street light **o candeeiro**
stretcher **a maca**
strike **a greve**
string **a corda**
stripe **a risca**
striped **riscado/a**
strong **forte**
student **o/a estudante**
studio **o estúdio**
to study **estudar**
stupid **estúpido/a**
style **o estilo**
styling mousse **a mousse para pentear**

subtitled **legendado/a**
suburbs **os arredores**
to succeed, be successful **ter êxito/sucesso** (ter, *see page 185*)
success **o êxito, o sucesso**
such **tal**
suddenly **de repente**
sugar **o açúcar**
sugar lump **o cubo de açúcar**
suit **o fato**
suitcase **a mala**
summer **o verão**
sun **o sol**
to sunbathe **tomar banho de sol**
sunburn **a queimadura solar**
sunglasses **os óculos de sol**

sunshade (*beach*) **o chapéu de sol**
sunstroke **a insolação**
suntan cream **o bronzeador**
supermarket **o supermercado**
supper **a ceia**
supplement **o suplemento**
suppose: I suppose so/not **suponho que sim/não**
suppository **o supositório**
sure **seguro/a**
surface **a superfície**
surname **o apelido**
surprise **a surpresa**
surprised **surpreendido/a**
surrounded (by) **rodeado/a (de)**
sweat **o suor**
sweater **a camisola**
sweatshirt **a camisola**
to sweep **barrer**
sweet **doce**
sweet (*dessert*) **a sobremesa**
sweetener **o adoçante**
sweets **os rebuçados** (*chocolates*) **os bombons** (*toffees*) **os caramelos**
swelling **o inchaço**
to swim **nadar**
swimming **a natação**
swimming pool **a piscina**
swimming trunks, swimsuit **o fato de banho**
switch **o interruptor**
to switch off (*light*) **apagar** (*engine*) **desligar**
to switch on **ligar**

how do you switch it on? **como é que se liga?**
swollen **inchado/a**
symptom **o sintoma**
synagogue **o sinagoga**
synthetic **sintético/a**
system **o sistema**

T

table **a mesa**
tablet **a pastilha**
table tennis **o ténis de mesa**
tailor **o alfaiate**
to take **tomar**
  (*bus, etc.*) **apanhar**
  (*time*) **demorar**
to take out **tirar**
taken (*seat*) **ocupado/a**
to take off (*remove*) **tirar**
  (*plane*) **descolar**
talcum powder **o pó de talco**
to talk **falar**
tall **alto/a**
tame **manso/a**
tampon **o tampão**
tap **a torneira**
tape **a fita**
tape measure **a fita métrica**
tape recorder **o gravador**
taste **o sabor**
tasty **saboroso/a**
tax **o imposto**
taxi **o táxi**
taxi rank **a praça de táxis**
tea **o chá**
teabag **a saqueta de chá**

to teach **ensinar**
teacher **o professor, a professora**
team **a equipa**
teapot **a chaleira**
to tear **rasgar**
teaspoon **a colher de chá**
teat (*for baby's bottle*) **a chucha**
tea-towel **o pano para a louça**
technical **técnico/a**
technology **a tecnologia**
teenager **o/a adolescente**
telegram **o telegrama**
telephone **o telefone**
telephone directory **a lista telefónica**
to telephone **telefonar**
television **a televisão**
to tell **dizer**
  I tell **digo**
  he/she/it tells, you tell **diz**
temperature **a temperatura**
  to have a temperature **ter febre** (**ter**, *see page 185*)
temporary **provisório/a**
tender **tenro/a**
tennis **o ténis**
tennis court **o court de ténis**
tennis shoes **os sapatos de ténis**
tent **a tenda**
tent peg **a cavilha**
tent poles **os ferros**
terminal, terminus **o terminal**
terrace **o terraço**
  (*of café*) **a esplanada**

terrible **terrível** (*pl.* **terríveis**)
terrorist **o terrorista**
thank you (very much) **(muito) obrigado/a**
that, that one **esse/a; aquele, aquela** (*see page 180*)
the **o, a;** (*pl.* **os, as**)
theatre **o teatro**
their/theirs **o seu, a sua;** (*pl.* **os seus, as suas**) (*see page 179*)
theirs **deles, delas**
them **os, as; lhes**
then **então** (*later on*) **depois**
there **ali**
there is/are **há**
therefore **portanto**
thermometer **o termómetro**
these **estes/as** (*see page 180*)
they **eles/elas**
thief **o ladrão**
thick **espesso/a**
thin **delgado/a**
thing **a coisa**
to think **pensar, achar**
 I think so/not **acho que sim/não**
third **terceiro/a**
thirsty: to be thirsty **ter sede** (**ter**, *see page 185*)
this, this one **este/a** (*see page 180*)
those **esses/as; aqueles/as** (*see page 180*)
thread **a linha**
throat **a garganta**

throat lozenges/pastilles **as pastilhas para a garganta**
through **por**
to throw **atirar**
to throw away **deitar fora**
thumb **o pulgar**
thunder **o trovão**
ticket **o bilhete**
ticket office **a bilheteira**
tide **a maré**
tidy **arrumado/a**
tie **a gravata**
to tie **atar**
tight **apertado/a**
tights **os collants**
till (*until*) **até**
time (*once, etc.*) **a vez**
time **a hora** (*see page 192*)
 there's no time **não há tempo**
timetable **o horário**
tin **a lata**
tin opener **o abre-latas**
tin foil **a folha de alumínio**
tinned **enlatado/a**
tip (*money*) **a gorjeta**
tired **cansado/a**
tissues **os lenços de papel**
to **a**
toast **as torradas**
toasted sandwich **a tosta**
tobacco **o tabaco**
tobacconist's **a tabacaria**
today **hoje**
together **juntos/as**
toilet **a casa de banho**
toilet paper **o papel higiénico**
toiletries **os artigos de toilette**

toilet water **a água de colónia**
toll **a portagem**
tomato **o tomate**
tomorrow **amanhã**
tongue **a língua**
tonic water **a água tónica**
tonight **esta noite**
too (*also*) **também**
too (*excessively*) **muito**
tool **a ferramenta**
too many **demasiados/as**
too much **demasiado/a**
tooth **o dente**
toothache **a dor de dentes**
toothbrush **a escova de dentes**
toothpaste **a pasta de dentes**
toothpick **o palito**
top (*hill*) **o cimo**
on top (of) **sobre, em cima (de)**
top floor **o último andar**
torch **a lanterna**
torn **rasgado/a**
total **total**
to touch **tocar**
tough (*meat*) **duro/a**
tour (*excursion*) **a excursão**
(*visit*) **a visita**
tourism **o turismo**
tourist **o/a turista**
tourist office **o posto de turismo**
to tow **rebocar**
towards **para**
towel **a toalha**
tower **a torre**
town **a vila**

town centre **o centro da vila/cidade**
town hall **a câmara municipal**
tow rope **a corda de reboque**
toy **o brinquedo**
track (*path*) **o caminho**
tracksuit **o fato de treino**
trade union **o sindicato**
traditional **tradicional**
traffic **o trânsito**
traffic jam **o engarrafamento**
traffic lights **os semáforos**
trailer **o atrelado**
train **o comboio**
by train **de comboio**
training shoes **os sapatos de ténis**
tram **o eléctrico**
tranquilliser **o tranquilizante**
to translate **traduzir**
translation **a tradução**
to travel **viajar**
travel agency **a agência de viagens**
traveller's cheque **o traveller's cheque**
travel sickness **o enjoo**
tray **o tabuleiro**
treatment **o tratamento**
tree **a árvore**
trip **a viagem**
trolley **o carrinho**
trousers **as calças**
trout **a truta**
true: that's true **é verdade**
to try (*attempt*) **tentar**
(*sample, taste*) **provar**

to try on **experimentar**
T-shirt **o T-shirt**
tube **o tubo**
tuna **o atum**
tunnel **o túnel**
to turn **virar, voltar**
to turn off (*light*) **apagar**
    (*engine*) **desligar**
    (*tap*) **fechar**
to turn on **acender**
turning (*side road*) **a
    transversal**
TV **a TV**
twice **duas vezes**
twin beds **duas camas**
twins **os gémeos, as
    gémeas**
twisted **torcido/a**
type (*sort*) **o tipo**
to type **escrever à máquina**
typewriter **a máquina de
    escrever**
typical **típico/a**

U

ugly **feio/a**
ulcer **a úlcera**
umbrella **o guarda-chuva**
uncle **o tio**
uncomfortable **incómodo/a**
under **debaixo de**
underground **o metro**
underneath **debaixo (de)**
underpants **as cuecas**
to understand **entender**
    I (don't) understand
    (não) entendo
underwear **a roupa
    interior**
underwater **subaquático/a**

unemployed
    desempregado/a
unfortunately
    infelizmente
unhappy **infeliz**
    (*sad*) **triste**
uniform **o uniforme**
university **a universidade**
unleaded petrol **a
    gasolina sem chumbo**
unless **a menos que**
unpleasant **desagradável**
to unscrew **desaparafusar**
until **até**
unusual **invulgar**
unwell **indisposto/a**
up **em/para cima**
upper **de cima**
upstairs **lá em cima**
urgent **urgente**
urine **a urina**
us **nos**
use **o uso**
to use **utilizar, empregar**
useful **útil** (*pl.* **úteis**)
useless **inútil** (*pl.* **inúteis**)
usual: as usual **como de
    costume**
usually **normalmente**

V

vacant **livre**
vacuum cleaner **o
    aspirador**
vacuum flask **o termo**
valid **válido/a**
valley **o vale**
valuable **de valor**
valuables **objectos de
    valor**

van o **furgão**
vanilla a **baunilha**
vase o **vaso**
VAT o **IVA**
veal a **vitela**
vegetable o **legume**
vegetarian **vegetariano/a**
vehicle o **veículo**
vermouth o **vermute**
very **muito**
very much **muito**
vest a **camisola interior**
vet o **veterinário**
via **via**
video cassette a **video-cassete**
video recorder o **gravador de video**
view a **vista**, a **panorama**
villa a **'villa'**
village a **aldeia**
   (*holiday*) o **aldeamento turístico**
vinegar o **vinagre**
vineyard a **vinha**
virgin a **virgem**
   Virgin Mary a **Virgem Maria**
visit a **visita**
to visit **visitar**
visitor o/a **visitante**
vitamin a **vitamina**
vodka o **vodka**
voice a **voz**
volleyball o **voleibol**
voltage a **voltagem**
to vote **votar**

W

wage o **ordenado**
waist a **cintura**
waistcoat o **colete**
to wait (for) **esperar**
waiter o **empregado de mesa**
   waiter! **faz favor!**
waiting room a **sala de espera**
waitress a **empregada de mesa**
   waitress! **faz favor!**
Wales o **País de Gales**
walk o **passeio**
   to go for a walk **dar um passeio**
to walk **andar**
walking stick a **bengala**
wall (*house*) a **parede**
   (*garden*) o **muro**
walls (*city*) as **muralhas**
wallet a **carteira**
walnut a **noz**
to want **querer**
   would like: I would like **queria**
war a **guerra**
warm **quente**
to wash **lavar**
washable **lavável**
wash-basin o **lavatório**
washing a **lavagem**
washing machine a **máquina de lavar roupa**
washing powder o **detergente em pó**
washing-up: to do the washing up **lavar a louça**

washing-up liquid o **detergente para a louça**
wasp a **vespa**
wastepaper basket o **cesto dos papéis**
watch (*wristwatch*) o **relógio**
to watch (*TV, etc.*) **ver**
watchstrap o **bracelete**
water a **água**
water-heater o **esquentador**
water melon a **melancia**
waterfall a **queda de água**
waterproof **impermeável**
water-skiing o **esqui aquático**
wave (*of sea*) a **onda**
wax a **cera**
way (*route*) o **caminho**
  that way **por ali**
  this way **por aqui**
  (*method*) a **maneira**
way in a **entrada**
way out a **saída**
we **nós**
weather o **tempo**
  what's the weather like? **como está o tempo?**
wedding o **casamento**
week a **semana**
weekday o **dia útil** (*pl.* os **dias úteis**)
weekend o **fim de semana**
weekly **semanal**
  (*each week*) **cada semana**
to weigh **pesar**
weight o **peso**
welcome **bem-vindo/a**
well (*for water*) o **poço**
well **bem**

278

as well **também**
well done (*steak*) **bem passado/a**
Welsh **galês, galesa**
west o **oeste**
western **do oeste, ocidental**
wet **molhado/a**
wetsuit o **escafandro**
what **que, o que**
what? **o quê?**
  what is . . . ? **o que é . . . ?**
wheel a **roda**
wheelchair a **cadeira de rodas**
when **quando**
when? **quando?, a que horas?**
where **onde**
where? **onde?**
  where is/are . . . ? **onde é/são . . . ?; onde está/estão . . . ?** (*see page 184*)
which **que**
which? **qual?** (*pl.* **quais?**)
while **enquanto**
whisky o **uísque**
  whisky and soda o **uísque com soda**
white **branco/a**
  (*with milk*) **com leite**
white wine o **vinho branco**
who **que, quem**
who? **quem?**
  who is it? **quem é?**
whole **inteiro/a**
wholemeal bread o **pão integral**
whose **cujo/a, cujos/as**
whose? **de quem?**

why? **porquê?**
why not? **porque não?**
wide **largo/a**
widow a **viúva**
widower o **viúvo**
wife a **mulher**
wild (*animal*) **selvagem**
  (*plant*) **silvestre**
win a **vitória**
to win **ganhar**
  who won? **quem ganhou?**
wind o **vento**
windmill o **moinho de vento**
window a **janela**
  (*shop*) a **montra**
windsurfing o **windsurf**
windy: it's windy **está**
  vento
wine merchant/shop a
  casa de vinhos
wing (*of bird*) a **asa**
  (*of building*) a **ala**
winter o **inverno**
with **com**
without **sem**
woman a **mulher**
wonderful **maravilhoso/a**
wood (*trees*) a **mata**
  (*material*) a **madeira**
wool a **lã**
word a **palavra**
work o **trabalho**
to work (*at job*) **trabalhar**
  (*function*) **funcionar**
world o **mundo**
world (*of the world*)
  mundial
  First/Second World
  War a **Primeira/**
  Segunda Guerra
  Mundial

worried **preocupado/a**
worry: don't worry **não se**
  preocupe
worse **pior**
worth: it's worth ... **vale ...**
  it's (not) worth it **(não)**
  vale a pena
would like (*see* to want)
wound (*injury*) a **ferida**
to wrap (up) **embrulhar**
to write **escrever**
writer o **escritor,** a
  escritora
writing pad o **bloco**
writing paper o **papel de**
  carta
wrong (*incorrect*) **errado/a**
  you're wrong **não tem**
  razão
  there's something
  wrong **há algo errado**

279

X

X-ray o **raio-X**

Y

yacht o **iate**
to yawn **bocejar**
year o **ano**
yellow **amarelo/a**
yes **sim**
yesterday **ontem**
yet **ainda**
  not yet **ainda não**
yoghurt o **iogurte**
you o **senhor,** a **senhora**
  (*formal*); **você; tu**
  (*informal*) (*see page*
  181)

young **jovem**
your(s) **o seu, a sua;** *(pl.)*
  os seus, as suas *(formal)*
  (see page 179)
youth **a juventude**
youth hostel **a pousada de**
  juventude

Z

zip **o fecho de correr**
zoo **o jardim zoológico**
zoology **a zoologia**

NOTES

NOTES

EMERGENCIES

(*see also* Problems and complaints, *page 166*; Health, *page 153*)

You may want to say

Phoning the emergency services

The police, please
A polícia, por favor
a pooleesya poor favohr

The fire brigade, please
Os bombeiros, por favor
oosh bohmbayroosh poor favohr

An ambulance, please
Uma ambulância, por favor
ooma amboolañsya poor favohr

There's been a robbery/
  burglary
Houve um assalto
ohv oom asaltoo

There's been an accident
Houve um acidente
ohv oom aseedayñt

There's a fire
Há um incêndio
ah oom eeñsayñdyoo

I've been attacked
Fui atacado/a
fwee atakahdoo/a

I've been mugged
Fui assaltado/a
fwee asahltahdoo/a

I've been raped
Fui violada
fwee veeoolahda

There's someone injured/ill
Há uma pessoa ferida/doente
*ah ooma pisoha fireeda/
  dooayñt*

It's my husband/son
É o meu marido/filho
e oo mayoo mareedoo/feelyoo

It's my wife/daughter
É a minha mulher/filha
e a meenya moolyer/feelya

It's my friend
É o meu amigo/a minha amiga
*e oo **mayoo** ameegoo/ a **meenya** ameega*

Please come immediately
Por favor, venha imediatamente
*poor favohr vaynya eemidyahta**maynt***

I am at . . .
Estou em . . .
*ishtoh ay** . . .*

I am at the . . .
Estou no/na . . .
ishtoh noo/na . . .

My name is . . .
Chamo-me . . .
shamoo-mi . . .

My telephone number is . . .
O meu telefone é o . . .
*oo **mayoo** tili**fon** e oo . . .*

Where is the police station?
Onde é a esquadra da polícia?
*ohñdee e a ish**kwah**dra da poo**lees**ya*

Where is the hospital?
Onde é o hospital?
*ohñdee e oo ohshpee**tahl***

At the police station/hospital

Is there anybody who speaks English?
Há alguém que fale inglês?
*ah ahl**gaym** ki **fahli** eeñ**glaysh***

I want to speak to a woman
Queria falar com uma mulher
*kireea fa**lahr** kohm ooma moolyer*

Please call the British Embassy
Por favor, telefone para a Embaixada Britânica
*poor favohr tili**fon** para a aymbiyshahda bree**tan**eeka*

I want a lawyer
Quero um advogado
*keroo oom advoo**gah**doo*

You may hear

When you phone the emergency services

Qual é o problema?
kwahl e oo prooblayma
What is the matter?

O que aconteceu?
oo ki akohñtisayoo
What has happened?

Diga o seu nome e morada
deega oo sayoo nohm ee moorahda
Tell me your name and address

Vamos enviar uma patrulha da polícia
vahmooz ayñveeeahr ooma patroolya da pooleesya
We will send a police patrol

Um carro da polícia vai/está a caminho
ooñ kahrroo da pooleesya viy/ishtah a kameenyoo
A police car is on the way

Um carro/tanque de bombeiros vai/está a caminho
ooñ kahrroo/tank di booñbayroosh viy/ishtah a kameenyoo
A fire engine is on the way

Envio-lhe já uma ambulância
ayñveeoo-lyi jah ooma añboolañsya
I am sending an ambulance to you now

The police

Como se chama?
kohmoo si shama
What is your name?

Qual é a sua morada?
kwahl e a sooa moorahda
What is your address?

O que aconteceu?
oo ki akohñtisayoo
What happened?

Onde é que aconteceu?
ohñdee e ki akohñtisayoo
Where did it happen?

Quando é que aconteceu?
kwañdoo e ki akohñtisayoo
When did it happen?

Podia descrever . . . ?
poodeea dishkrivayr . . .
Can you describe . . . ?

Venha comigo/connosco à esquadra
vaynya koohmeegoo/ kohnoshkoo ah ishkwahdra
Come with me/with us to the police station

Está preso/a
ishtah prayzoo/a
You're under arrest

The doctor

Onde lhe dói?
ohñd lyi doy
Where does it hurt?

Tem de ir para o hospital
taym di eer para oo ohshpeetahl
You/he/she will have to go to hospital

Há quanto tempo está assim?
ah kwañtoo taympoo ishtah aseeñ
How long have you been like this?/How long has he/she been like this?

Emergency shouts

Help!
Socorro!
sookohrroo

Help me!
Ajude-me!
ajoodi-mi

Police!
Polícia
pooleesya

Stop!
Pare!
pahri

Stop thief!
Agarra que é ladrão!
agahrra ki e ladrowñ

Look out!
Cuidado!
kweedahdoo

Fire!
Fogo!
fohgoo

Danger! Gas!
Perigo! Gás!
pireegoo gahsh

Get out of the way!
Saia do caminho!
sahya doo kameenyoo

Call the police
Chame a polícia
shami a pooleesya

Call the fire brigade
Chame os bombeiros
shami oosh bohṁbayroosh

Call an ambulance
Chame uma ambulância
shami ooma aṁboolañsya

Get a doctor
Traga um médico
trahga ooṁ medeekoo

Get help quickly
Traga auxílio depressa
trahga owseelyoo dipresa

It's an emergency
É uma emergência
e ooma imirjayñsya

Emergency telephone numbers

The emergency number throughout Portugal is **115**, though this may change to **112**, the European emergency number.

ALL-PURPOSE PHRASES

Hello
Olá
ohlah

Good morning/Good day
Bom dia
bohm deea

Good afternoon/evening
Boa tarde
boha tahrd

Good evening/Goodnight
Boa noite
boha noyt

Goodbye
Adeus
adayoosh

Yes
Sim
seem

No
Não
nowñ

Please
Por favor
poor favohr

Thank you (very much)
(Muito) obrigado *(if you're male)*
(mweeñtoo) ohbreegahdoo
(Muito) obrigada *(if you're female)*
(mweeñtoo) ohbreegahda

Don't mention it
De nada
di nahda

I don't know
Não sei
nowñ say

I don't understand
Não entendo
nowñ ayñtayñdoo

I speak very little Portuguese
Falo muito pouco português
*fahloo mweeñtoo pohkoo
poortoogaysh*

Pardon
Como?
kohmoo

Could you repeat that?
Podia repetir?
poodeea rripiteer

More slowly
Mais devagar
miysh divagahr

Again, please
Outra vez, por favor
ohtra vaysh poor favohr